Baseline

Lean is about building and improving stable and predictable systems and processes to deliver to customers high-quality products/services on time by engaging everyone in the organization. Combined with this, organizations need to create an environment of respect for people and continuous learning. It's all about people. People create the product or service, drive innovation, and create systems and processes, and with leadership buy-in and accountability to ensure sustainment with this philosophy, employees will be committed to the organization as they learn and grow personally and professionally.

Lean is a term that describes a way of thinking about and managing companies as an enterprise. Becoming Lean requires the following: the continual pursuit to identify and eliminate waste; the establishment of efficient flow of both information and process; and an unwavering top-level commitment. The concept of continuous improvement applies to any process in any industry.

Based on the contents of *The Lean Practitioners Field Book*, the purpose of this series is to show, in detail, how any process can be improved utilizing a combination of tasks and people tools and introduces the BASICS Lean® concept. The books are designed for all levels of Lean practitioners and introduces proven tools for analysis and implementation that go beyond the traditional point kaizen event. Each book can be used as a stand-alone volume or used in combination with other titles based on specific needs.

Each book is chock-full of case studies and stories from the authors' own experiences in training organizations that have started or are continuing their Lean journey of continuous improvement. Contents include valuable lessons learned and each chapter concludes with questions pertaining to the focus of the chapter. Numerous photographs enrich and illustrate specific tools used in Lean methodology.

Baseline: Confronting Reality & Planning the Path for Success focuses on change management and how to manage and accelerate change. The authors also outline how to get ready to implement lean, how to baseline your processes prior to implementing Lean, and how to create a value stream map of processes. This book also discusses Lean accounting.

BASICS Lean® Implementation Series

Baseline: Confronting Reality & Planning the Path for Success
By Charles Protzman, Fred Whiton & Joyce Kerpchar

Assess and Analyze: Discovering the Waste Consuming Your Profits
By Charles Protzman, Fred Whiton & Joyce Kerpchar

Suggesting Solutions: Brainstorming Creative Ideas to Maximize Productivity
By Charles Protzman, Fred Whiton & Joyce Kerpchar

Implementing Lean: Converting Waste to Profit
By Charles Protzman, Fred Whiton & Joyce Kerpchar

Check: Identifying Gaps on the Path to Success
By Charles Protzman, Fred Whiton & Joyce Kerpchar

Sustaining Lean: Creating a Culture of Continuous Improvement
By Charles Protzman, Fred Whiton & Joyce Kerpchar

Baseline
Confronting Reality & Planning the Path for Success

Charles Protzman, Fred Whiton, and Joyce Kerpchar

Routledge
Taylor & Francis Group

A PRODUCTIVITY PRESS BOOK

First published 2023
by Routledge
605 Third Avenue, New York, NY 10158

and by Routledge
4 Park Square, Milton Park, Abingdon, Oxon, OX14 4RN

Routledge is an imprint of the Taylor & Francis Group, an informa business

ISBN: 978-1-032-02911-5 (hbk)
ISBN: 978-1-032-02910-8 (pbk)
ISBN: 978-1-003-18577-2 (ebk)

DOI: 10.4324/9781003185772

Typeset in Garamond
by KnowledgeWorks Global Ltd.

This book series is dedicated to all the Lean practitioners in the world and to two of the earliest, my friend Kenneth Hopper and my grandfather Charles W. Protzman Sr. Kenneth was a close friend of Charles Sr. and is coauthor with his brother William of a book that describes Charles Sr. and his work for General MacArthur in the Occupation of Japan in some detail: *The Puritan Gift: Reclaiming the American Dream amidst Global Financial Chaos.*

Charles W. Protzman Sr.

Kenneth Hopper

Contents

Acknowledgments

There are many individuals who have contributed to this book, both directly and indirectly, and many others over the years, too many to list here, who have shared their knowledge and experiences with us. We would like to thank all of those who have worked with us on Lean teams in the past and the senior leadership whose support made them successful. This book would not have been possible without your hard work, perseverance, and courage during our Lean journey together. We hope you see this book as the culmination of our respect and appreciation. We apologize if we have overlooked anyone in the following acknowledgments. We would like to thank the following for their contributions to coauthor or contribute to the chapters in this book:

- Special thanks to our Productivity Press editor, Kris Mednansky, who has been terrific at guiding us through our writing project. Kris has been a great source of encouragement and kept us on track as we worked through what became an ever-expanding six-year project.
- Special thanks to all our clients. Without you, this book would not have been possible.
- Russ Scaffede for his insight into the Toyota system and for his valuable contributions through numerous e-mail correspondence and edits with various parts of the book.
- Joel Barker for his permission in referencing the paradigm material so important and integral to Lean implementations and change management.
- Many thanks to the "Hats" team (you know who you are).
- I would like to acknowledge Mark Jamrog of SMC Group. Mark was my first Sensei and introduced me to this Kaikaku-style Lean System Implementation approach based on the Ohno and Shingo teachings.
- Various chapter contributions by Joe and Ed Markiewicz of Ancon Gear.

For the complete list of acknowledgments, testimonials, dedication, etc. please see The Lean Practitioner's Field Book. The purpose of this series was to break down and enhance the original Lean Practitioner's Field Book into six books that are aligned with the BASICS* model.

Authors' Note: Every attempt was made to source materials back to the original authors. In the event we missed someone, please feel free to let us know so we may correct it in any future edition. Many of the spreadsheets depicted were originally hand drawn by Mark Jamrog, SMC Group, put into Excel by Dave O'Koren and Charlie Protzman, and since modified significantly. Most of the base formatting for these spreadsheets can be found in the Shingo, Ohno, Monden, or other industrial engineering handbooks.

About the Authors

Charles Protzman, MBA, CPM, formed Business Improvement Group (B.I.G.), LLC, in November 1997. B.I.G. is in Sarasota Florida. Charlie and his son, Dan along with Mike Meyers, specialize in implementing and training Lean thinking principles and the BASICS® Lean business delivery system (LBDS) in small to fortune 50 companies involved in Manufacturing, Healthcare, Government, and Service Industries.

Charles has written 12 books to date and is the coauthor of Leveraging Lean in Healthcare: Transforming Your Enterprise into a High-Quality Patient Care Delivery System series and is a two-time recipient of the Shingo Research and Professional Publication Award. He has since published *The BASICS® Lean Implementation Model* and *Lean Leadership BASICS®*. Charles has over 38 years of experience in materials and operations management. He spent almost 14 years with AlliedSignal, now Honeywell, where he was an Aerospace Strategic Operations Manager and the first AlliedSignal Lean master. He has received numerous special-recognition and cost-reduction awards. Charles was an external consultant for the Department of Business and Economic Development's (DBED's) Maryland Consortium during and after his tenure with AlliedSignal. With the help of Joyce LaPadula and others, he had input into the resulting DBED world-class criteria document and assisted in the first three initial DBED world-class company assessments. B.I.G. was a Strategic Partner of ValuMetrix Services, a division of Ortho-Clinical Diagnostics, Inc., a Johnson & Johnson company. He is an international Lean consultant and has taught beginner to advanced students' courses in Lean principles and total quality all over the world.

Charlie Protzman states, "My grandfather started me down this path and has influenced my life to this day. My grandfather made four trips to Japan from 1948 to the 1960s. He loved the Japanese people and culture and was passionate and determined to see Japanese manufacturing recover from World War II."

Charles spent the last 24 years with Business Improvement Group, LLC, implementing successful Lean product line conversions, kaizen events, and administrative business system improvements (transactional Lean) worldwide. He is following in the footsteps of his grandfather, who was part of the Civil Communications Section (CCS) of the American Occupation. Prior to recommending Dr. Deming's 1950 visit to Japan, C.W. Protzman Sr. surveyed over 70 Japanese companies in 1948. Starting in late 1948, Homer Sarasohn and C.W. Protzman Sr. taught top executives of prominent Japanese communications companies an eight-week course in American participative management and quality techniques in Osaka and Tokyo. Over 5,100 top Japanese executives had taken the course by 1956. The course continued until 1993. Many of the lessons we taught the Japanese in 1948 are now being taught to Americans as "Lean principles." The Lean principles had their roots in the United States and date back to the early 1700s and later to Taylor, Gilbreth, and Henry Ford. The principles were refined by Taiichi Ohno and expanded by Dr. Shigeo Shingo. Modern-day champions were Norman Bodek (the Grandfather of Lean), Jim Womack, and Dan Jones.

Charles participated in numerous benchmarking and site visits, including a two-week trip to Japan in June 1996 and 2017. He is a master facilitator and trainer in TQM, total quality speed, facilitation, career development, change management, benchmarking, leadership, systems thinking, high-performance work teams, team building, Myers-Briggs® Styles, Lean thinking, and supply chain management. He also participated in Baldrige Examiner and Six Sigma management courses. He was an assistant program manager during "Desert Storm" for the Patriot missile-to-missile fuse development and production program. Charles is a past member of SME, AME, IIE, IEEE, APT, and the International Performance Alliance Group (IPAG), an international team of expert Lean Practitioners (http://www.ipag-consulting.com).

Fred Whiton, MBA, PMP, PE, has 30 years of experience in the aerospace and defense industry, which includes engineering, operations, program and portfolio management, and strategy development. He is employed as a Chief Engineer within Raytheon Intelligence & Space at the time of this book's publication.

Fred has both domestic and international expertise within homeland security, communications command and control intelligence surveillance and reconnaissance sensors and services, military and commercial aerospace systems, and defense systems supporting the US Navy, US Air Force, US Army, US Department of Homeland Security, and the US Intelligence Community across a full range of functions from marketing, concept development, engineering, and production into life cycle sustainment and logistics. Fred began his career as a design engineer at General Dynamics, was promoted to a group engineer at Lockheed Martin, and was a director at Northrop Grumman within the Homeland Defense Government Systems team. As vice president of engineering and operations at Smiths Aerospace, he was the Lean champion for a Lean enterprise journey, working closely with Protzman as the Lean consultant, for a very successful Lean implementation within a union plant, including a new plant designed using Lean principles. Prior to joining Raytheon, Fred was a senior vice president within C4ISR business unit at CACI International and prior to joining CACI was the vice president and general manager of the Tactical Communications and Network Solutions Line of Business within DRS Technologies.

Fred has a BS in mechanical engineering from the University of Maryland, an MS in mechanical engineering from Rensselaer Polytechnic Institute, a master's in engineering administration from The George Washington University, and an MBA from The University of Chicago. He is a professional engineer (PE) in Maryland, a certified project management professional (PMP), served as a commissioner on the Maryland Commission for Manufacturing Competitiveness under Governor Ehrlich, as a commissioner on the Maryland Commission on Autism under Governor O'Malley, and as a member of the boards of directors for the Regional Manufacturing Institute headquartered in Maryland and the First Maryland Disability Trust.

Joyce Kerpchar has over 35 years of experience in the healthcare industry that includes key leadership roles in healthcare operations, IT, health plan management, and innovative program development and strategy. As a Lean champion, mentor, and Six Sigma black belt, she is experienced in organizational lean strategy and leading large-scale healthcare lean initiatives, change management, and IT implementations. Joyce is a coauthor of Leveraging Lean in Healthcare: Transforming Your Enterprise into a High-Quality Patient Care Delivery System, Recipient of the Shingo Research and Professional Publication Award.

She began her career as a board-certified physician's assistant in cardiovascular and thoracic surgery and primary care medicine and received her master's degree in Management. Joyce is passionate about leveraging Lean in healthcare processes to eliminate waste and reduce errors, improve overall quality, and reduce the cost of providing healthcare.

Original Authors

We would like to acknowledge Chris Lewandowski, Steve Stenberg, and Patrick Grounds as original authors of The *Lean Practitioner's Field Book*.

Introduction

This book is the first of the six books BASICS Lean® Implementation Series and was adapted from The Lean Practitioner's Field Book[1]: Proven, Practical, Profitable, and Powerful Techniques for Making Lean Really Work. In Book 1, we discuss the Lean philosophy and provide a Lean Overview where we explore batching, the BASICS Lean® Business Delivery System, how to conduct Lean assessments, and preparing for a Lean Implementation (Kaikaku). We then begin with the B in the BASICS Lean® Implementation Model, which is BASELINE.

The books in this BASICS Lean® Implementation Series take the reader on a journey beginning with an overview of Lean principles, culminating with employees developing professionally through the BASICS Lean® Leadership Development Path. Each book has something for everyone from the novice to the seasoned Lean practitioner. A refresher for some at times, it provides soul-searching and thought-provoking questions with examples that will stimulate learning opportunities. Many of us take advantage of these learning opportunities daily. We, the authors, as Lean practitioners, are students still thirsting for knowledge and experiences to assist organizations in their transformations.

This series is designed to be a guide and resource to help you with the ongoing struggle to improve manufacturing, government, and service industries throughout the world. This series embodies true stories, results, and lessons, which we and others have learned during our Lean journeys. The concept of continuous improvement applies to any process in any industry.

The purpose of this series is to show, in detail, how any process can be improved by utilizing a combination of tasks and people tools. We will introduce proven tools for analysis and implementation that go far beyond the traditional point kaizen event training. Several CEOs have shared with us; had they not implemented Lean, they would not have survived the Recession in 2008 and subsequent downturns.

Many companies prefer we not use their names in this book as they consider Lean a strategic competitive advantage in their industry, and some of these companies have now moved into a leadership position in their respective markets; thus, we may refer to them as Company X throughout the series. We explain to companies that Lean is a five-year commitment that never ends. Eighty to ninety percent of the companies with whom we have worked have sustained their Lean journeys based on implementing our BASICS® Lean approach that we will share with you in this book.

The BASICS Lean® Implementation Series discusses the principles and tools in detail as well as the components of the House of Lean. It is a "how to" book that presents an integrated, structured approach identified by the acronym BASICS®, which when combined with an effective business strategy can help ensure the successful transformation of an organization. The Lean concepts described in each book are supported by a plethora of examples drawn from the personal experiences of its many well-known and respected contributors, which range from very small machine shops to Fortune 50 companies.

The BASICS Lean® Implementation Series has both practical applications as well as applications in academia. It can be used for motivating students to learn many of the Lean concepts and at the end of each chapter there are thought-provoking questions for the reader to help digest the material. The investment in people in terms of training, engagement, empowerment, and personal and professional growth is the key to sustaining Lean and an organization's success. For more on this topic, please see our book Lean Leadership BASICS®. Lean practitioners follow a natural flow, building continually on previous information and experiences. There is a bit of the Lean practitioner in all of us. Hopefully, as you read these books to pursue additional knowledge, as a refresher or for reference, or for academia, it can help expand your knowledge, skills, and abilities on your never-ending Lean journey.

Note

1. The Lean Practitioner's Field Book 1st Edition by Charles Protzman (Author), Fred Whiton (Author), Joyce Kerpchar (Author), Christopher Lewandowski (Author), Steve Stenberg (Author), Patrick Grounds (Author), Productivity Press; 1st edition (April 4, 2016).

Chapter 1

Lean Philosophy and Foundations

No one has more trouble than the person who claims to have no trouble.

Taiichi Ohno

Father of the Toyota Production System (TPS)

Brief History

There are literally hundreds of books that address Lean thinking and the Lean production system. However, very few explain how to implement the tools we will share with you. Lean is a term that describes a way of thinking about and managing companies as an enterprise. Becoming Lean requires the following:

- The continual pursuit to identify and eliminate waste
- The establishment of efficient flow of both information and process
- Unwavering senior leadership team commitment
- The continual development and engagement of your team members

The term Lean was coined by John Krafcik in his paper "Triumph of the Lean Production System" for his master's thesis at Massachusetts Institute of Technology (MIT) Sloan School of Management in 1988.[1] It was introduced by James Womack and Dan Jones in their book titled Lean Thinking[2] after a five-year MIT study of the automotive industry described in a book titled The Machine That Changed the World.[3] In the book and on the Lean Enterprise Institute (LEI) website,[4] Lean is described as the five-step process for guiding the implementation of Lean techniques as easy to remember, but not always easy to achieve:

1. Specify value from the standpoint of the end customer by product family.
2. Identify all the steps in the value stream for each product family, eliminating whenever possible those steps that do not create value.

DOI: 10.4324/9781003185772-1

1

3. Make the value-creating steps occur in tight sequence to ensure the product flows smoothly toward the customer.
4. As flow is introduced, let customers pull value from the next upstream activity.
5. As value is specified, value streams are identified, wasted steps are removed, and flow and pull are introduced. Begin the process again and continue it until a state of perfection is reached in which a perfect value is created with no waste.

Lean has its roots in the United States. Such notables as Frank and Lillian Gilbreth, Frederick Taylor, and Henry Ford all practiced principles that make up Lean today. The 1970s oil crisis and then New United Motor Manufacturing, Inc. (NUMMI), the California-based joint venture between General Manager and Toyota, put Lean on the map. The Toyota Production System (TPS) has become synonymous with Lean; however, Lean is not just for automotive companies. This system will work for any company, healthcare organization, service industry, or government/military entity. Since many of our processes are unique and every company's culture is distinctive, one must adapt the principles and tools to the environment in which one implements. This methodology has produced significant results for many companies.

Lean will sustain, but only if implemented properly and with ongoing training and people development. Lean must be rolled out enterprise-wide (not just shop floor) requiring an overall transformational change within the company. It must be championed and driven from the top of the organization. It must include all functional areas (i.e., finance, sales, marketing, HR, information systems [IS], operations), at all levels, from the board of directors to the person on the front line on the shop floor or in the office. It must include all value streams from the supply chain to the customers to recycling within the overall enterprise system framework.

Lean will not be successful if it is directed only at the frontline staff, promoted by someone within middle management, or if it is measured by the number of point kaizen events conducted each year. Today we find most companies have pockets of excellence[5] or what we call Lean lite and have struggled to sustain or had to relaunch Lean multiple times. Some feel they have completed their Lean implementations or have improved enough.

Implementing Lean requires a counterintuitive paradigm shift in thinking to offset the ever-prevalent resistance to batching inherent in the current system. This includes the need to adopt new accounting techniques and potentially instituting significant structural organizational changes. In short, developing a new way of thinking.

A consistent theme throughout this series (see Figure 1.1) is the balance and integration required between philosophy and tools. Learning to implement the task portion of is often not difficult; however, the people and philosophy piece which is emergent and always the most challenging. We cannot overstate the importance of separating these two pieces and implementing and integrating them together to achieve a complete Lean implementation. All the chapters in this series have been reviewed or written by leading experts in their fields and practicing internal company and external consulting Lean practitioners.

We Need a New System: The BASICS Lean® Business Delivery System!

When you finally make the decision to embark on a Lean journey or you decide to restart your Lean journey, you must realize and be willing to admit how little you may know about your processes or how to improve those processes. Remember, all the problems you have today are the

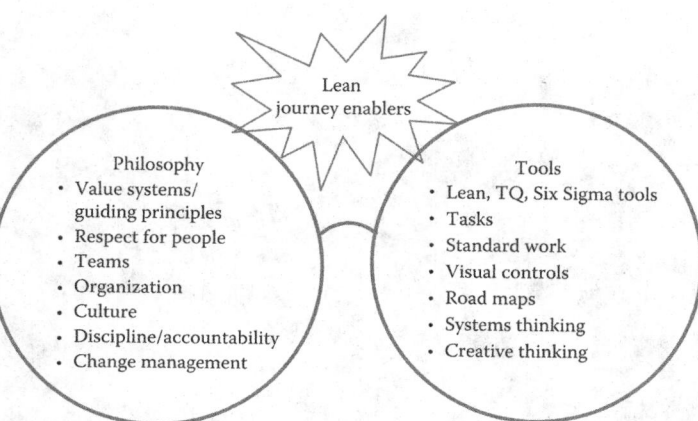

Figure 1.1 Lean journey enablers.

result of changes you or someone prior to you made in the past and these are the most difficult to change. Listed below are stories and anecdotes associated with our Lean journey.

Dock to Stock[6]—A Manager's Experience[7]

While I didn't know it at the time, my business experience with Lean began with at that time a new general manager (GM) named Dave Passeri at our Bendix Communications Plant. I had recently been promoted to dock-to-stock manager, which meant I managed all supplies and materials shipped to the plant. I was responsible for receiving, overseeing inspection, the stockroom and issuing parts kits to the manufacturing floor. At the time we could not ship our product due to significant material shortages. When I first toured the department, I found, in a large storage area, boxes of materials piled literally to the ceiling of the receiving holding area, averaging three to four months with some having birthdays, bottlenecking the production on the shop floor.

Dave invited some of us to meet with him and brought in a change agent named Jonno Hannifin[8] to work with us for several months, working on brainstorming ideas and process changes to start our production system moving again. We became known as the "hats" team.

With this new assignment to the dock-to-stock process, Dave gave me specific instructions to issue only one box at a time to the inspection department. I didn't understand how this would help our severe backlog; if anything, it seemed counterintuitive and would only slow things down further. Another new manager of quality assurance, Curtis McTeer, his staff, and I worked together along with many others to barcode and create a simple access database to log every item which was log jammed in the dock-to-stock process.

When we first entered the inspection department, there were boxes of parts everywhere and literally no room to walk. Each inspector had grabbed the easiest to inspect boxes and stashed them at their station (Figure 1.2). Meanwhile, the harder to inspect boxes sat, piled high in shelves in the storeroom. Prior management was considering expanding the incoming (receiving) inspection area due to the constant complaints about the lack of space.

We proceeded to remove every box from the inspection area and move it back into the holding area. We then, as directed by our GM, issued one box at a time (some already having been partially inspected) to each inspector to process individually. Once they completed the work, they could come back for another box. As each box was issued, we logged it into the database we created.

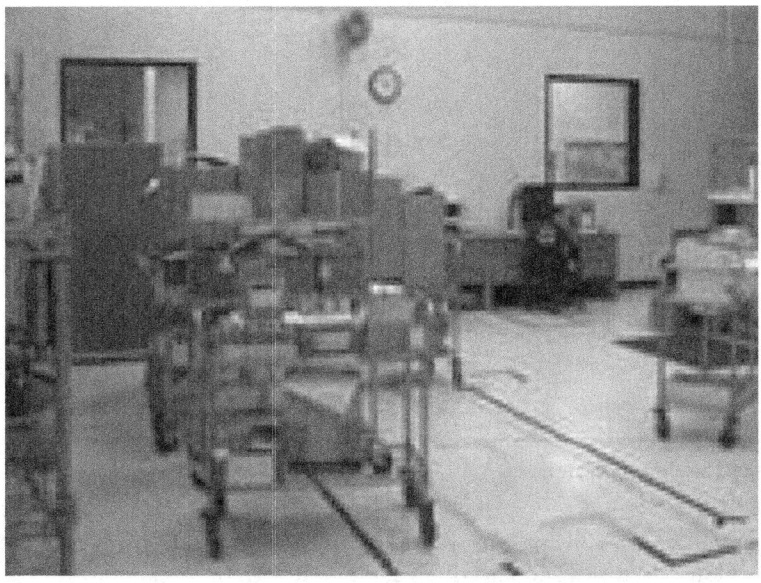

Figure 1.2   Inspection department—Working in batches.

When we cleaned out the inspection area, each station was full of various lots of materials the inspectors were working on. Instead of finishing one lot, they would take each lot and run it through one of the inspection operations, then run all the lots through the second operation, etc., until they were all completed. As a result, all the delinquent lots would sit until the last operation was completed for the lot. A significant amount of time was lost moving boxes of parts around the inspection area due to lack of space. It was difficult to find where a particular lot was located as there was so much material in inspection. Every day, this led to greater amounts of expediting and searching by supervisors and managers trying to track down and expedite this material. The management staff turned into day-to-day firefighters and high-paid expediters

Suddenly, something amazing started to happen. Over a two-week period, we cut our backlog from an average of 16 weeks to 6 weeks! In addition, we found there was plenty of space in the inspection department once we removed the excess inventory. During this effort, since parts were assumed to be lost by the planning department, we realized that we had double or even triple ordered much of the same material waiting for inspection. No one bothered to get up from their comfortable office chairs to look for the material, and if they did, there was so much material; it was just easier to order more than to look for it in the disorganized holding area.

Within four weeks, we were down to a two-week backlog and within six weeks, we caught up. Once we caught up, everyone tried to go back to the old way of doing it; however, we wouldn't let them. We freed up a tremendous amount of space not only in inspection but also in the holding area as well. Everything now smoothly flowed through the dock-to-stock process. This is when we first learned the true power of one-piece flow (now called Lean); however, we still didn't understand the breadth or true vision of it at the time.

When we went back to analyze the root cause of the problem, we discovered the reason we were so far behind was because we were batching the items through inspection. Batching, in this case, meant the inspectors would go into the receiving holding area filled and take four or five lots of material. Since they could pick and choose which boxes to work on, they would naturally look for the easiest things to work on first and leave the harder items for someone else.

Lesson learned: Batching environments are fraught with waste, lack of space, and delays. Batch environments always create the perception of the need for more space. In a batch environment, people usually take the easiest piece to work on first instead of using FIFO, the first in first out or EDD earliest due date principle. We also find it easier to reorder something instead of having to conduct an endless search for it. You cannot always depend on what others tell you. You must get up out of your chair and "go see" for yourself to identify the problems.

Once you "Lean out" an area, the supervision of the area becomes much easier, thus creating time to work on small improvements. Space which seems initially to be at a premium turns out to be "excess" space. Results can be obtained quickly within a specific area or process. Root cause analysis and management-by-fact may initially solve the problem, but you cannot switch back to the old ways of doing things if one wants to avoid reoccurrence of the problem.

Carousels[9]

As part of my new position in the dock-to-stock process, I inherited a capital request from the prior director to install two brand-new carousels (like the system shown in Figure 1.3) on the second floor of our stockroom to replace all the shelves of material. We already had two robotic retrieval systems on the first floor with which we always had problems. For example, if the power went out, we couldn't pick parts and would shut down assembly. We always had to have someone trained

Figure 1.3 Carousel material handling system.

and available to operate them. Parts would get lost and servicing them was expensive. It was going to be several hundred thousands of dollars (not including installation and ongoing maintenance) and justified with a rather large return on investment (ROI) analysis. I was told to finish up interviewing the various suppliers and provide a recommendation. It occurred to me after some Lean training that we were going to spend all this money to manage a bunch of inventory that was now considered evil. So, my recommendation was to cancel the capital appropriation request.

My eventual goal became to eliminate the need for my job, and within three years of my assignment which I achieved. We had successfully vacated the separate two-story stockroom building and moved the material to the production floor at the point of use where it belonged. Not only did we save hundreds of thousands of capital expenditure dollars, but we also eliminated picking, counting, and kitting parts to the floor. When we cleaned out the old robotic system in the stockroom, we found hundreds of previously lost parts that were misallocated and reordered.

Lesson Learned: Installing carousels and automated material storage equipment makes it much harder to implement Lean. Once it is purchased, accounting wants it used so they can depreciate it. The goal should be to eliminate stockrooms along with all the waste they create. The next time you look at an automated material storage device, make sure it is not just adding cost to store material you don't want in storage. We also learned and embraced the idea of removing waste by always working to eliminate our own jobs.

Slide Line[10]

The next experience with Lean involved the use of slide lines. Our division manufactured electronic circuit boards and systems equipment primarily for the military. We invested significant capital in machines that sequenced transistors and diodes (Figure 1.4), so they could be put onto another

Figure 1.4   Diode and transistor sequencing machine.

machine, which put those parts into circuit boards. The boards would then move to another set of functionally laid out equipment because all our "like" machines were placed together in the same functional area or work center that would insert integrated circuit chips into the circuit boards. We would issue parts kits pulled from the first and second floor of our stockroom (sometimes for hundreds of boards), which then were transported across a large parking lot to the manufacturing building. Sometimes, cars would get dented when the racks accidentally slipped away from the stockroom material handler.

The kits would slowly move from machine to machine and operation to operation. We were doing significantly large amounts (100–250 or more piece kits) of batching. We had an army of material, inventory, and production control people to track all this material being batch processed through the factory, providing daily updates for sometimes 2- to 3-hour long production status meetings. It was not unusual to receive daily calls from the floor supervisors saying they were short parts in the kits we sent down.

When we made mistakes, we found the problem too late in the process. Since we released up to a week's worth of kits to the floor at a time, if the shop floor operator had a problem with a part, or lost a part, they would simply steal it from the next kit creating a new shortage in an unrelated kit. This would cause constant arguments between the stock room and the shop floor over whose fault it was. In addition, if scrapped parts were not entered into the material requirements planning (MRP) system (or batched up whenever the supervisor had time to enter them), we would run out of parts since the system thought we had them creating shortages.

The longer it took to change a machine over from one lot to the next, the larger the batch of boards we would run through it. The batch process was considered more efficient, and we were mainly measured on machine utilization and earned hours. There was a sea of rolling racks of various board types on the floor in corresponding unfinished stages as it progressed through the shop, making it very difficult to track down a specific customer order (Figure 1.5). As the batches grew,

Figure 1.5 Batched up electronics assembly area.

Figure 1.6a Dip inserters.

Figure 1.6b Wave solder machine.

the time it took to move the boards through the factory grew as well. It would take so long to cycle the boards through; we would fall far behind on our delivery dates, which then required frequent and long production meetings where we would pick and choose the lots we had to expedite, based on the most vocally upset customers, or the lots we thought we could get processed the quickest so first-in-first-out (FIFO) was completely lost. This created constant problems on the shop floor as they were told to stop one order in midstream and work on another super-hot one.

After all the parts were inserted (see Figure 1.6a), the boards were wave soldered (Figure 1.6b) on a massive machine (monument), and then inspected by several people, to fix all the problems

Figure 1.7   Slide line.

the machines created. Some boards were so bad we sent them to what we called the hospital or rework area to be fixed. Many manufacturers have specially designated areas where parts or products are reworked, and they build hospital areas into their processes or what some call virtual rework cells into their factory layouts. We create "hospital areas" because we assume we can't fix the design or root cause problem, so we plan for rework in our schedules and parts issued to the floor. When the schedule and quality became really, really, bad and we were so far behind, we would be sitting in a production meeting and the production manager would say, "Let's set up a slide line!" (Figure 1.7).

When we first heard this, we all asked, "What's a slide line?" He explained that a slide line was a temporary line we put together with stand-up/walking workstations. The line had two adjustable tracks that ran down the length of the line. The circuit board would fit in these tracks and slide from person to person. Each person had four- to six-parts bins they would pull from and insert into the board and then slide it to the next person.

The fascinating part of this story is we could produce boards so much faster this way than using all these expensive machines. Many times, we would catch up our customer orders within two to three weeks. This line also had virtually no rework and thus did not need the hospital area. We didn't know it at the time, but we were utilizing what we now know as one-piece flow or what is today called a Lean line.

Of course, once we caught up with our production schedule, the team would go back to batching all the parts through the machines again. When I look back, I now realize how inefficient that was. Once we fell behind on production again, someone would suggest during a production meeting that we set the slide line up again. Why did we do this? Why didn't it occur to us to just keep the slide lines set up and running?

In retrospect, it was because we had a significant investment of time and money in the old equipment and systems. The finance team would never let us abandon equipment that had not even been fully depreciated. We had to meet machine utilization and overhead absorption metrics. The accountants didn't want us to make significant reductions to inventory at the time because it would hurt our profitability. In addition, previous managers had spent significant time developing

ROIs to justify all the capital equipment purchased and they weren't ready to abandon it, including job descriptions, training, and reporting all built around this type of batch process system. It was our investment in these capital-intensive systems that prevented standardizing the slide line type of assembly.

During this time, there was a video released in 1989 called <u>Business of Paradigms</u>,[11] by Joel Barker. And in 1991, <u>The Machine That Changed the World</u>[12] was published by Jim Womack and Dan Jones. It was a five-year MIT study of the automotive industry. After all our managers read this book and watched the paradigm video, we started to realize we could make changes to our processes and obtain significant improvements. In the end, we created a model Lean site that was benchmarked by Harley Davidson and other companies for high-performance work teams (HPWTs) and Lean systems.

Results: One-piece flow works much better than batch. One-piece flow resulted in eliminating hundreds of carts, and we no longer needed to store inventory. This improved our productivity by over 40%, reduced our throughput time by 90%, and freed up more than 50% of our space in manufacturing. We also eliminated the two-floor stockroom building, stopped issuing kits which had to ride up and down the elevator, and had room to put all the materials on the floor reducing searching, firefighting, and expediting. We managed 80% of our shop floor production outside the MRP system.

Lesson Learned: We don't always realize when we are thinking Lean, and if we do, it doesn't always occur to us to standardize on it. Our current accounting and measurement systems often prevent us from considering one-piece flow. Large batch sizes result in longer lead times and increased work in process (WIP) inventory. It is often difficult to identify defects in products in batch systems, and when one is found, it requires finding and checking the rest of the batch that is normally bad as well. Don't let the old batch systems, MRP, enterprise resource planning (ERP), financial systems, or batch philosophy prevent implementing Lean systems.

Counter Bagger Story[13]

This story involved an expensive piece of capital equipment that automatically counted out screws for the kits issued to the floor and then automatically put them in plastic bags and sealed them. It was called a counter bagger machine. A year or so prior, the previous director put an ROI together and convinced upper management to purchase this equipment. The eight-foot high, six feet by six feet wide counter bagger was purchased and installed in the only area it would fit, which was on the first floor of the stockroom.

In the ROI justification, the plan was to save a person and speed up operations. However, since the machine wasn't in the main flow, only one person really knew how to run it, and it frequently broke down or did not work properly; it virtually was never used. It was already in need of maintenance with no money in the budget to fix it, and the person it was supposed to save ended up standing and watching the machine run in case it broke down, jammed, or occasionally sent parts flying everywhere.

The machine wasted a lot of valuable space and required the stockroom person to pull the boxes of hardware, put them on a cart, transport them down the elevator, move them to the counter bagger, and then wait for the person to run the machine. He would then have to take all the parts back up the elevator to match up the bagged parts with the kits and then put the boxes of hardware away in the stockroom. Once the kit was completed, it had to be taken back down the elevator to the Mini-Trieve robot picker area and wait for the final parts to be pulled.

When the process was analyzed, we discovered we could count and bag the parts faster by hand. We decided to request the machine be sold or scrapped. The previous director heard of our request and protested to management. He could not understand why no one wanted to use this time-saving machine. Finance determined it could not be scrapped or sold as it wasn't depreciated enough to be written off. I was then threatened with the loss of my job by this director if I continued down this path.

Since the first rule of a change agent is to survive, I decided to keep the machine, but it was never used. I ended up running several point kaizen events in the stockroom but finally discovered we were wasting our time as the end goal was to simply eliminate it. Eventually, as the factory transitioned to a Lean environment, the whole stockroom went away, and we eventually sold the machine.

Lesson Learned: Introduction of automation and new software does not always solve the problem. Automation does not always free up people and in some cases results in more people. Don't add machines wherever they will fit; put them where they belong in the flow. We should never have to stand and watch a machine to make sure it doesn't break. The first rule of a change agent is to survive. You can't make change happen if you get fired! "Pick the hills you want to die on!" Point kaizen events can often be avoided when one takes time to step back and review the overall system.

Dealing Directly with Toyota[14]

During my time at AlliedSignal, back in the TQ days, there was a story about our spark plug division. They wanted to sell their spark plugs to Toyota. Toyota insisted on receiving samples prior to deciding whether to utilize them as a supplier. The company pulled the best samples out of its production lot and sent them to Toyota. Toyota analyzed the samples and told them they would not purchase their product because their overall quality system was poor. They asked if any of the spark plugs failed to meet the specs. Toyota said they all met the specs. So, what was the problem?

Toyota responded the problem was found when they completed testing of the random sample of spark plugs. From the testing results, they were able to determine the order in which they were produced. They also noticed that the process was not under control owing to the deviations of each individual part to the centerline of the spec. This means that the process capability was poor and the spark plugs at any time could have gone out of spec. The sample showed that they were far from a process that was under control and could maintain zero defects and thus too risky for Toyota.

Lesson Learned: Batch systems typically have little control over their processes. The emphasis is placed on meeting a specification using inspection, experience, or statistical process control (SPC) versus developing a capable process with a combination of people, material, and machines designed to make good parts all the time with zero defects.

Placing Orders with a Japanese Supplier[15]

During my time at AlliedSignal, we ordered parts from a Japanese supplier. One of the normal purchase orders clauses-imposed quality criteria, which stated lots of parts shipped had to be 97% good parts. The Japanese supplier shipped 3% of the parts in a bag labeled bad parts. When asked why, the Japanese supplier said they did this to meet our 97% acceptable parts criteria.

Lesson Learned: Be careful what you ask for. Insist on a 100% defect-free product.

United States versus Japan: How They Deal with Quality with a Tier 2 Supplier[16]

A company located in the Chicago area, which was a tier 2 automotive supplier, experienced problems with their production line, which supplied critical engine components. The problem turned into delinquent deliveries and broken promises to their customers. One of the customers was at the time a big three US automotive company and the other was Honda. Both customers scheduled visits with the company to find out firsthand what the problem was and how they were going to resolve it. Several of company staff were charged by senior management with preparing a first-class PowerPoint™ presentation designed to get them out of this mess.

The US customer arrived and was taken to a conference room filled with delicious, assorted breakfast items. The Company presented their PowerPoint™ to the US customer, describing the problems with late deliveries and the corrective actions planned. The customer was given lunch followed by a quick tour of the line and returned home satisfied with the explanation received and root cause and corrective action items the company was undertaking.

Honda visited the next day. The company took them to the conference room filled with the same delicious breakfast spread and stated their intentions to go through the same PowerPoint® presentation. Honda told them to forget the presentation and take them to the floor to show them the cause of the problem. The company really didn't know the root cause of the problem and that became obvious as Honda ran them through the 5 whys tool. Honda found what the company claimed to be the root cause of the US customer, was just a symptom of the problem. Honda worked with this company for three days to discover the true root cause, suggested countermeasures, and then helped the company implement corrective actions to fix the problem so it would not come back.[17]

Lesson Learned

- You can't fix problems with PowerPoint® presentations, by reviewing reports in your office, or by listening to what someone else thinks are the problems. This is known as death by PowerPoint.[18]
- If you want to understand what is going on as a manager or leader, you must experience the problem firsthand by going to the floor (throughout the book, we refer to the shop floor or where the action is happening as the Gemba) to see the problem firsthand.
- Use the 5 whys (described later in this book) to challenge assumptions and separate the symptoms from the real cause of the problem.
- You will know when you have fixed the root cause if the problem never returns.
- Supply chain managers must visit suppliers to certify that their processes are under control, and they follow a problem-solving model based on fact.
- Suppliers should continuously work on innovative solutions to reduce inventory and project costs.

Toyota #1

Toyota dethroned General Motors as the world's number one automaker in worldwide vehicle sales in 2008[19]; however, Toyota has then been plagued with a series of recalls. They were exonerated for their most publicized recall by NASA in February 2011,[20] which was unintended acceleration, but the recalls continued showing that even the number one implementer of the Lean production system is not totally there yet. They were also cleared from the acceleration problem caused by an improper floor mat installed at a Toyota dealership. Toyota takes these recalls very seriously.[21] This book is not about Toyota but focuses on the business and production system that Toyota has best exemplified. The Toyota Production System has been proven very effective for all companies that have properly implemented it; however, Toyota will readily admit that they still have much room for improvement. We encourage companies not to try to copy Toyota as it will not be successful. However, understanding and implementing the principles works. They have since dethroned GM as the #1 manufacturer in the United States.[22]

Big Company Disease

The stories outlined earlier show that, prior to implementing Lean, manufacturing entities were ignorant about their processes. In many cases, the processes were poorly documented, if at all. They do, however, show that Lean solutions result in significant improvement. Most batch-based organizations are designed in functional silos where executive leadership is located far from the manufacturing floor with most of their time spent in meetings. The leaders have no time left to walk the floor (Gemba) where the value creation takes place.

Most leadership teams we visit do not have a clear understanding of their business delivery systems (value streams) or the interconnectivity of their processes and have difficulty giving tours by themselves. In today's literature, this is referred to as big company disease. The following are the worst symptoms of this disease[23]:

1. Employees do not know who their customers are or, if they do know, may not think of the external customer as their number one priority. They are more concerned with internal politics and pleasing their boss. Employees don't realize their customer is the next process with specific expectations.
2. People can't do anything because they are always in meetings. Meetings are not run effectively, people show up late, don't come to any conclusions, actions aren't recorded, and there is little or no follow-up.
3. The company has more than five layers from the front line to the president and is slow to respond to any type of challenge, leadership initiative, innovation, or customer feedback. People laugh, when new goals are announced, as being impossible to meet. The overall organization lacks structure and accountability.
4. The company hires consultants to do all their strategic planning.
5. Companies hire consultants to identify, solve problems, and facilitate large change initiatives.
6. The budgeting process takes over a week and, in some cases, three to six months, with long email strings, and in the end, finance dictates the budget resulting in thousands of wasted hours of analysis and meetings throughout the company.
7. The company reacts to its employee's opinions and assumptions and makes shoot-from-the-hip (based on historical data or many times inaccurate information) decisions versus taking the time to go to the floor to discover the true facts and collect data. It is common for leaders to have to retract or revise something said to their boss about a problem or situation incorrectly explained to them from a lower level subordinate.
8. Complacency sets in as managers focus on the past and present instead of focusing on the future. These companies average less than one suggestion per month or even year per

employee or simply don't know their suggestion implementation rate per employee or they "mandate" so many suggestions per employee per month. Employee engagement/empowerment is not regarded as important as this is management's job. There is no feedback or follow-through on suggestions.

9. It is easier to order a new part than try to find it on the shelf, in the cabinet, on the line, or in the stockroom. In the office, you run out of room to store all your office supplies and your desk is overflowing with paperclips. You need to order another file cabinet or hard drive to store your emails. It takes you longer than 10 seconds to find a specific file on your computer.

10. Authority, accountability, discipline, company loyalty, and respect are all replaced by the desire for power at the expense of your employees and customers. In this environment, employees (many times middle or upper management) are not customer focused. Managers are extremely territorial and on occasion intentionally sacrifice a customer's shipment to make another manager look bad or to get revenge.

11. People are seen as expendable, and the company lays people off as a way of controlling capacity or reacting to spikes in customer demand.

12. Build mezzanines, add warehouse space, or install carousels to store your inventory and you physically count it once a year or more.

13. Contract a service to water your plants.

14. Have a minimum percentage outsourcing policy which must be adhered to regardless of the cost.

15. Measure your Lean progress by how many point kaizen events you have each year, and you can become a certified Lean master after participating in and/or leading a certain number of kaizen events. The Lean master is responsible for all Lean results and to implement all the Lean projects and activities. In some cases, improvements wait to be implemented until a point kaizen event is scheduled.

16. Employees start late, leave the plant early, and come back late from breaks.

17. Weeks are spent preparing for the president's visit or the Team clean up just before a senior leader arrives and creating a path through the factory for the president to travel.

18. Salesmen are paid commission on sales dollars only—there is no margin component. The true product costs are not known, as many costs are hidden.

19. Competition is not benchmarked. Business metrics, such as product costs, market share, and win rates are not known or tracked.

20. You have finally completed your Lean initiative.

We hypothesize that big company disease starts at the point where leaders switch from running a small company, where they all know each other and each is wearing many hats, to running a company that grows to a point where one hat is assigned for a specific department, and they no longer perceive they are responsible for multiple hats or the overall value stream. This normally starts between 5 and 15 employees.

The goal with Lean is to get back to basic management fundamentals. We need to restore the core values of company loyalty based on employees gaining domain knowledge of the business, where supervisors are training their team members how to do the job, we develop our leaders by promoting mostly from within, and start insourcing versus outsourcing our products and services.

In the words of Professor Feng Chen[24] of Jiao Tong University: Lean is a systematic and long-term management philosophy rather than large ROI projects. Successful

Lean activities never come from standard textbooks and must depend on problem-solving by expert teams involving internal staff from different departments and different levels, and external consultants who have many experiences from other companies.

"Toyota fears complacency and Big Company Disease above all else. They constantly challenge the status quo each day and worry about who is going to catch up and if they can't figure out about whom to worry, they worry they can't worry."[25] In Japan, they call it "the arrogance that comes from success which leads to complacency and ultimately corporate failure."[26]

Lesson Learned: Toyota embraces their no layoff policy as a fundamental operating principle. This policy is not guaranteed but is only in place because of every team member's daily continuous improvement. Visitors to Toyota plants often write stellar trip reports regarding what they have seen. Lean practitioners realize it is the system behind what we see at Toyota that must be studied and understood. It is this system which makes Toyota successful, and every employee understands and practices this.

Lifetime Employment

Many companies sponsor plant visits and most of the companies show well in tours. However, is any US company willing to go back to the days of lifetime employment, develop leaders with a watchful eye, continually pull 80% of improvement ideas from the front line, and spin off employee big idea teams that meet on their own time and report to the board of directors, and not be totally dependent on bankers? If not, can any company really succeed at installing a system and reap results like Toyota?

We asked Russ Scaffede[27] former plant manager and VP of Toyota for his opinion on this subject:

As for lifetime, employment it is interesting. No, I do not think a management team needs to offer lifetime employment to be successful, however, I do think they need to offer some form of understanding as to what it would take to keep lifetime employment. What I found interesting when I joined Toyota directly was a statement given to every employee when we joined during our assimilation week.

Nate Furuta[28] told us, "I know you have all been told the Japanese have Lifetime employment. Well let's be clear, that could not be further from the truth. What we, Toyota offer (this was in 1988 so not sure today) was if the company is making a profit, you have a lifetime employment opportunity. But understand clearly, if at any time the company is not making a profit all bets are off. There is no company in the world that can offer lifetime employment when they are not making a profit. Therefore, when you leave this week's assimilation the more you contribute to continuous improvement and use the TPS to foster waste elimination, the more you will have a job for life and so will your sons and daughters."

This is a far different contract with the team than most US companies make with their employees. Most say no one will lose their job by working to eliminate waste or reduce over processing. This sounds good; however, it leaves the door wide open for the first downturn or non-improvement reason, and the company can downsize even if still making a profit.

If I am not mistaken, Toyota has gone well above and beyond. Even during these last downturns, I do not think they have had a layoff. They have utilized several short work weeks and sent people to school and other industries; however, I have not heard of one layoff in the United States.[29]

The other element along with this I find even more critical is the 100% promotion from within on the floor up to and including at least the plant manager and most of the manufacturing engineers. This is the only way to keep a great system learned and fully understood. Learn as a team member, team leader, group leader, assistant manager, etc.

Again, most US companies use the floor as a training ground or look for college graduates that are always changing. In fairness to the Big Three, there was a labor agreement back in the 1970s that had floor people begin losing seniority if they went to a management position. The main motive of this system was to gain seniority, so if we have a layoff, I am up the totem pole far enough to keep my job. Most of the great floor leaders began refusing to fill supervisory positions so going to the outside was the only option.

The late James Bond, former college professor and Toyota recruiter stated: "Toyota strives to identify and develop great people within the organization who will gain skills (technical and soft or "task vs. people" which is a central theme to this series) necessary to meet the next challenges for them within the organization. Many courses are offered to enhance required skills for the current or next challenge."[30]

How Does Toyota Handle Downturns?

Listed in the following text are some anonymous posts during the great recession in 2008 from LeanBlog.org.[31]

I work for Toyota (TABC) in Long Beach, California. Production was down by more than 50% and to some departments even more. The extra manpower is undergoing training and skills upgrade which they say would benefit Toyota in the long term. Everybody hopes there would be no layoffs in the future though we know the economy has still to see its worst. As for Toyota, "adversity doesn't create character, it reveals it." Let's see what the company is really made of.

Another anonymous post from LeanBlog.org[28]

I am also a Toyota employee in Indiana, and we are all highly aware Toyota will have to make difficult decisions and take purposeful steps to protect the overall health of the company. Speaking only for myself, even as an hourly wage earner, I would rather take an equivalent pay cut than see any of our team laid off. There is still a bonus program in place, and I think that would be the first logical reduction to make before even considering shedding employees. Toyota has won a lot of loyalty from employees by retaining them amidst the constant negative news from other manufacturers, and the economic downturn. Priceless loyalty could just as easily be lost if the leadership decides to reverse all their frequent statements of company commitment to our employment security. There are many options TMC is currently considering, and from what I have seen in my seven years of employment at Toyota they will make the choice that best benefits the company and its employees.

Toyota Philosophy

The Toyota philosophy is embodied in the following[32] four principles:

1. Customer first.
2. People are our most valuable resource.

3. Kaizen (daily activities that cause improvement).
   a. Create a learning organization.
   b. Create a problem-solving environment.
   c. Surface problems quickly with swift solutions and countermeasures.
   d. Standard work (there cannot be improvement without a standard in place).
4. Go and see.
   a. Shop floor focus.
   b. Everyone in the organization is a resource that supports the floor (Gemba).
   c. Build and encourage a supportive culture.

CEO and Lean Results

Many large US-based manufacturers utilize Lean techniques, however, there's much room for improvement, according to the results of the following survey[33]:

- Overall, 73% of the US manufacturers actively deploy Lean or Six Sigma.
- Overall, 49% of senior manufacturing executives are satisfied with their Lean programs.
- Overall, 44% of senior execs believe their Lean programs are effective.
- Overall, 5% of senior execs rate their Lean programs as extremely effective.
- Overall, 22% of the US manufacturers don't use either Lean or Six Sigma methodologies.

The statistics are interesting and difficult to come by. The problem with these statistics is they don't tell the whole story. Lean and Six Sigma are not the same. Six Sigma is a collection of tools designed to improve quality and reduce variation in processes. These tools were first popularized by Americans: Shewhart (who worked at Bell Labs, aka Western Electric), Deming (who interned at Bell Labs), and Juran (who worked at Bell Labs), and formerly known in the United States as total quality or in Japan as total company-wide quality. Lean is a totally different tool set that emphasizes zero defects, one-piece or small lot flow, and total waste elimination. Companies cannot obtain zero defects with just Six Sigma and SPC.

In the statistics earlier, over 49% of the 73% (35%) of the companies are satisfied with their Lean programs, and only 44% of the 73% (32%) believe their programs are effective. We continuously emphasize that Lean is a journey. As stated earlier, we say "Lean is a five-year commitment that never ends." Some companies have tried Lean or Six Sigma and had bad experiences, which is unfortunate as it tends to hurt their overall improvement efforts. Many companies have started with Six Sigma tools and while enjoying, some solid results have had difficulty reducing costs, variation, and overall cycle time. In general, this is due to preeminence of batch systems with few standardized or even stabilized processes. Our experience in the United States is as follows:

- Over 20% of companies are either not exposed to Lean or struggle with it, dabble with it, or choose not to try it.
- Overall, 20% of companies try it and fail.
- Overall, 40% of companies will make ongoing attempts with Lean and may have pockets of excellence where several point kaizen events have been implemented and only some have sustained, or they are still batching within their Lean lines. We call this Lean lite.

- Overall, 15% of companies will try it with some level of success.
- Overall, 5% will truly embrace the transformation required to develop a successful Lean or continuous improvement culture.

Although these statistics may leave some asking why even attempt the Lean journey, we have found that organizations that engage in any Lean activities tend to achieve results that exceed traditional process improvement initiatives that provide a competitive advantage.

Lesson Learned: An analogy helps to drive the point. To manage his farm, the farmer must make sure he prepares the soil properly to receive the seeds. Once the seeds are planted, he must water and fertilize the plants and allow time to grow. Once the crops are grown, they must be harvested with care and then transported and sold at market. Too often, CEOs don't want to take the time to prepare the field, don't want to spend the money to fertilize or water the crops, and want the crops harvested twice as fast as the last time we grew them. Just as it is with crops, Lean needs a properly prepared field rich in nutrients to sow the seeds. Once planted, the seeds need to be nourished and developed. They must be watered and cared for. If you try to rush the Lean process, you end up with rushed results. Just as with the harvest, Lean needs cultivation as it is a shift in culture, and cultural change takes time. Lean results incurred by doing each implementation twice as fast as the prior one result in poor performance and end up dying. Lean practitioners must understand their place in the organization and what the future holds for them as they often do not receive much support from their peers who feel they are "doing all this to them!"

Supporting versus Leading

CEOs tend to support the Lean initiative rather than lead them, at least until they can see the positive outcomes for themselves. The initial part of the Lean journey generally results in pockets of excellence or about a 50% success rate from various point kaizen events spread across the organization. If the CEO does not recognize the gains obtained while learning the value of Lean and start leading by example with Lean principles and establishing a Lean culture, the organization will have a difficult time sustaining because even the best-intentioned CEO will unknowingly be driving the same old traditional yet wrong behaviors. Listed in the following are three cases:

1. If you have a CEO and board of directors that are knowledgeable in Lean principles where pull is created in the line organization for Lean results, the business will see excellent returns.
2. The CEO must buy in and lead by example to be successful. In this environment, employees look forward to sharing the improvements they have made with the CEO since his last visit.
3. If you have a CEO and board of directors that support Lean and put some of their best people into the effort, they will initially see good results but struggle to sustain them.
4. If you have a CEO and board of directors that do not understand Lean or support it properly and put people on it that are easiest to free up, they will see spotty results, not sustain them, and then blame the Lean practitioner(s) and Lean for their poor results.

Lesson Learned: Once you start down your Lean journey, every problem incurred, regardless of how old the problem may be, will be Lean's fault. The CEO must provide the unwavering commitment to Lean by leading by example, participating in kaizen, and driving the continuous improvement culture.

Process-Focused Data

The best results are recognized in organizations that develop a standard method for collecting process-focused data to monitor gains that ensure sustainment and ultimately adopt a culture of continuous improvement in accordance with the BASICS® and plan–do–check–act (PDCA[34]) models and must be coupled with leadership accountability to ensure an organization's success.

If the CEO buys in and drives Lean as part of the strategic plan and incorporates Hoshin policy deployment or bottom-up planning, they will see excellent results in bottom-line improvement. Results will be direct cost savings and significant cost avoidance. We define cost savings as those that directly hit the bottom line, whereas cost avoidance refers to items that would have increased costs had we not alleviated the need for them. In addition, the elimination of waste will decrease the process steps and reduce the opportunities for errors, thereby improving customer satisfaction and, ultimately, quality. As this Hoshin approach is rolled through the entire organization, everyone in the organization can see the value of their contribution to both the internal and external customer.

We have had companies and hospitals that, over the first five years, save literally millions of dollars, avoided hiring significantly more labor, combined, and freed up significant space, and avoided major construction projects. Notice that we quantified these results over the first five years. Many times, companies don't see huge bottom-line improvements immediately, as it takes time to embed Lean throughout the overall system: however, some projects can quickly result in large gains. Quality and service can be improved substantially. Customer and employee satisfaction improve as well. There is an investment required to implement Lean properly, but it should be more than offset (sometimes up to a 10× payback) by the benefits. Eventually, overtime is eliminated, and overhead personnel can be reduced by up to 30% or more.

Lesson Learned: Lean is not a venture to be entered into lightly. It takes a tremendous amount of training and perseverance and sometimes brute force to implement. CEOs must lead and drive Lean utilizing their best resources to obtain the best results.

What Results Can You Expect?

The authors implemented or participated in thousands of point kaizen events and system Lean implementations where companies have dramatically improved their overall order entry to cash business delivery systems. Companies that implement Lean experience the following common results:

- Reduce direct labor by 50% or more.
- Increase output to 50%–70% or more resulting in similar productivity gains (hours per unit).
- Reduce time from order entry to cash and concept to market that we also call throughput time, by up to 80%, sometimes days or weeks to hours.
- Reduce hospital emergency department wait times by 90% and increase physician productivity. Surgeons increase their cases per day in less time.
- Reduce changeover times by 50% or more, many times to less than 3 minutes or even eliminating them altogether.
- Free up millions of dollars of cash by increasing inventory turns.
- Reduce monthly accounting closings from weeks or days to hours.

We have seen:

- landscapers increase their customers per day with the same number of employees.
- reductions in indirect labor of over 30% or more.
- government, state, and local agencies provide more services with the same staff.

Lesson Learned: The results received from implementing Lean strategies are directly proportional to the investment in Lean training, tools, and culture the business invests. Lean companies eventually figure out that the real value in Lean comes from the small, yet everyday improvements from the shop floor and frontline office staff.

Organizational Philosophy

Team Leader and Group Leader versus Supervisor

At Toyota, there is a position known as the Team Leader. In the United States, this is sometimes referred to as a working Team Leader. This person is dedicated and more of a facilitator and is in a nonmanagerial position. This means he/she is responsible for training team members and making sure they follow the standard work; problem-solving; and encouraging ideas as well as implementing improvements. Fifty percent of his/her time is spent on solving day-to-day issues and the balance on continuous improvement. He/she is not responsible for discipline, pay decisions, evaluations, etc. The team leader typically manages five- to eight-team members. The supervisor in the United States would be comparable to a group leader at Toyota who manages five- to eight-team leaders.

Author's Note: There are rare instances in the United States where the teams will take on managerial duties including hiring, firing, etc., for example, Johnsonville Sausages. These became known as HPWTs. Toyota does not use HPWTs as such.

Trust and Respect for People[35]

The following examples illustrate the benefits of creating an environment of trust and respect for people within an organization. Is it easy to create this environment of trust and respect? Definitely not! It requires dedication and follow-up; however, the results are very gratifying on many levels from an organizational perspective to a passion to do the right thing. This approach creates an environment of openness and honesty and transparency in which problems are identified immediately and fixed, so they never come back.

One day there was extensive damage on a passenger door in his area. When asked what had happened, the employee indicated he was unsure. However, he did offer a potential cause. He said he may not have properly latched the door (he was very open about volunteering this information). This information was offered freely as an environment of trust and respect had been developed within my teams. Today this is called psychological safety. What can we do in the process (process focus not person focus) to prevent this I asked? The team member thought for a few moments and said, "well I could check by just pulling on the door before it left my station." Are you able to complete this extra task during takt time I asked? The team members said yes. Building consensus, I discussed this with all the other members of the team on other shifts who also agreed. Then we proceeded quickly to make changes to the standardized work and retrained everyone and this then became the new standard.[36]

I arrived at a client's facility to create a model area by applying Lean principles. After my initial discussions with the senior leadership, I went to the floor to observe the current condition. Neither my presence nor my roles or responsibilities had been communicated to the floor. As a result, there was some initial resistance (an opportunity). I immediately took all the time required to talk to every employee on all shifts in the model area and explained I was here to help them make their jobs easier and I wanted to understand the available opportunities in their areas. This took several days and long hours to complete. An environment of respect and trust began to develop. With this trust came open and honest communication that resulted in not only the surfacing problems but potential solutions as well. Observations included lack of timely leadership support and process understanding, lack of daily management interaction, and follow-up with floor operators. The floor team members had some possible solutions to some concerns they had raised which they now discussed with the senior leadership team. As part of my discussion with the senior leadership, I indicated that as systems and processes are developed, one must concurrently involve the leadership team by developing a management accountability system to ensure sustainability of these systems and processes within the organization. This accountability system is highly dependent on discipline and visual controls.

As I left, the Director of this organization said to me "James, I finally got it" and he did truly understand the Lean principles. More importantly, he realized that it's all about the people as it is the people who will provide the innovation and knowledge the organization requires to be successful.

Lesson Learned: Some people in an organization become disillusioned for a variety of reasons. One must understand first that there is a concern and then an opportunity to turn that negative into a positive. My goal has always been to create an atmosphere of trust and respect with everyone in my group and beyond. With this comes transparency and openness. I remember that there was a person with a bad attitude in my group having a negative impact on the team's morale. I spoke with this individual to try to understand what had caused this attitude to manifest itself. He told me his story in detail because of the trust and respect that developed between us. "Can't change the past" was my response. "However, you can change your own future." With empathy and support and some additional training, that person became very positive, was promoted, and became the best programmer/troubleshooter for a specific piece of equipment in the area. This individual worked with maintenance to collaboratively solve problems.[37]

Right Seat on the Bus

Unfortunately, there will be casualties, as not everyone will buy in to Lean, resulting in a need to place people on different "seats on the bus," or a different bus altogether.[38] Some people, no matter how much time you spend training and working with them, fundamentally are never going to buy in to Lean. We refer to these folks as concrete heads. As you Lean out the lines, they become very visible and can no longer hide. Generally, they are moved to another area instead of dealing with the problem head-on; essentially rewarding their behavior. They outwardly fight the effort first and then fight it behind the scenes resulting in overall reduced morale.

The benefits of dealing with these people quickly are extremely rewarding. The longer you wait to move these people to a place where they can benefit the company as an individual contributor, or off the bus completely, the less chance of success your Lean journey will have.

Many times, Lean practitioners are asked their opinion of where a person is on their Lean journey and whether they will ultimately buy in to Lean. After gaining experience in implementation, one can determine if a person is a skeptic (which is good) or a cynic (which is bad) and if they will buy in simply by the questions they ask.

So many times, we hear "you were right, I should have moved that person years ago; we lost so much time because of them." Moving someone or suggesting that it may no longer be the best company for them to work is a difficult step and should not be undertaken lightly. However, some people are just never going to accept the new Lean system. (i.e., concrete heads). They undermine Lean implementations, disrupt adoption of new processes and tools, and are like weeds and thorns growing in our field (from the earlier analogy).

Lesson Learned: The weeds and thorns must be pulled, or they will strangle and jeopardize (poison or choke) the harvest of new crops.

Author's Note: This decision should be significantly vetted. Keep in mind that a person labeled as a concrete head is still fighting the effort even after significant coaching and one-on-one sessions to work on solving their objections to the new system. If you can coach them and turn them around, they tend to become Lean zealots.

Why Implement Lean?

With all the uncertainty today, if business institutions are to survive, they will have to implement Lean. The auto industry is a good example. You can see what has happened to the companies that did not or were late to adopt Lean.[39] The auto companies started implementing Lean and Six Sigma back in the 1980s, aerospace and the military in the 1990s, and healthcare in the 2000s and now government agencies have begun to embrace Lean thinking. Even presidential candidates are beginning to use continuous improvement as part of their platform.[40] As competition increases, customers look for the best value, which embodies high quality at a lower price. Lean is about focusing on customer value and the elimination of waste. Companies leverage Lean to improve their business gaining the competitive edge by providing the highest value product at the lowest cost.

Results: A company located in Ohio was producing a large metal ring. They used to produce large batches of rings from processing the flat stock through the roller machine, then the welder and then the flanger that shaped the ring into a concentric circle. For years, they had trouble with the parts being "out of round." When they set up their first cell and switched to one-piece flow, they noticed suddenly their out-of-round problem went away. What we found was since the parts were still hot from the welder and then immediately flanged, the flanger was able to make perfect concentric circles. In addition to increasing productivity 50%, by implementing OPF they also fixed the root cause of a stubborn quality problem that had plagued them for years.

Lesson Learned: This tends to be an amazing yet normal side effect of Lean Implementations. Sometimes just by stabilizing the process and moving immediately to the next operation one piece at a time, root causes of past quality problems disappear. Remaining problems come right to the surface and must be dealt with, or the line stops.

Don't Let Government Requirements Be an Excuse

Results: In 1995, AlliedSignal (now Honeywell) made gyros for missile systems in a clean room environment (Figure 1.8). The units were produced in large batches, generally 250 pieces or more. The units went from bench to bench traveling across the clean room in no order. We were met with several challenges. We had to convince the workers to perform their jobs standing and walking versus sitting. To accomplish this, we had several operators first do their jobs sitting down (across several workstations) and then doing the same jobs standing and walking. First, we heard that very small delicate hand aerospace soldering could not be done standing up. We disproved this rather quickly. Then we watched the videos of sitting versus standing and walking. We found, analyzing the sitting versus standing videos side by side, a 30% improvement just by going from sitting to standing and walking. This convinced them to try it. Overall, we realized a 67% improvement in productivity. We also realized a bonus in quality. In the past, they had a rather large lot failure rate. The specification said that if more than two parts failed the 250-piece lot sampling requirement, they had to 100% test the entire lot. The 100% test was pretty much standard. However, after implementing one-piece flow on the entire line (which took about ten weeks), we decreased the rework to zero and started passing every lot sampling test. It was so successful, after taking the customer on a tour and showing them that we now had our processes under control, the government waived the 250-piece lot sampling requirement which allowed us to reduce the batch size. The conclusion we reached regarding the past high failure rate was that prior to one-piece flow, the parts spent about six weeks exposed to the open air. Even though it was a class 10,000 clean room (less than 10,000 particles per million) under the hoods, a small piece of dust or FOD (foreign object debris) could create problems in the unit. Now, the parts spent no more than one to two days in this environment before they were sealed. We attributed this reduction in throughput time to solving the root cause of the contamination.

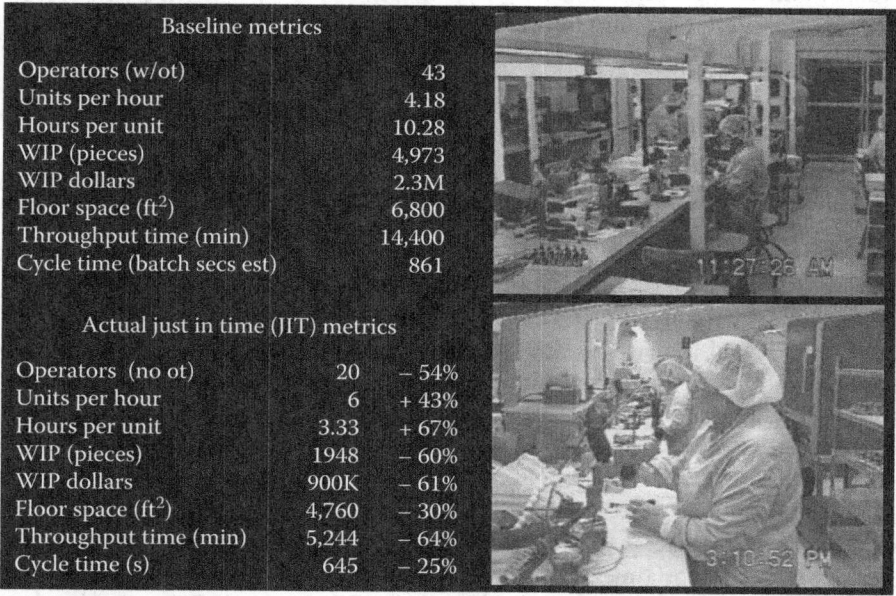

Baseline metrics		
Operators (w/ot)	43	
Units per hour	4.18	
Hours per unit	10.28	
WIP (pieces)	4,973	
WIP dollars	2.3M	
Floor space (ft^2)	6,800	
Throughput time (min)	14,400	
Cycle time (batch secs est)	861	
Actual just in time (JIT) metrics		
Operators (no ot)	20	− 54%
Units per hour	6	+ 43%
Hours per unit	3.33	+ 67%
WIP (pieces)	1948	− 60%
WIP dollars	900K	− 61%
Floor space (ft^2)	4,760	− 30%
Throughput time (min)	5,244	− 64%
Cycle time (s)	645	− 25%

Figure 1.8   Results from lean implementation.

We could keep on going with hundreds of examples of these types of results that are typical with Lean projects. We have saved companies millions of dollars in cost avoidance and hard savings by cancelling already requisitioned capital equipment, merging multiple buildings of production into one building, and eliminating the need for expensive plant expansions and the list goes on and on. While these projects sound impressive, you will learn that the real power behind Lean is in the creation of the culture that drives small improvements by the front line in the workshop or in the office, which are implemented every day.

Never Let a Good Crisis Go to Waste?

We witnessed one team in Europe that fought the Lean effort for several months after the implementation. This was the first line implemented in the plant. They shared their problems, suggested improvements, reviewed the videos with us, were trained in Lean principles and simulations, and were involved in every step of the way before and after a difficult implementation.

While the line outperformed the batch system immediately by about 18%, it took six months to work through all the problems, many of which were engineering, and design related. Numerous safety, TPM, and 5S improvements were made along the way. The line made some additional marginal improvement and realized a 25% increase in productivity. We then implemented a second line with extremely good results.

It was not until the president of the company toured the area and had a private chat with the Group Leader that their behaviors changed. The president indicated to the Group Leader that if they did not change their behaviors, he would close the plant. While we do not condone fear as a motivator, the president's comments showed the team his commitment and passion for Lean. Three months later the Group Leader had bought into the system and was actively participating in Leader as Teacher activities. Sometimes, as Taiichi Ohno stated, we have to brute force the system. Now, the line is producing 500 units per day versus an average of 255 per day in batch mode with the same number of people but with the addition of several operations not part of the batch line (i.e., washing, welding, drilling) (see Table 1.1). The team has also generated several hundred improvement ideas since the implementation.

ROI and Implementing Lean

Achieving a ROI is very important to organizations but is a very short-sighted approach. Unfortunately, many organizations utilize financial savings or the elimination of labor (bodies) as the only metric to gauge the success of their Lean implementation. However, using a financial ROI in and of itself can be a very misleading metric and is not the true goal of any Lean practitioner. While in most cases freeing up labor is a result, the ROI should include balanced metrics based upon improving customer value and eliminating waste. Since the goal of Lean is to improve process-focused metrics versus results-focused ROI type metrics, there is an immediate conflict of interest for the Lean practitioner.

Lesson Learned: However, if you get the process-focused metrics right, the results-focused metrics will take care of themselves. This is a very difficult "leap" for most executives to take since there is so much pressure on short-term results. No one wants to admit it, but in many organizations, product and office process velocity, flow, quality, safety, and inventory all take a backseat to labor dollar savings. Many times, as Lean consultants, we are asked up front, during the proposal stage, sometimes even before the first meeting, by CEOs and CFOs to stipulate how many employees we are going to take out.

Table 1.1 Lean Line Results: Batch to Flow—Month by Month Results Utilizing Process-Focused Metrics

First Implemented Line	Before	December (Adjusted)	January	February	May–August	Variance (%)
Operators	6.8	6.5	5.7	6.0	5.0	−26.5
Cell lead	0.8	0.8	0.8	0.8	0.5	−37.5
Water spider/ warehouse	–	1.0	1.0	0.5	0.5	−50.0
Total people	7.6	8.3	7.5	7.3	6.0	−21.1
Unites per day	320.0	432.0	421.0	414.0	481.0	50.3
Paid minutes per unit	11.4	9.2	8.6	8.5	6.0	−47.5
Throughput time working days	1.9	0.117	0.020	0.020	0.019	−99.0
Cycle time (minutes— estimated batch)	1.5	1.0	1.0	1.1	0.979	−34.7
Space (m²)	300.0	90.0	116.0	116.0	116.0	−61.3
Travel distance (m)	40.0	12.0	13.0	13.0	13.0	−67.5
WIP #	574.0	54.0	9.0	9.0	9.0	−98.1
Units per shift per person	42.1	52.0	56.1	56.7	80.2	90.4
Second Lean Line Implemented	Before	December	January	February	Variance (%)	
Operator + cell lead	1.9	1.9	1.5	1.8	3.7	
Units per day	145.0	222.0	193.0	216.0	49.0	
Paid minutes per unit	6.2	4.1	3.8	4.0	35.4	
Throughput time working days	3.7	0.018	0.021	0.019	99.5	
Cycle time (minutes– estimated batch)	3.0	2.0	2.3	2.0	32.8	
Space (m²)	80.0	40.0	40.0	40.0	50.0	
Travel distance (m)	19.0	9.0	9.0	9.0	52.6	
WIP #	554.0	4.0	4.0	4.0	99.3	
Units per shift per person	77.5	117.5	125.3	120.0	54.8	

Source: BIG archives.

It is extremely frustrating for Lean practitioners to go into organization after organization and be asked to stand behind an up-front-quoted ROI for implementing Lean in an area. The ironic part is that even though they are interested in implementing Lean, know they need it, they are keenly aware of their broken processes, escalating internal costs, and skyrocketing inventories, with a goal of future survival, understanding the ROI still always becomes front and center. When we as Lean practitioners ask this question, their answer can immediately plot where that company is on the Lean maturity path. Companies that truly comprehend Lean don't go after ROIs; they go after improving the process, which they know will result in improvements in quality and in financial savings to the bottom line ROI.

ROI also comes in the form of hard-dollar savings such as labor productivity, improved quality (i.e., less defects and scrap), reduced overtime, initial reduction in and then later increased use of temporary labor (for handling spikes in demand), operational savings such as a reduction in throughput time, waste in over processing, and increased cash flow via inventory reduction.

ROI can come in the form of soft results like shop floor and general improvements in organization, reduced searching, safety, morale, less absenteeism, employee retention, service and increases in market share, and customer satisfaction. Additional soft-dollar savings in the way of cost avoidance are realized by avoiding new construction costs, doing more in the same or less space, avoiding or cancelling new equipment purchases, or gaining capacity increases (which can only be recognized if the organization has a plan in conjunction with Lean to grow their business). Other soft-dollar savings may be achieved in rework reduction, higher quality products as perceived by the customer, and customer retention and/or growth.

If ROI is going to be your only main objective, we recommend that all projects engage a financial analyst (at least part time) to assist in calculating the financial ROI so it will be accepted by the organization as ROI savings in general tend to be a moving target and most companies have poor process-related baseline data. For instance, if the initiative is anticipated to provide the opportunity to increase capacity, marketing must be engaged simultaneously to develop and execute a plan to drive more business to backfill the available time freed up because of the elimination of waste; otherwise, real value will not be achieved. However, using ROI as the only measure of improvement leads to a foolhardy journey, which will not result in sustaining Lean.

One of the most challenging facets is coming to an agreement on what the ROI should be. Generally, the financial department of the organization is only interested in the bottom line, in other words, "how many employees can we lay off?" or labor savings and "when can they adjust the department's budget and show bottom-line reductions?" Executives must keep an open mind and be willing to challenge those who believe that employees must be laid off or each initiative must yield hard-dollar savings. We cannot emphasize enough; hard-dollar savings will be achieved but may not be an immediate return or immediately visible on every project. Some value streams have a longer time horizon, for instance, perioperative (surgical) services in hospitals or single product large capital equipment producers.

As organizational proponents begin to engage in Lean deployments, all eyes will be on the Lean initiative. One reason ROI is emphasized is everyone has heard of the potential improvements and successes in other industries and other service organizations. Executives rightly want to make sure that the initiatives they are sponsoring yield success. If they are hiring consultants, they want to justify the price they are paying for their services.

Lesson Learned: Organizations must realize there will and should be successes on each Lean initiative; however, the correct infrastructure and budget must be in place to train, implement, and sustain the gains. The most successful ROIs are recognized when there is a cultural shift and the entire organization, both vertically and horizontally, buys into Lean. Seeing and eliminating waste becomes how everyone in the organization does business. We must leverage our Lean tools, such as leader standard work, incorporating Gemba walks (go to the workplace and see), PDCA, operator and supervisor standard work, mistake proofing, and visual management systems, measure, and targets (key process indicators [KPIs]), as well as information and communication flows are implemented. We are often asked how long it takes to see results. There should be immediate results in flow and productivity within the scope of the effort being implemented while some overall financial results may lag.

Lesson Learned: You will know you are further down the Lean culture path when building a culture of ongoing continuous improvement every day outweighs the insistence on implementing only those perceived large ROI projects first! Large ROI projects may require large resource commitments that most organizations are not able to free up.

Short Term versus Long Term

Paybacks in the United States tend to be short-term focused. Paybacks within a year are normally prescribed. We are always worried about the next quarter's results. While the short term is important, we must convert our decision-making to a long-term focus if we are going to survive. Toyota has a long-term focus; some companies, among them Toyota, SC Johnson, Medtronic, and Unigen Pharmaceuticals, are rumored to have 100-year business plans.[41] A good example is to consider the individual purchase of solar panels. Paybacks (even with government incentives of 30%, energy credits and grants) generally span 7–12 years. If individuals used the corporate mentality of no more than one-to-two-year paybacks, there would not be one solar panel installation in the United States today.

Lesson Learned: The solution to this sole ROI focus is simple yet takes great patience to achieve. Ultimately, it is the efficiency of the process and layout that dictate how many FTEs[42] are required. Once waste is removed, the process and the layout, designed for flexing, define what one needs to effectively run that operation.

Results: In Company X, Lean lines went from eight people, 8 hours per day to three people for 4 hours per day of working time. In this case, management was accountable and worked hard to continuously improve the system after it was installed. It took more than a year to achieve the desired results and ultimately the system became more productive than even the early Lean proposals predicted.

Lesson Learned: If one focuses on improving the process, the ROI will take care of itself. Once reductions are identified, management must have the fortitude to act on facts and make the changes without laying off permanent team members.

For CEOs, patience and perseverance is the key. What is really required is upper level executive leadership to drive culture change, adoption, and deployment. Toyota did not get there in a month! It took many decades to implement TPS, and they are still working on perfecting it today. As organizations embark on their multiyear Lean journey, they will need to determine if they need or what they will accept as their ROI and how to articulate the benefits of Lean across the enterprise and to the board members to sustain ongoing cycles of continuous improvement.

Lesson Learned: Companies that are Lean no longer use ROI as the main decision-making tool or keep track of ROIs. They implement Lean because focusing on continuous process improvement is the right thing to do for their organization's survival.

Theory of Root Cause Analysis

We should introduce here the concepts of baseline, entitlement, and benchmark. The baseline process is the original process with which we start. Entitlement is when, theoretically, we have reached the best possible outcome with this process (normally considered 3× value-added time) and benchmarking is changing the fundamentals of the process, that is, instituting a new paradigm.

Toyota has a multistep approach, which included two countermeasures: (1) a temporary countermeasure, which allowed flow to continue without any impact on customer requirements or downstream processes, with employee safety always the first consideration; (2) a permanent countermeasure would be developed within a specific time frame to eliminate the observed constraint at that point in time using a structured framework that includes root cause analysis to discover that permanent countermeasure. The fact that the problem has been eliminated is because the control part of the PDCA cycle confirms that prior condition does not exist or has been eliminated. Root causes can also be eliminated as part of a paradigm shift where a new benchmark type process that changes the rules of the old process is created. (For instance, on reel to reel or cassette tapes, we had to move through the entire tape to get to a song. Now, with digital formats, we can just select the song. Since the problem no longer exists, the root cause no longer exists and the corrective action, i.e., developing a new process, has eliminated the problem. An organization moving forward to maintain their competitive advantage and survive must adopt this continuous learning by embracing this as a new way of thinking.)

We all also concur with Dr. philosophy that no problem (within the current process parameters, i.e., short of a paradigm shift) can necessarily be fixed permanently. We may install a corrective action, for example, some type of mistake-proofing device, but in the future discover how we can improve that device or implement another mistake-proofing solution upstream in the process eliminating the need for the downstream device. This does not mean that we should ever waver from our goal of zero defects.

Any type of problem-solving (i.e., PDCA) cycle is still considered under the continuous improvement umbrella. No process is ever perfect. Just as we say it is never possible to completely "Lean out" a process, that is, there is always a better way, Lean is never finished, etc. Furthermore, it should always be a goal not to just fix the process (i.e., root cause) so the problem never comes back but to, in fact, work to improve the process at the same time. Therefore, we favor the PDCA cycles over the Six Sigma DMAIC model approach.

Summary[43]

Lean is about building and improving stable and predictable systems and processes to deliver to our customers the high-quality products/services on time by engaging everyone in the organization. Combined with this, we need to create an environment of respect for people and continuous learning. It's all about people. People create the product or service, drive innovation, and create systems and processes, and with leadership buy-in and accountability to ensure sustainment with this philosophy, employees will be committed to the organization as they learn and grow personally and professionally. An integrated framework is required to ensure that Lean initiatives are successful. The components for this integrated structure would include the following:

■ Visual management
■ Information flow

- Management process (leadership)
- Measurables and targets
- Standards
- Process focus

Chapter Questions

1. What is the five-step thought process for Lean?
2. Where did Lean thinking begin? Where are its roots?
3. What results can you expect from implementing Lean?
4. What role does the CEO play in Lean transformations?
5. Explain the impact or ROI on Lean transformations.
6. What is big company disease? Does your company have it?
7. What are some differences between batch and one-piece flow?
8. Where can one apply Lean principles and tools?
9. What are five principles of the Toyota philosophy?
10. What is important to remember as a Lean practitioner?
11. What did you learn from this chapter?

Notes

1. http://rk2blog.com/2010/03/08/the-etymological-origin-of-Lean/ "In fact, it is well known that Lean was coined by John Krafcik in his 1988 Sloan Management Review article." Triumph of the Lean production system query." It is less well known that Krafcik adopted the term late in his academic career. In his early academic papers, including "Learning from NUMMI" (1986), an internal working paper of "MIT's International Motor Vehicle Program," through his 1988 MIT master's thesis, he didn't call it Lean. He called the production system used by Toyota and a small number of other Japanese automakers fragile query."
2. Lean Thinking, James Womack & Daniel Jones, ©1996 Simon and Schuster.
3. The Machine That Changed the World, James Womack, Dan Jones & Daniel Roos, ©1990, Harper Collins.
4. http://www.Lean.org/WhatsLean/Principles.cfm.
5. Pockets of excellence is an expression that refers to a line or part of a line that is far down the Lean path but overall, the plant is not Lean.
6. Dock to stock means the manager is responsible from the receipt of order on the loading dock to when the product is put away in the stock room and then when it is pulled from the stockroom to when it is issued to the floor.
7. Story by author Charlie Protzman.
8. https://www.jonnohanafinassociates.com/.
9. Story by author Charlie Protzman.
10. Story by author Charlie Protzman.
11. Video by Joel Barker, The New Business of Paradigms, ©2001. Joel Barker—Original Business of Paradigms, 1989, Charthouse International Learning, Distributed by Star Thrower.
12. The Machine That Changed the World, James Womack, Dan Jones & Daniel Roos, ©1990, Harper Collins.
13. Story by author Charlie Protzman.
14. Story by author Charlie Protzman.
15. Story by author Charlie Protzman.
16. Story by author Charlie Protzman.

17. It should be noted that problems can always come back which is why we have the CHECK in PDCA. However, the goal should be always to go after corrective actions/countermeasures that fix the problem so it never comes back, understanding that technically any problem can resurface.

18. All references to Microsoft Office products are trademarked to Microsoft Corporation.

19. Toyota holds the top spot as world's number one carmaker, The Guardian—"Toyota holds the top spot as world's number one carmaker," Associated Press, guardian.co.uk, Monday January 24, 2011, 03.47 EST.

20. NASA's Toyota study released by the Department of Transportation, February 8, 2011.

21. Toyota under Fire, Jeffrey Liker, McGraw-Hill, 2011.

22. https://www.caranddriver.com/news/a38664893/toyota-beats-gm-us-sales/#:~:text=Toyota%20and%20General%20Motors%20announced,in%20the%20fourth%20quarter%20alone.

23. Influenced by Tsuyoshi Kawanishi, legendary former CEO of Toshiba Semiconductor, Chip Management, Ten Symptoms of Big Company Disease, as compiled by Professor Yoshiya Teramoto of Meiji Gakuin University and influenced by Bob Norton, "Big Company Disease is Most Often Fatal for Startup Companies. The Top Ten Signs a Company has 'Big Company Disease,'" http://www.clevelenterprises.com/articles/big_company_disease.html.

24. Personal e-mail correspondence from Professor Feng Chen, Jiao Tong University.

25. MIT Lecturer Steve Spear who worked on the Toyota Line, CBS Sunday Morning, "Under the Hood" Reported by Anthony Mason June 24, 2007.

26. Leading the Lean Enterprise Transformation, George Koenigsaecker, CRC Press, ©2009, p. 19.

27. Correspondence with Russell Scaffede Tuesday, February 7, 2012, 7:25 PM, who is the owner of Lean Manufacturing Systems Group, LLC and Management Consulting, Vice President of Manufacturing at Toyota Boshoku America, past General Manager/Vice President of Toyota Motor Manufacturing Power Train, and past Senior Vice President, Senior Vice President of Global Manufacturing at Donnelly Corporation. Russ is co-author of the book, The Leadership roadmap: People, Lean & Innovation, along with Dwane Baumgardne.

28. Nate Furuta was appointed chairman and CEO of Toyota Boshoku America, Inc. in 2008. (TBA), headquartered in Erlanger, Kentucky. TBA is a Toyota Boshoku company and member of the Toyota Group of companies, http://mbs.cargroup.org/2008/content/view/95.

29. Toyota has not laid off one person in any country except, as of this writing, one layoff of permanent employees in Australia Altona Plant in Melbourne http://www.theaustralian.com.au/news/nation/toyota-to-march-workers-off-altona-plant-as-job-cuts-take-effect/story-e6frg6nf-12327486781, confirmed in personal correspondence with Beck Angel, 1/14/2013 20121123_Toyota Australia Media Release_FINAL.pdf, since 1950. However, temporary employees have been cut (which is why they are utilized), executives have had pay cuts, and wage freezes have been used along with attrition and buy out packages. http://www.torquenews.com/106/toyota-offering-buyout-options-us-employees—may need to revise.

30. Personal correspondence with Professor James Bond, December 8, 2012. James Bond, college professor, Toyota retiree and current international Lean consultant.

31. http://www.leanblog.org/2009/01/report-toyotas-first-layoffs-since-1950/ site and blog by Mark Graban, public domain, http://usatoday30.usatoday.com/money/autos/2009-01-23-toyota-considers-cuts_N.htm?csp=34, http://www.manufacturing.net/news/2009/02/toyota-canada-cuts-production-pay-to-avoid-layoffs.

32. Speech by Gary Convis to MWCC, 2008 annual meeting.

33. http://www.industryweek.com/companies-amp-executives/Lean-results-Lean-programs-numbers. Source: PricewaterhouseCoopers LLP based on 2008 data.

34. The BASICS® model is copyrighted by Charlie Protzman and will be explained in this book. The PDCA model stands for plan–do–check–act and is credited to W. Edwards Deming but is now believed to be credited to the CCS pre-Deming as Deming stated he didn't know where PDCA came from. Moen, R., and Norman, C., "The History of the PDCA Cycle." In Proceedings of the 7th ANQ Congress, Tokyo 2009, September 17, 2009, https://honoringhomer.net/documents/ccs-memos/.

35. Personal correspondence with James Bond dated December 5, 2012.

36. Story furnished by Professor James Bond during chapter review January 2013.
37. Story furnished by Professor James Bond during chapter review January 2013.
38. Good to Great: Why Some Companies Make the Leap… and Others Don't, Jim Collins, ©2001, Harper Collins.
39. How Toyota Became #1: Leadership Lessons from the World's Greatest Car Company, David Magee, Penguin Group, ©2007.
40. Newt Gingrich Promotes Use of Lean Six Sigma Business Strategy, https://xray-delta.com/2012/01/22/newt-gingrich-jane-jacobs-and-lean-six-sigma/.
41. Brian Gongol, 100-Year Business Plans, http://www.gongol.com/research/economics/100yearplans/.
42. FTE is full-time equivalent. It converts part-time bodies (people) to full-time equivalent bodies based on the number of hours they work. That is, 40 hours × 52 weeks = 2080 hours or one full-time equivalent body.
43. Submitted by James Bond. James Bond, college professor, Toyota retiree and current international Lean consultant—personal correspondence December 5, 2012.

Additional Readings

Balle, F. and Balle, M. 2005. The Gold Mine. Cambridge, MA: Lean Enterprise Institute.
Drucker, P. 2002. Managing in the Next Society. New York: St. Martin's Press.
Goldratt, E. and Cox, J. 2004. The Goal. Croton-on-Hudson, NY: North River Press.
Henders, B.A. and Larco, J.L. 1999. Lean Transformation. Richmond, VA: The Oaklea Press.
Iverson, K. 1997. Plain Talk. New York: John Wiley.
Jennings, J. 2002. Less Is More. New York: Penguin group.
Liker, J.K. 2005. The Toyota Way. New York: McGraw-Hill.
Liker, J.K. 2011. Toyota Under Fire. New York: McGraw-Hill.

Chapter 2

Lean Assessment and Health Check

> It's difficult to appreciate the value of others when your own self-assessment is overvalued.

Author unknown

This chapter gets at the "heart" of why we wrote this series. So many companies think they are "Lean" today and aren't even close. It is common to hear, "Oh, we have improved enough! We don't need Lean anymore." Many have checked off the Lean box and are looking for the next fad. Many companies are repackaging Lean (like Six Sigma did with Total Quality) under different names such as World Class Manufacturing but there is no world beyond Lean. Even the Shingo organization, the highest recognition one can receive today, realized it needed to revise its model to focus more on building a Lean culture, learning organization, and sustaining. It is a journey many have been on since the early 1980s with only a few having something to really show for it. For those that really understand it, it is a journey of continuous improvement that never ends. We hope you will take time to really think as you read this chapter, uncheck your Lean completed box, and reflect on your true opportunities that lay ahead.

Lean Assessments

Assessment can be defined broadly as an appraisal or evaluation with respect to worth. There are many facets to assessing or evaluating the adoption or deployment of Lean. Whether your organization has just embarked on the Lean journey or has been at it for several years, most organizations find that they want to assess where they are on the Lean maturity curve and the benefits they still have left to achieve. The purpose of this chapter is not to be prescriptive but to make you think.

There are some simple assessment tools one can use to begin the process. Our experiences are that many companies, worldwide, talk Lean but are not truly Lean. Normally, it is a check-off

DOI: 10.4324/9781003185772-2

box on someone's list so they can say that they completed their Lean objective for the year. In the words of Professor Feng Chen[1] of Jiao Tong University:

> Many first- and second-tier companies now implement Lean, not because they believe in Lean but because their customers want them to do Lean. Their big bosses (executives) really don't know how to implement Lean, and some can't keep Lean going year after year. Many big bosses prefer BIG ROI projects instead of continuous improvements. Most of these companies lack clear performance goals and motivational plans, which reduces their growth and the number of employees especially frontline workers. Therefore, people worry that they won't have a big salary increase or career development year after year. At a lot of companies, people are more dependent on the Lean guys for standard answers from Lean, instead of working with the Lean guys and finding out the answers themselves; therefore, frontline people end up trusting more on their experience and working habits instead of real standard work.

Lesson Learned: My experience is that any sensei worth his or her salt will never tell you how much they know about Lean but will tell you how much they have yet to learn.

Take the Lean Assessment Quiz Below

1. Do you plan, predict, and measure your production output? On an hourly basis? How well do you perform? Are you 100% accurate?

   It is surprising how many companies do not measure their real production output each day much less to the hour. If they do measure it, seldom can we narrow it down to the individual product line, and even if we can, it is often impossible to determine the true amount of direct and indirect labor tied to each line. It is very difficult to get to total labor hours per unit or units per day per operator (especially if operators are moved between lines).

2. Do you continuously improve your manufacturing standards? Do you have real standards? Written down? With times for each step? How often do you revise them weekly? Monthly? Quarterly? Yearly?

   A true standard has three components: sequence of operations, cycle time, and standard work in progress. If one is continuously improving, the (written) standards should be changing at the same rate. Note: This is not the same as traditional cost accounting standards, i.e., earned hours.

3. Do you have 100 inventory turns each year? Do you have 20? Do you have 6? Do you even have four?

   Most companies average four to eight inventory turns. We shoot for 12 the first year for a Lean line, then 20 the next year. However, if one is heavy into aftermarket-type sales, we would expect the finished goods inventory to run much higher (i.e., until the company could supply parts the same day to the customer directly). We would also expect to have safety stock for critical components.

4. Do you have >20% total overall productivity gains per year? How about 6%? How about 1%?

   World-class companies tend to average 6%–8% year-over-year productivity gains. This may come from supplier price decreases, from joint value engineering with suppliers, or through shop floor or office continuous improvement. Are your suppliers' true partners with you in the marketplace? Do you use design for assembly techniques to reduce cost? Lean starts with engineering and product development.

5. Is your operator (shop floor or office worker) morale over 90%? How about 50%? Do you even measure it? What is your perfect attendance percentage? What is your average absenteeism percentage? Have you created an environment where employees look forward to coming to work every day?

   There is a tool available from the Cynefin Company called Sense Maker® which can help find out what your employees are really thinking. It doesn't measure morale or culture and it will provide much more valuable feedback to help change the culture versus a typical employee survey.

6. Do your employees provide two to four suggestions or more each month for small improvements? Can your operators work on the line without needing supervision? Would they recommend your workplace to their family members? Do your operators (shop floor or office workers) have control over 20% of their pay? 10%? 6%? Do they know your current business outlook? Do they know your latest three to six months booking status? Do they know the industry trends?

   The idea for this is to determine if your operators get some sort of return based on their overall improvement ideas, company performance, and work ethic exhibited.

7. Do you have >95% customer satisfaction? Do you measure it? Do you know if your customer is telling you the truth or are they telling you what you want to hear?

   This question should be self-explanatory. However, we find that most companies don't really measure customer satisfaction. Many companies, especially websites, have all sorts of surveys but the true measure of customer satisfaction, assuming there is competition, is do they come back to buy or use your product or service, and do they recommend you to their friends? These companies don't need surveys as they know they are doing a good job. Do you have products customers really want to buy? Do you engage your supply chain in engineering the products?

8. Do you have 100% on-time delivery? If yes, is it to the customer's requested date? Or you're mutually agreed to date? How is your quality? Do you ever sacrifice quality to get your delivered product out the door? (Whether it is a physical product or information?) How do you measure quality? Is it to the customer specification or is it to what the customer expects or both? What are your internal defects? Do you really measure them? What is your first time through or right the first-time yield? Do you measure it? On any process in the organization? Is quality more important on the floor or in the office? How is your customer service? Do you have a customer service department? (Isn't everyone in your organization really a customer service provider?)

   Lean companies measure their own time delivery based on their customer required date, not the negotiated delivery date. If the customer really wanted it yesterday, they would try to figure out how they could meet that expectation.

9. Could you react instantaneously to a 20% increase (or decrease) in customer demand? How many full-time permanent people would you have to lay off?

   This question delves into your supply chain, risk planning, and purchasing practices.

10. Is your production system flexible enough to reprioritize customer orders? Within the same day?

    This question investigates how close your system is to just in time (JIT) along with its flexibility.

11. Can you walk around the office or production floor and immediately know what is going on? Do you know if they are on plan (i.e., meeting the schedule)? without asking anyone.

Do you know if there is a problem anywhere in the organization? without asking anyone. Are people accountable in your organization? Do you have to constantly follow up?

In many organizations, people are just not held accountable. There are no positive or negative consequences for their actions. Blame is easily shifted, and excuses are abundant. Lean organizations do away with excuses and focus on doing what they say they are going to do. Accountability starts within each of us, individually, first. We should never feel entitled or that the company owes us something. We should earn our pay each day and be loyal to our companies. I remember looking around the office and being the only one left there still working. I used to ask myself why am I the only one here? I concluded that I was being held accountable, but I wasn't holding my direct reports to the same level of accountability.

12. Do you have a written policy and procedures, that is, standard work or work standards, for everything you do? (To the extent it makes sense.) When was the last time they were updated? Is everyone trained in them? How often are they updated? When was the last time you updated them?

    The only way to create a learning organization is to document everything you do. Otherwise, when individuals leave, their knowledge goes with them. A Lean system can only sustain if it can outlive the departure of key individuals, including the CEO. If you are continuously improving, your procedures should be constantly adapting as well.

13. Does your frontline employee know what the organization's top five goals are? Do they know your top five customers? Do they know your top two competitors? Do they have goals that are directly tied into (connected to) your goals? How vested are your employees in the organization's goals and your objectives? Are they part of the family? Do you trust them? They should be working with you and have goals and actions directly tied to the CEOs, so they know how what they are doing is contributing to the overall good of the company.

14. Do you have discipline in your organization? Do you have a chain of command? Do people follow it? Can your people, the next management layer down, take you to the next level your organization is shooting for? If not, do they know? Do they have a one-, three- or five-year development plans with necessary actions to fill any gaps in their knowledge, skills, or abilities?

    If you don't have discipline everyone does whatever they want to do or how they want to do it. Many companies lack discipline. Employees come and go as they please. They leave early for breaks and get back late. They line up at the time clock 15 minutes early. They let mistakes go unnoticed. They don't follow the standard work and prefer to do things their way. This leads to firefighting. It makes it very difficult to run a company.

    Discipline is not a bad word. Discipline means we follow company policies and standards (the assumption being they are all meeting legal requirements).

15. Do you still push for end-of-the-month numbers? Do you pull orders in from future months to make the numbers? Do you have separate numbers you report to corporate? (If you are a corporate staff reading this, it should tell you something.)

    With Lean, we strive to level load the business. Therefore, we work to meet the end of the day or end of each hour numbers versus end of the month. This way, we can react real time to problems, implement countermeasures, and make the numbers versus living with the bathtub curve (Figure 2.1). This gives us shipment linearity. The bathtub curve is a vicious cycle. Every month, we ship very little out in the first two to three weeks and then push to get it all out at the end of the month. We ship everything that can be possibly shipped. To do this, we end up pulling in parts and orders from the next month. Then when we make the end-of-the-month numbers, we spend the next two to three weeks building our inventory backup to start the process all over again.

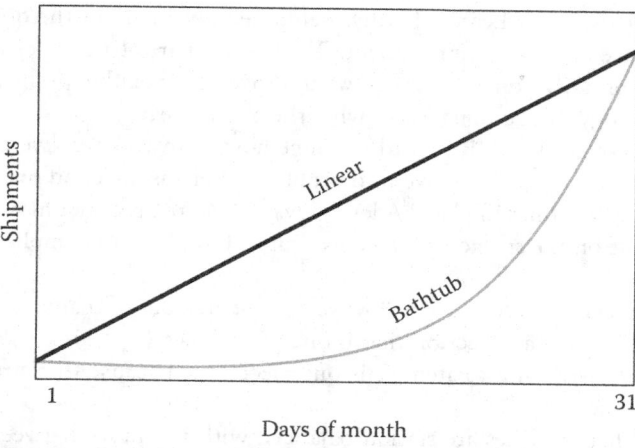

Figure 2.1   Bathtub curve.

16. Do you use the plan–do–check–act (PDCA) cycle or some other problem-solving model religiously? Do you truly root cause problems/mistakes so they never come back?

    Integrating PDCA and A3 Thinking into the organization is the only way to get rid of the vicious firefighting cycle.

17. Have you completed your Lean initiative? Did you reach your goal to have 80% of your sites Lean in three to five years? If not, when will you be done?

    If you answered yes to any of these questions, you are not exhibiting true Lean thinking. Lean is a journey that never ends. It is not an initiative or project. It is a culture of continuous improvement, and daily development and engagement of your people.

18. Do you know the three components of standard work? Do you have leader standard work that you personally follow? How much time do you personally spend on the floor when you are in a plant? 100%, 75%, 50%, 25%, or do you get your debriefings via PowerPoint presentations?

    If you don't know the answer to the first question, you have no basis for improvement in the organization, much less any chance of creating a learning organization. The only way to really status a plant is to walk around and observe what is really happening. The financials can be reviewed anywhere nowadays with the Internet. To sit in a meeting reviewing the financials just doesn't make sense anymore. If you want to know what is really going on, you must go to the floor, office, area, etc., and see what is really going on. If you walk into an area and must ask someone what is going on, you are not Lean yet.

19. Do you listen to your employees' ideas, or do they go into a suggestion box? If you are the CEO, can an employee or a customer get a hold of you directly?

    If the answer to this question is you have a suggestion box, you are most probably not Lean. Some of the best ideas have died in suggestion boxes. If a customer cannot reach you directly, you are not Lean. How can you know how you are doing without direct first-hand feedback? Hearing how a customer feels about you from a salesperson is secondhand information. Every handoff is an opportunity for error and for information to be tainted. Remember the telephone game?

20. Do you have a culture where your employees feel they can speak up and give their opinions without retribution? Do you consider your employees team members?

Please notice that the word Lean is hardly mentioned anywhere in the questions above. Are you Lean? Do you have room for improvement? The hardest part of any assessment is being honest. But if we are not brutally honest, how can we improve? The next big problem with every Lean assessment is terminology. If you don't know what the words mean (i.e., visual controls, heijunka, mistake proofing, one-piece flow), it is hard to gauge how Lean you are. Even with the level 1–5 scales with descriptions for each level, we find problems. For instance, on one evaluation, it said do you have one-piece flow lines in place? A level 5 was where the product moved from batch one-piece flow lines. While on the surface, this seems simple, but it is very complicated. For instance,

- Does it mean every line is one-piece flow versus one line out of many?
- Does it mean the line has a section that is one-piece flow?
- Some people honestly think batching is one-piece flow because they are only working on one piece at a time.
- Does it mean that the lines are station balanced with inventory between each station? Or are they bumping?

We see this problem even with the term Lean. I can't tell you how many times I have heard "oh yes, we are Lean, we don't have nearly enough people we need to do the job!" We have seen companies score very high on Lean self-assessments that should have scored much lower. However, there is no real benefit in scoring unless one has a very objective measure to score against. We prefer assessments that can easily be answered with yes or no questions. When one introduces values and scores, people are more concerned about gaming the system then focusing on real improvement.

The Showcase Company

Many companies never progress much further on their Lean journeys than 5S (see Figure 2.2a) and (Figure 2.2b) and many have difficulty even sustaining this activity! (See Figure 2.3.) Other companies set up cells or what we call the illusion of Lean cells where production may at one point have flowed but now operators are batching up within the cells thus what we call fake flow or Lean batch. The areas may look good (5S) and may have production boards in place that show their output to the casual uninformed Lean observer. However, when one scrutinizes the area, one sees that there is little or no flow, operators are sitting down (see Figure 2.4) and there is significant batching, no in-process metrics, no standard work, and lots of excess inventory. Immediate signs of problems include operators going to shelves to get their own materials or moving their parts to an aisle for inspection. What seems to be very prevalent are sit-down assembly jobs where the work is totally imbalanced.

Why Assessments Are Needed

Leaders often think they understand what needs to be improved; however, the assessment will provide an objective view of the company, from an independent auditor's viewpoint. Most companies use external auditors to perform financial audits during the yearly business cycle and for ISO 9000 compliance costing US corporations billions of dollars; yet many firms are reluctant to spend funds for a Lean assessment that could provide insight to additional savings, higher inventory turns, faster cash conversion, and ultimately better customer and stakeholder satisfaction.

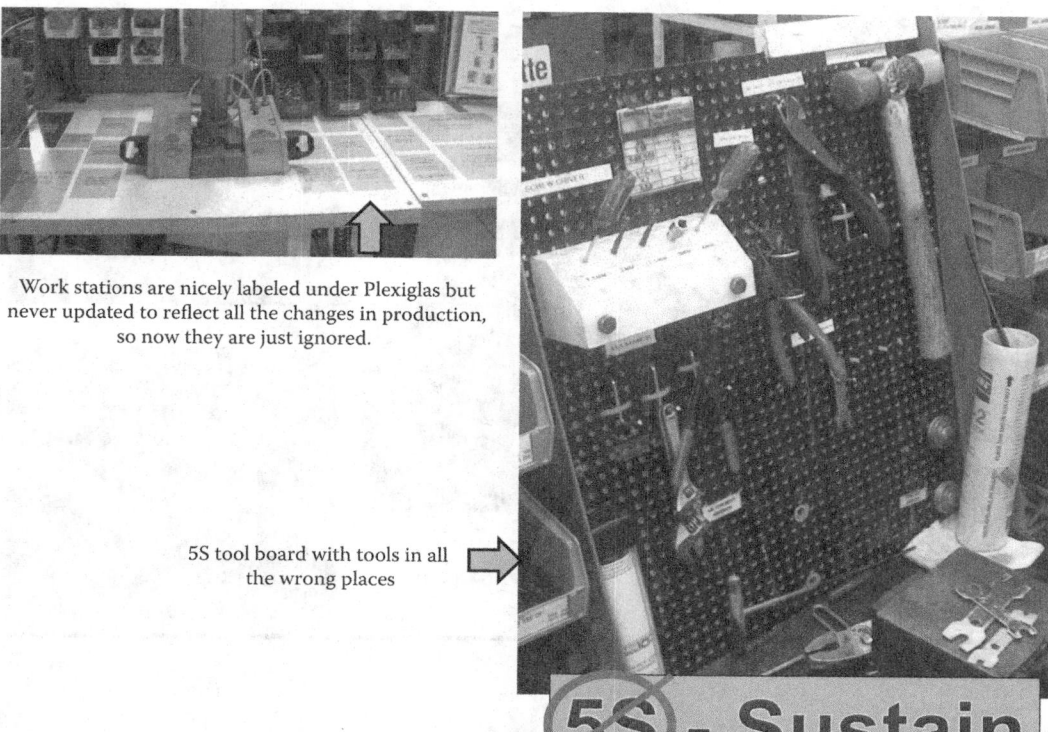

Work stations are nicely labeled under Plexiglas but never updated to reflect all the changes in production, so now they are just ignored.

5S tool board with tools in all the wrong places

Figure 2.2a   How not to do 5S.

Looks good but no labels for each tool... what goes where? Am I missing any? Some shelves labeled by machine, others have no labels.

Looks good... lots of banners, yet why are there trash bins there? What looks like machining cells are set up like isolated islands. Utilities are not flexible.

Figure 2.2b   What's missing?

Figure 2.3 Poor 5S examples.

As one moves from one Lean company to another Lean company, we find that no two companies are the same. There are many causes that drive the success of becoming a Lean organization. There is not a one-size-fits-all assessment methodology to determine the level of Lean maturity within an organization. Even though organizations and consultants have devised many ways to determine the effectiveness and pervasiveness of Lean adoption, we must caution most

Figure 2.4 What's wrong in these pictures.

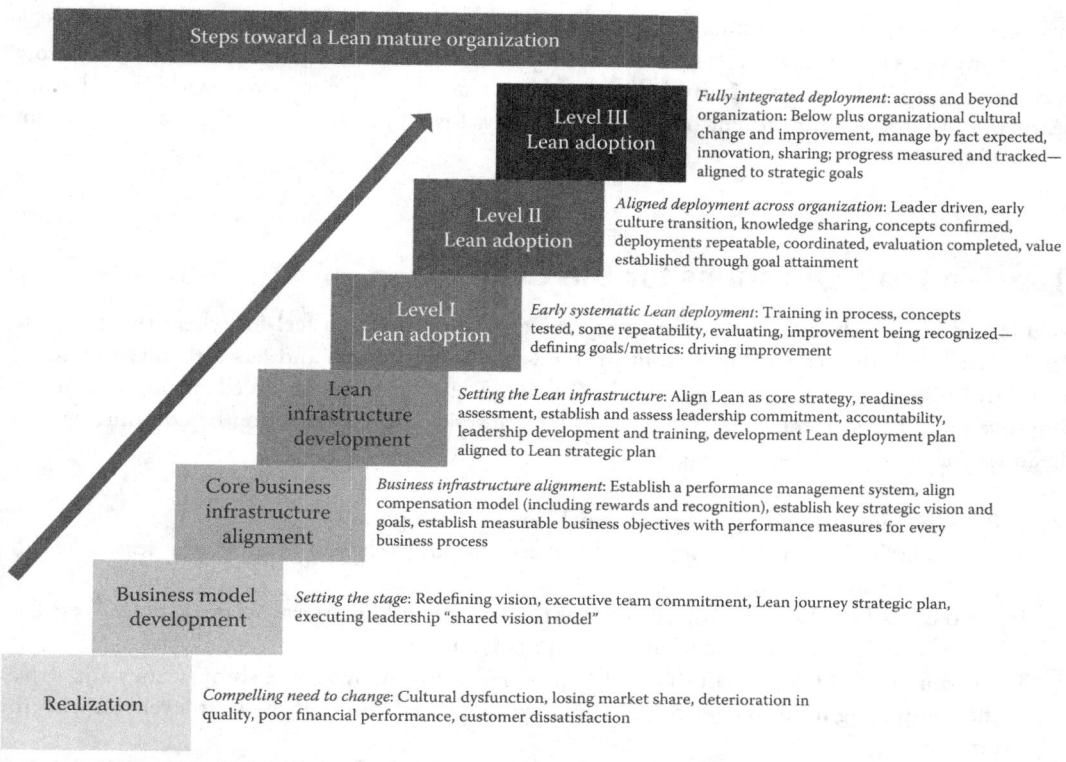

Figure 2.5   Lean maturity path.

organizations to believe that they are further down the Lean maturity path (LMP) (see Figure 2.5) than what they really are.

Lesson Learned: The farther we progress in our individual Lean journeys, the lower we tend to score ourselves on the assessments because prior to that, we find we did not even understand the criteria.

For example, at one company, the Lean specialist graded the company low on their 5S assessment because all their equipment was not freshly painted, and everything was not taped out. However, the 5S criteria for shine—calls for it to be clean (not freshly painted) and store (set in order)—says everything has its place. The fact that it was labeled versus having a tape outline really does not matter. In the opposite direction, the Lean practitioner graded the cell high on standard work because they saw forms labeled with standard work at the top of them hanging in the cell and they wanted everyone in the cell to feel good because they believed it was part of the respect for humanity principle. However, the standard work was not being followed, everyone was batching, and the standard work did not have cycle times on it; therefore, it was not true standard work anyway.

Lesson Learned: Audits should not be designed to make people feel good; they should be designed to highlight areas for ongoing improvement. This is what should make people feel good!

We run into this repeatedly. This is not meant to discourage new organizations; however, even organizations further down the LMP often find they only have pockets of excellence with the rest of their company lacking compliance. Leaders must understand that Lean is a journey and, even after many years of work, will always have more opportunities to achieve and sustain. Even Toyota has taken over six decades to attain the level of Lean maturity it has achieved, with many lessons learned and setbacks even recent ones, along the way. Listed below are some typical assessment categories:

Top Ten Lean Questions for the CEO

CEOs and leaders should carefully examine the company to gain a feel for where the company is. The company that is making a profit in line with industry peers and has difficulty providing a positive response to seven or more of the following questions has an excellent opportunity to improve margins, accelerate cash flows, and increase stakeholder satisfaction by committing to a Lean journey:

1. Rate your understanding of Lean from 1 (low) to 5 (high).
     Note: To answer the balance of the questions positively you must have at least a level 5 understanding of Lean.
2. Who owns Lean? Are Lean goals part of the annual and long-term strategic objectives? Do you have a Lean implementation roadmap? Is it current?
3. Do you utilize Hoshin planning techniques? How do you overcome complacency and drive the compelling need to change? Do you have a detailed vision of the next level you wish to obtain?
4. Do you drive Lean through the line organization or a kaizen promotion office (KPO)? Do you have a communication plan, training plan, and resource plan?
5. Is your company in the top 10% of peers in terms of financial performance? Are all major business systems, to include HR, quality management system, finance, and IT, integrated with Lean?
6. Are incentives plans aligned with Lean objectives? Do they drive ongoing continuous improvement activities?
7. Do you have a learning organization? Is standard work built into your ISO documentation?
8. Is a continuous improvement process in place and supporting the company vision? Are employees trained in continuous improvement and Lean principles? Are employees engaged in improvements at all levels?
9. Are Lean principles integrated in products and services delivered to the customers?
10. Does the leadership team fully support Lean or are they engaged and driving it?

For almost a year, the authors struggled to come up with a very simple ten-question assessment any CEO could take. The idea was that the CEO did not have to ask anyone for data or any type of information. They did not have to be familiar with any Lean terminology. But the questions would show that no matter how long they had been working on Lean, whether it is never or for decades, they had opportunities for improvement. It turned into a very difficult task based on the reasons mentioned earlier in the chapter. The underlying assumption is you must have some fundamental knowledge of Lean to even answer the questions. You don't know what you don't know.

Evaluating or Assessing a Company

When evaluating how a company is performing in Lean, one must look at assessing Lean within an organization in three categories of activities:

1. Strategic
2. Core operations that are subdivided into learning to see and work process improvement
3. Knowledge sharing and performance. Do they have a system for creating, storing, and transferring knowledge?

Author's Note: It is important to separate philosophy from tools. This goes back to our people versus task theme. The philosophy should be a constant, including the values, the mission, and the driving forces. This includes the change management aspect of the Lean roadmap. The company must eat, live, and breathe these values.

Strategic (Philosophy)

The strategic category encompasses the components that impact the organization's strategic design and is the impetus for the why behind engaging in Lean. These include evaluating the following activities:

- The system behind their Lean system. Is it robust yet flexible? Will it force ongoing continuous improvement forever?
- What is the leadership's engagement in Lean?
- Overarching purpose of why the organization is engaged in Lean.
- Overall effectiveness of Lean throughout the organization.
- The movement of the organization to offering, developing, and improving products and/or services based upon customer value-added propositions or value-based products.
- Does the organization's think in terms of Lean, i.e., takt, flow, pull?
- The focus of driving quality in delivering products and services.
- Walking the walk: setting expectations traversing from leadership to frontline staff—with a -bottom-up planning approach.
- Problem-solving focused on eliminating blame (process focused) and driving quality—elimination of defects.
- Lean becomes the way we do things and is a common language and not flavor of the month.
- Standardization is a prevalent methodology in the overall company (not just the shop floor).
- Continuous improvement strategy with the elimination of waste is driven throughout the organization, that is, the use of kaizen, PDCA, or other problem-solving methodologies.
- Leadership development, leader as teacher, promoting a learning organization.
- The organization implements training and skill development plans with a focus on cross-training and people development including succession planning.

Core Operations (Tactical)

The next category core operations include Lean activities that impact the operational performance of the organization and how effectively the organization leverages Lean concepts and tools in improving the delivery and overall value of the service or product based as defined by the customer.

Learning to See

- The use of value stream maps
- Visual management
- Mistake proofing
- Workplace organization
- Techniques for waste reduction
- How to see

Work Process Improvement

- Process flow-driven line and facility layouts
- Single-piece flow
- Standard work
- Level loading or balanced production
- Scheduling production toward build to order
- Setup/changeover reduction
- Kanban and supply chain management
- Total productive maintenance

Knowledge Sharing and Performance (Building the Learning Organization)

The final category of knowledge sharing and performance covers evaluating the company's measurement systems. How do they assess the overall performance of the organization and how does the company reinforce continual improvement and performance to avoid complacency? Does the measurement system lend itself to determining the effectiveness of the organization with respect to the original reason or purpose for engaging in Lean? This would include the following:

- System to ensure updating of standard work and knowledge transfer of same
- Use of Scorecards—organizational and departmental, work process (see Figure 2.6). We prefer scorecards with yes / no vs. numerical ratings. People will tend to "game" the ratings.
- The method for defining, assigning, documenting, and monitoring organizational objectives such as Hoshin planning that is like catchball[2] utilized by Bridgestone, Fuji, Texas Instruments, AT&T, Boeing, IBM, Motorola, and Toyota[3] used to create and align goal flows from top to bottom
- Audits
- Process stability
- Defect elimination
- The use of Gemba walks as a leadership development tool
- Idea and suggestion programs
- Some types of gains sharing program

Regarding Assessments: Do You Know What You Need to Know?

We have sat in meetings and listened, while managers outright lied to their executives about how things are happening on the factory floor or in the office. So, we ask you the reader if the manager never leaves his or her office and how will he or she ever know about the actual problems on the

		Task from Leadership Roadmap Book			Detailed Leadership Model	
Right Job	A1	Develop & Approve Mandate	0%	Right Job	The Mandate	0%
	A2	Develop & Approve Strategic Business Plan	?		The Strategic Plan	?
	A3	Develop & Approve Actual Operating Plan With A.I.M.S.	5%		Annual Operating Plan	5%
The Business Model	B1	CEO Commitment Decision	20%	The Business Model	CEO assesses reality and determines need for change	20%
	B2	Executive leadership Team Commitment	15%		CEO commits to the Roadmap	15%
	B3	Board Commitment Decision	5%		Executive Leadership Team commits to roadmap	5%
	B4	Basic Model Elements	10%		Executive Leadership Team develops basic model elements	5%
	B5	Basic Model Review	10%		Board reviews basic model elements	0%
	B6	Build Understanding & Ownership	15%		Leaders deepen the understanding and ownership	10%
	B7	Organization Wide Roll-Out	15%		CEO presents roadmap to the whole organization	5%
	B8	Total Deployment of Base Elements	10%		Teams deploy the basics model elements	10%
	B9	Ongoing Performance Reviews	5%		Leaders implement a systematic performance review process	5%
People Systems	C1	Leadership Roadmap Navigation Course	5%	People Systems	Create a belief system	5%
	C2	Performance Management Systems	5%		Conduct Leadership Audit Survey	0%
	C3	Compensation System	0%		Institute a course in Leadership Roadmap Navigation	0%
	C4	Leadership Development System	5%		Develop Performance Management Systems	5%
					Develop and Equitable Compensations System	5%
					Plan for leadership development and succession	5%
Lean Systems Structure Development	D1	Lean Expert Leadership	15%	Lean Systems Structure Development	Identify lean expert leadership / resources	15%
	D2	Organization Unique Lean Production System	10%		Develop organization-unique lean production system	10%
	D3	Lean Goals & Strategies	15%		Conduct early plant/ office audit	5%
	D4	Lean production System Office	20%		Develop goals and strategies for the organization	20%
	D5	Education Process for Lean Tools	20%		Establish a lean production system office	20%
	D6	Lean Recognition	0%		Develop an educational process for lean tools	10%
					Recognize and reinforce lean enterprise	0%
Lean Implementation	E1	Executive Education	10%	Lean Implementation	Educate Executives (including Board members)	5%
	E2	Lean Operations Leader	15%		I.D. Lean leader	15%
	E3	Design Organization Lean System	10%		Design Organizational Lean System and create a visual	10%
	E4	Introduction to Entire Organization	40%		Introduce entire organization to new lean system	20%
	E5	Form Line Staff Level Lean Implementation	30%		Form a lean implementation steering team	10%
	E6	Implement Basic Training	35%		Implement basic training	35%
	E7	Draw Current & Future State Desired Layouts	30%		Establish hospital clinic overall flow (current and future state)	30%
	E8	Achieve Future State Layout	10%		Select a model line	25%
	E9	Select Model Line/Cell for Application of Lean	25%		VSM Model Line	25%
	E10	Establish Value Stream Map of Target Area or Cell	40%		Implement Lean Tools	25%
	E11	Introduce lean Tool Functionality to All Team Members	20%		Expand to other lines	10%
	E12	Expand lean Application Around Organization	10%		Expand to other suppliers	5%
	E13	Expand Lean Applications to All Departments & Suppliers	5%		Audits (my addition)	5%
Innovation System Structure Development & Implementation	F1	Executive Education	0%	Innovation System Structure Development & Implementation	Educate executives	0%
	F2	Innovation Leader	10%		Identify an executive champion for innovation	0%
	F3	Design Organization's Innovation System	0%		Design an organization unique innovation system	0%
	F4	Innovation Goals & Strategies	5%		Establish goals and strategies for innovation	5%
	F5	Implement Innovation System	0%		Implement the innovation system	0%
	F6	Innovation Recognition & Reinforcement	0%		Formally recognize and reinforce innovation	0%
					Conduct an innovation audit survey	0%
				Sustain (our addition)	Ongoing education for and by leadership	5%
					Performance management system (HOSHIN)	0%
					Business succession planning	0%
					Annual Reality Reviews	0%
					Audits on People, Lean and Innovation	2%
					Reset Operational objectives and STRAPP	5%
					Quarterly Reinforce with leadership and Board	5%
					Constantly raise standards and expectations	5%

Figure 2.6 Lean scorecard. (The Leadership Roadmap, By Dwane Baumgardner, Russell Scaffede, Taylor and Francis 2019, first published 2008.)

floor or in the office, the lack of progress being made, or if what is reported is even the truth? How reliable is the information transferred from layer to layer up to the CFO, CEO, or board of directors? How many layers do you have? Many times, audits and assessments are created or scored to make the company, area, or department look or feel good! This is not the purpose of a Lean assessment. Lean assessments should be all about surfacing problems, eliminating waste, and driving continuous improvement.

Lesson Learned: Beware! There is only one way to know what you need to know. You must get out of your comfortable chair, divorce yourself from your inbox, skip that next meeting, leave your office, and go to the floor!

Remember that an assessment is a snapshot in time; its importance lies in its objectivity and truth. Assessments should be leveraged to provide a roadmap to grow, learn, and improve. It is critical that organizations have internal mechanisms to audit and gauge what is going on in real time within the organization to walk the walk and continually improve and progress as they embark in deploying Lean.

Chapter Questions

1. What are the main benefits of an assessment?
2. What is an LMP?
3. Name and describe five of the ten assessment categories.
4. Can assessment be performed in the office areas? What should be considered when conducting such assessments?
5. Who should conduct the assessments?
6. What is a self-assessment? What is the value?
7. What should management do with the results from an assessment?
8. What is a pre-Lean assessment? What is the information used for?
9. What did you learn from this chapter?

Notes

1. Personal e-mail correspondence from Professor Feng Chen, Jiao Tong University.
2. Catchball refers to catching the goal and then includes a one-on-one discussion between levels as to how best to meet that goal. It includes the description of the metric to understand what objectives are to be met, their timeline for completion, and the owner (accountable individual) of the metric. The company goals (no more than five) are long term (three to five years) and, along with the mission and vision, remain unchanged. Catchball ensures alignment from top to bottom.
3. Create a high-performance culture with Hoshin Kanri by Frank Deno.

Additional Readings

Baumgardner, D. 2019. Russell Scaffede, The Leadership Roadmap. Taylor and Francis, first published 2008.
Becker, B.E. 2001. HR Scorecard. Boston, MA: HBR Press.
Collins, J.C. 1997. Built to Last. New York: Harper Business Press.
Collins, J.C. 2001. Good to Great. New York: Harper Business Press.
Kaplan, R.S. 1996. The Balanced Scorecard. Boston, MA: HBR Press.
Rother, M. 2010. Toyota Kata—Managing People for Improvement, Adaptiveness and Superior Results. New York: McGraw Hill.
Swartz, J.B. 1994. The Hunters and the Hunted. Portland, OR: Productivity Press.

Chapter 3

Our Misguided Allegiance to the Batching Paradigm

I truly believe one piece flow is better than batching; but what you don't understand is the volume on all our parts is too low to do one piece flow!

An anonymous Lean Practitioner

Even if the order is for one piece, we build ten at a time no matter what… It is our company policy! We don't care about the inventory costs.

Owner of Company located in South Baltimore during a Factory Tour

Process Definition

Anything with an input that is transformed into something else representing the output is defined as a process (see Figure 3.1). An input can start with raw material from the ground or from the brain. It is then converted as part of the process to the output desired (or sometimes not desired, i.e., defect). It can be physical or mental; it can be a manufacturing step for a product or a series of manufacturing steps. It can be cocoa turned into hot chocolate or hot chocolate where milk and/or marshmallows are added to it to make it creamier and more delicious. A process can be information that is transformed into a different output by a particular input. When we take a patient's history in an emergency department (ED), we have an input of information from the patient that produces an output, which is the beginning of a medical chart. Writing an email or text is a process. Writing this book was a process.

Types of Processes

There are several different types of processes. They range from batching to continuous flow.

- Batching processes are created by adding the same input to several parts in sequential order and then adding a second input to each of the parts sequentially until the parts are completed.

DOI: 10.4324/9781003185772-3

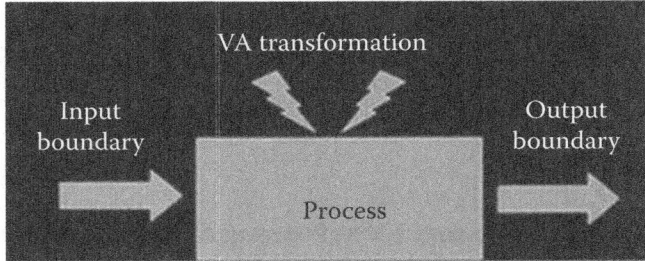

Figure 3.1   Process transformation.

- One-piece flow (OPF) is adding each input sequentially to one part until it is completed.
  - If the line is set up correctly, OPF can be set up for any process from high-volume low mix to low-volume high mix even with high variation.
  - Group technology processes line up operations in order and then produce products in "families." These families typically then feed multiple lines. Group technology can support variations in mix and volume.
- Continuous flow processes are one-piece or multiple-piece flow processes in parallel where each input is added sequentially on an assembly of manufacturing line.
  - Continuous flow processes are generally high-volume low mix or low variation but can be high variation if setup changes are reduced to zero, for instance, a line that reads barcodes to change colors or composition of materials based on programing preset in the machines on the line.
- Lights-out (automatic) processes can run unattended.

Batching Processes and Systems

Batching systems and processes and their resulting variations are the hidden enemies of Lean Thinking. It is this batching mindset that makes sustaining the OPF philosophy so difficult. This mindset is always present and unconsciously lurking in the background ready to disrupt Lean practitioners (LPs) at any time. As we proceed through the chapter, we will investigate the:

1. What
2. Where
3. Why
4. When, and
5. How we drive the batching process

Andy McDermott states: "Batch systems are also known in the Lean world as 'PUSH' systems. There was a quote which is said to have come from Dwight D. Eisenhower which is as follows: Pull the string, and it will follow wherever you wish. Push it, and it will go nowhere at all."[1] Batching systems are analogous to pushing the string. This is because products are pushed via a material requirement planning (MRP) system or just introducing many lots of material to the floor (generally scheduled based on parts availability vs. the customer schedule), which move from work center to work center, are expedited, and eventually completed. The goal of Lean is to create a "PULL" system where products move through the factory in a seamless fashion.

What Is Batching?

What is batching? The word batch[2] comes from Old English and originally meant to bake or something that is baked. Today, we still tend to bake things that are mostly made in batches. What sounds better than a freshly baked batch of cookies or a triple batch of cupcakes? (see Figure 3.2.). We define a batch system as one where one step is done to multiple items at a time before the next step is started or before the next process begins. This process is repeated until all steps are completed for each part. So, one doesn't see the first completed piece until the first (or sometimes last) piece of the entire batch or lot is done.

Therefore, for those cupcakes, the ingredients are all mixed to form the batter that is spooned into the cupcake pans, and all baked together at the same time. When they are cooled, the frosting is piped on each one and the edible confetti is sprinkled over the top of the whole batch. What results is an entire tray of the finished product. However, the downside of this process is we must wait until the last one is iced before we can eat our first one.

Batching also includes things one may not realize. When we go to the copy machine, we normally collect all the things we want to copy first. If we are getting drinks for several people, we will put the ice in all the glasses first. If we are making several sandwiches (see Figure 3.3) and have room, we will lay out the bread first, then put the ham on each one, then put the cheese on each one, then the final piece of bread, then we cut them all, and finally on to plates or we put them all in baggies and into our children's lunch boxes.

- Traffic lights are batch.
- Traffic circles are flow.
- Highways (with no traffic lights) flow with parallel lanes (until you get too many cars).
- Elevators are batch. Escalators are Flow.

Centralizing is a hidden word for batching. As soon as we centralize something, we need to schedule it and create processes for working within and around the process, department, or system. The centers of excellence (basically creating a monopoly at one site) concept where one plant does an entire product line (e.g., circuit boards, for every other plant in the division or company)

Figure 3.2   Batching cupcakes.

Figure 3.3 Batching sandwiches.

is another form of batching on a large scale. Batching occurs even in many Lean or OPF lines where there are work in process (WIP) caps or Kanban squares containing process parts or bins of partially assembled parts between operators (Figure 3.4). Batching occurs when operators build ahead because someone called in sick or there are part shortages for the next assembly or simply because they can. Beware! Batching is all around us, every day.

In process kanban
between stations

Figure 3.4 Between process Kanbans.

Where Do We Find Batching?

Batching is prevalent in every company we visit all over the world (Figure 3.5). The batching paradigm is so strong within all of us, that we find everyone, everywhere, batching all the time. Watch anyone working on two or more of something at a time and you will normally see them utilizing a batch process. Batching can be observed in all types of organizations, at restaurants, fast-food establishments, banks, insurance companies, government agencies, hospitals, airports, and directing traffic. Batching occurs at the hardware store when making keys or by teachers preparing newsletters for school children, stores wrapping packages, or a company processing invoices.

Most firms batch the back office or administration processes, for example, having all employee evaluations due in December, end-of-the-month closings, yearly budgeting processes, and accounting check runs. Even the US government has all tax returns due on the same date, April 15th. This forces companies that do taxes to hire many temporary employees for three months and then let them go or accounting firms to work overtime and weekends during tax time. If you look hard enough, you will see batching can and does occur somewhere at every level within every company. You just need to know what to look for!

Batching in Volunteer Service

There were two separate groups of volunteers working with a women's shelter. We watched as the first group of volunteers served food to the tables. They were looking to improve their process that

Figure 3.5   Batching production.

Figure 3.6 Flow sandwich line.

had been to plate the food in advance and place the plates under food warmers until the women arrived. Sometimes the food did not fit properly under the warmers and was either cold or over-cooked and had to be thrown out. They were not happy with the scrap and the fact that it had to be replated.

Now the food is plated one at a time from a steam table (Figure 3.6) as each plate is made when the woman enters the dining room. The food is never returned now, and the volunteers and the women really like the new system. Recently, a second group of three new volunteers brought in fresh fruit to serve the women. They began washing and cutting the fruit at about 12:30. Then they placed all the cut-up fruit on one platter and wheeled it through the dining room to each table. One day, the trio arrived so late, the women in the dining room had started to leave. The first group suggested they bring out whatever was already cut up and washed. Instead, the trio stuck to the original system and continued cutting up the bananas and apples to finish their platter. When they came out to the dining room, only 12 of the 75 women were still there. Instead of serving more women with what they had already prepared, they insisted on finishing their batches of fruit. Not only did they miss out on serving more women, but they were also left with food that would not even keep until the next meal and had to be thrown away!

Why Do We Batch?

So why do people batch? Whether we are 10 years old or 80 years old, our minds seem to be programed to believe working on more than one piece or activity at a time is better. We don't know why this is; maybe it is in our genes, but it certainly seems innate based on our experiences across the globe. Ask anyone and they will vehemently defend their batching behavior as being the most efficient and hence the most productive way to do the job. They reason that they should continue to do the same operation to all the other pieces before moving onto the next operation. Inherent in batching is the illusion we are working faster and more efficiently. This illusion is so prevalent that it drives most of the eight wastes in our factories, hospitals, government, retail industries, and service sectors.

Do not underestimate the power of the batching paradigm. It is an extremely difficult mindset to overcome, and most Lean initiatives are destroyed by it. It is a hard sell and almost impossible to convince people otherwise. They just cannot see why OPF makes any sense and how can it possibly hurt to make a few extra. They take joy in their defiance of OPF just to prove their point and convince you that you are wrong. None of us are immune. Even those of us who are LPs sometimes find ourselves batching, for instance, doing chores around the house. Once we suddenly realize we are batching, we just don't care; we do it anyway.

Lesson Learned: If you don't figure out a way to deter people from batching and convince them OPF is better, it will be virtually impossible to sustain Lean in the long run. This is where you will hear LPs refer to people as finally "getting it." Do you "get it?"

Ohno's Cowboy Metaphor

We borrow a metaphor of a cowboy driving his herd of cattle across the plains. A smaller herd is much easier to keep together. As a few head of cattle begin to wander off at the edges, the cowboy can herd them back toward the middle. In the case of human beings, one would think that our superior intelligence and sophisticated communication methods would help us to align with the team (rejoin our herd) quicker, but often the opposite is true. We (the herd) use our intelligence and communication skills to defend our position, or to try to bring the cowboy to our way of thinking. So, it takes more time to persuade people.

The concept of batching initially seems logical and sensible until one is taught and truly understands the OPF or Lean paradigm. Operating a line using a batch process takes up significant amounts of valuable resources, time, space, and inventory. The partially assembled inventory is called WIP (Figure 3.7) and is essentially stored labor that cannot be converted to cash until it is shipped to the customer. Batching can create a lack of overall process controls, lack of standardization, and poor quality. If a defect occurs, it is not discovered until the end of the process where the entire batch becomes defective. In OPF, we can discover the defect immediately after the first piece is completed, and in a truly Lean system, we never pass on a bad part.

Quantity Discounts—The #1 Waste of Overproduction

When you purchase a large quantity of the same product, you expect a discount. This concept has spilled over into the manufacturing process and further gives credit to those embracing batch.

Demonstrated with Lean (first pass)

Operators   20   – 23%
Units per day   109   + 18%
DL mins per unit (9 hour day) 99   – 43%
Throughput time (hour)   2.5   – 83%
Cycle time   8   – 20%

43% Increase in productivity

Demonstrated with Lean (second pass)

Operators (goal is 14)   18   –11%
Units per day (9 hour day)   120   +9.2%
DL mins per unit   81   –26.4%
Throughput time (hour)   1.4   –44%
Cycle time   8   –0%

26.4% additional increase in productivity from first pass
53.7% increase in productivity from batch base and realized
$187,500 unburdened labor savings annually

Figure 3.7   Before and after results.

They rationalize it must be efficient to produce in batches; otherwise, the firm would not offer quantity discounts. So, we all are programed to order more than what we need and before we need it to save costs. However, do discounts really save us in the long run? How many of you shop at a Costco, Sam's Club, or similar type stores?

- How many of you had to purchase an extra refrigerator or freezer and find more space or build a larger pantry to store the three months' worth of groceries and sundries you purchased?
- How many of you have food at the bottom of your freezer which is now six months to a year or more old? In addition, how often have you put off defrosting the freezer because there was too much inventory in the freezer.
- How much food have you had to throw away (scrap) because of freezer burn?
- How much money do you have tied up in inventory? If you bought it on a credit card, you may be paying interest on it as well. Was your food labeled? Did you use it based on first in first out?
- How often have you purchased something at the local store which you had already purchased at the big box store but didn't have time to look for it or forgot you already had it?

This discount principle applies to businesses as well. In the factory, when the marketing/sales department offers a discount or promotion, the factory must work around the clock and overtime to get the product out. Then when the sale is over, the factory must cut back the hours. This artificial demand is a by-product of batching.

There is a cost to purchasing a large quantity before you need it. We have seen companies with stock items or shelves full of finished goods (FG) (Figure 3.8) that were the result of large quantity buys. The theory was if the machine is set up, then all these extra pieces are free. We just must store them until someone calls us, or maybe we can rework them and deliver them quicker than starting from scratch.

Figure 3.8　Finished goods stock—Just in case.

However, most of the time, the calls never come! And no one checks to see if any can be reworked because it takes too much time. The parts sit collecting dust and quickly becoming excess and obsolete (E&O). When we make more than what we need, we often must sell it at a discount. The exception to this rule is the stores that offer discounts every day or have sales all the time, which in essence level loads their demand. We have affectionately coined the term batchards to describe people displaying this batching behavior or mindset. Batchards are also those who have been introduced to OPF but refuse to follow it. These are the stuck-in-the-mud types who won't give up batching!

Elementary Batching

Parent Teachers's Association (PTA) volunteers at an elementary school published the school's newsletters. They copied, collated, and distributed it to the children. The volunteers always batched this process. Each stack of the different newsletter pages was set out on the table (four of five of them). The volunteers would fold each stack separately and place in piles and then pick up one of each to put into the envelopes. Then they would take the envelopes out to distribute them to the children as they were leaving. One day, they arrived late, and it was suggested they do OPF. They all said it would not be as efficient and continued to batch the newsletters as always. Since they had to wait until all the steps were done for the first one to reach the envelope, none of the children received newsletters. One day a new volunteer suggested they stuff the envelopes in OPF. They did it and the results were amazing. Every child went home with a newsletter because so much time and space were reduced.

Lesson Learned: LPs are always on the front lines in the battle for OPF and waste elimination. The batchards are always numerous, lurking in hidden, sometimes protected, and unexpected, places and constantly in the wings waiting to attack and push back the LP's steady advance.

When Do We Batch?

The general answer to this question is, as human beings, we batch whenever possible if we have not been introduced to Lean thinking. We have found during initial Lean assessments that many companies think their product lines are Lean and flowing, yet we constantly see batching throughout the lines. We have witnessed companies that have implemented Lean, in some cases for years or even decades, which do not realize they are still batching within their lines or offices. They honestly think their lines are Lean and are proud to show them off to customers and trade organizations. They think their lines are flowing when they are nowhere close to the level possible. Some companies have even told us "We have improved enough" or they have already finished implementing their Lean initiative and "You can't possibly think there is anything you can help us with!"

Batch environments create the perception of the need for more space and more people (Figure 3.9) since we need room for all that WIP, and it does take up a lot of room. This is flawed thinking, and clearly, this is not thinking Lean. In addition, if people have a choice, they will always take the easiest things to work on first in a batch environment. We also batch when we don't have a choice and batching is mandated by our policies and procedures. Many times, batching gets written into ISO 9000 procedures, and then, ISO is used as an excuse not to do OPF when, all we must do is change our procedures to reflect OPF.

Lesson Learned: Batching is innate. Our minds seemed to be programed to batch. We all tend to batch whenever we can. We have never run into a situation where we had to ask someone to switch from OPF to batching! We don't innately consider OPF as the first thought when setting up our processes. We don't know exactly why this is, but we do know that it is! My niece, a Junior,

Batch baseline metrics		
Operators	13	
Units per day (includes OT)	35	
Hours per unit	2.97	
WIP (pieces)*	46	
WIP dollars	$36k	
Floor space (ft^2)	4000	
Throughput time	63 minutes	
Cycle time (est. batch)	11.4 minutes	
After Lean metrics		
Operators	8	−32%
Units per day	35	+0%
Hours per unit	1.82	−35%
WIP (pieces)	7	−85%
WIP dollars	$11k	−69%
Floor space (ft^2)	2,500	−38%
Throughput time	3.6 minutes	−94%
Cycle time (minute)	11.4 minutes	−0%
35% improvement in productivity		

Figure 3.9 Before and after results.

was assisting with a research study for a math professor at McDaniel College and during our conversation I found out she was batching her process, so we ended up discussing Lean and OPF at some length. A week or two later in a note she sent me she added at the bottom: P.S. "Uncle Charlie—I think about batching now basically every time that I do something." I smiled to myself and thought "Yes, she gets it."

Batching in Manufacturing

A Visit to Lean Factories

Batch to Lean Results: In the words of the Toledo Metal Spinning Vice President Craig Fankhauser,[3] "I do remember the lead-time issue. See Table 3.1 In January 1999, shortly after

Table 3.1 Weld Department Before

Before		Eliminated need for production facility 10 miles away Freed up and sold capital equipment Significant reductions in inventory in first six months Reduced headcount through attrition Reduced factory labor overhead Reduced setup times from 3 hours to 6 minutes
Operators	3	
Units per day (includes OT)	69	
Output per hour per person	2.5	
DL hours per unit	0.4	
Floor space (ft²)	2500	
WIP	Lots	
Throughput time (working days)	35 days	
Cycle time (seconds) estimated	1327	
Distance traveled	10 miles	

Weld Department After

After actual			Some investment was required Annual savings = better than 10 × consulting fees 61% increase in productivity
Operators	1	−66%	
Units per day (includes OT)	62	−104%	
Output per hour per person	6.5	+160%	
DL hours per unit	0.153	−61%	
WIP	0	−100%	
Floor space (ft²)	504	−80%	
Throughput time	554	−99%	
Cycle time (seconds)	554	−56%	
Distance traveled (ft)	42	−99%	
Cut 38 week late backlog to 2 weeks early—in 8 weeks			

our Lean training, the weld department's lead time was running 12–16 weeks for simple rolled, seam-welded, and flanged cylinders. We had more work than we knew what to do with and we were challenged to keep up with customer demand. We incorporated a Lean initiative in the department, and over the next few weeks, we rearranged the welding equipment and process flow. By April, we were all caught up and shipping parts on time with a four- to six-week planned delivery. Currently, this department can produce parts in one to two weeks if the customer demand is there. The cell can also run with one man instead of two or three, depending on customer takt time (TT)."

Prebuilding and Outsourcing Are Forms of Batching!

During our Lean training classes, the batching paradigm becomes extremely evident. We conduct an OPF Lean exercise in which there is a discussion on acceptable improvement ideas. The number one idea/suggestion for improvement is always "Can we build up the subassemblies ahead of time?" Most people don't feel building ahead is batching. The next question is "Can we have a supplier build them and ship them in pre-built?" The participants don't understand that pre-building is, in fact, batching and this desire to outsource comes so easily. But note that outsourcing takes people's jobs off the line. Does this mean the supplier should be able to do it better than you can? If the process involves very specialized, expensive equipment, the answer may be yes, but otherwise, it should be cheaper to build it in-house once you understand the Lean paradigm. Once you outsource the product, you lose control over it and quality may suffer. "Without due diligence and appropriate controls, outsourcing could end up being much costlier than in-house manufacturing or services (especially once you have applied the Lean tools), resulting in high defect rates, late deliveries, poor service, and customer dissatisfaction."[4]

Batch to Lean Results

This biotechnology company, Life Technologies, used to prepare (batch up) buffer stock solutions in advance for their scientists. This was performed in a large room called a buffer kitchen. In this kitchen, triple batches of solutions were prepared and stored in very large plastic containers that sat waiting just in case someone would need them. The thought process was if we prepare these ahead of time, it will speed up preparation of the final solutions. When we studied the process, we found, most of the time, the buffer stocks were only partially used and the balance had to be disposed of because it expired, which meant another batch had to be prepared. We changed the process to build to order, which meant we started making the final solutions according to just what was needed in the buffer kitchen OPF. The results were as follows:

- We eliminated the buffer stock solution containers and storage space (several hundred square feet).
- We reduced the size of the buffer kitchen.
- We reduced the size of the equipment required.
- We saved thousands of dollars a year in unused buffer stock solutions.
- We freed up additional capacity for the buffer kitchen (this was the opposite of what they expected).
- We improved the quality of the final solutions.
- We eliminated the need to audit the expirations dates or the opportunity to fail an audit due to expired dates (since the buffer stock was eliminated).

Lesson Learned: Time gained by batching (where there is a lot of variation) is lost due to extra handling of the parts and lost time waiting at the machine for each work center.

How the Batch Process Occurs: Sometimes We Have to Batch ... Right?

We constantly get told by companies they have no choice other than to batch. We must point out there are times when batching products or paperwork is more efficient than OPF. Some of you are smiling right now and thinking "Yes ... I knew it." However, you can always trace the reason back to one of the reasons listed as follows:

Eight Reasons Leading Us to Batch

We have found eight major reasons that drive us to batch. These are as follows:

1. Our minds (brains)
2. Setups/changeovers
3. Travel distance
4. Equipment
5. Processes
6. Idle time
7. Space
8. Variation

Our Minds

The single biggest incentive to batch comes from our minds. Humans, for some reason, are made to batch. We have never run into people who objected to batching; but after many years of objections to OPF, one can assuredly deduce that batching must be an innate quality we all possess, and for some reason, we are all hardwired to think batching is better. If it was not for this, I think most companies would naturally already be OPF. My claims for this line of thinking are as follows. Have you ever had a discussion with someone not exposed to Lean (and in many cases, it doesn't matter anyway) where you did not have to defend OPF and work very hard to explain why it is better? I'm sure some of you think we are crazy. We are born thinking batching is the one best way.

So, consider the following analogy. We had a 12-year-old male Bichon Frise. We only fed him dog food all his years, except for some French vanilla cake of which he is quite fond. One day, we gave him a big ham bone, almost bigger than him. Now, please keep in mind we had this dog since he was eight weeks old. He never had a bone! Our dog took this bone and chewed on it until it was bare and then immediately went down to the backyard, started digging in our garden, and buried the bone. Five minutes later, he knew exactly where it was and dug it up again. Now, I ask you, why did this dog bury the bone? He had never even seen a bone before, had never been trained by his mother to bury a bone, never dug up the dirt before, and yet still buried and dug up this bone. He started digging up other places to bury it, and we finally had to take it away and give him a bath.

So, what about this batching thing? I believe we are all just like the dog burying the bone. None of us were taught to batch, we just come by it naturally. Therefore, we believe this is one reason why Lean fails so often, and it is so easy to undo once it's implemented.

Many times, it may be part of your organizations' vision that drives batching (i.e., We've always done it that way) resulting in a natural cultural resistance to change. For example, a new CEO who knows nothing about Lean or flow can easily kill the progress with or the Lean program without even knowing or realizing. We see this happens repeatedly. If it is not somehow truly interwoven into the culture, it will not sustain because all of us are constantly trying to undo it with our minds!

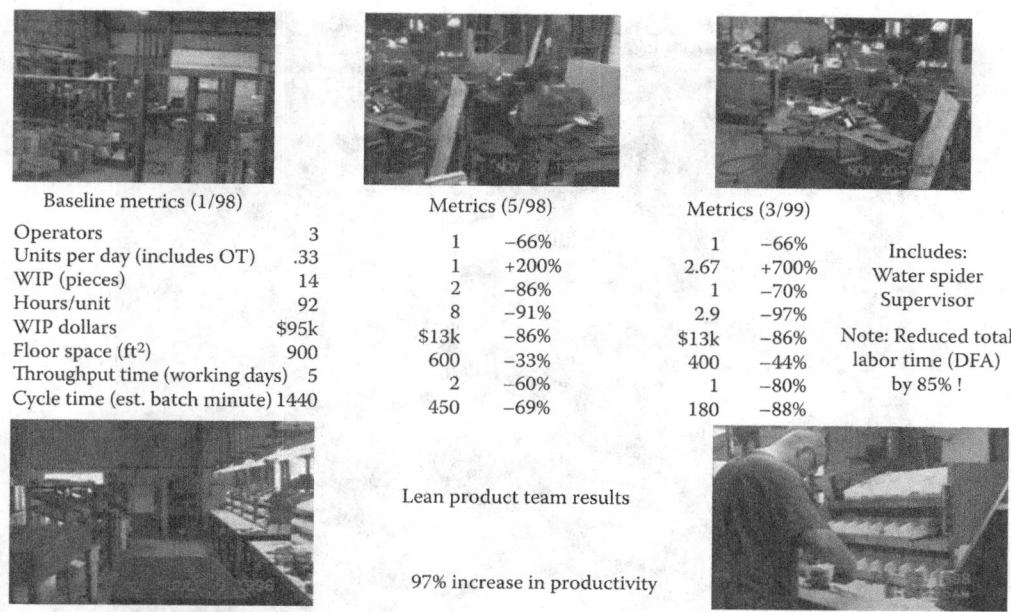

Baseline metrics (1/98)		Metrics (5/98)		Metrics (3/99)	
Operators	3	1	−66%	1	−66%	Includes:
Units per day (includes OT)	.33	1	+200%	2.67	+700%	Water spider
WIP (pieces)	14	2	−86%	1	−70%	Supervisor
Hours/unit	92	8	−91%	2.9	−97%	
WIP dollars	$95k	$13k	−86%	$13k	−86%	Note: Reduced total
Floor space (ft²)	900	600	−33%	400	−44%	labor time (DFA)
Throughput time (working days)	5	2	−60%	1	−80%	by 85% !
Cycle time (est. batch minute)	1440	450	−69%	180	−88%	

Lean product team results

97% increase in productivity

Figure 3.10   Before and after results.

Lesson Learned: And that is what batching is all about, Charlie Brown.[5,6] Our experience is 99% of people are not born to think Lean. People don't just figure this stuff out.

Batch to Lean Results (Figure 3.10): This company used to assemble this product to make sure the parts fit together, then disassemble the product to paint it, and then assemble it again and then pack and ship it. We used video analysis and the design for assembly (DFA) analysis tool to build it just once, revised all the drawings, created standard work, and improved productivity by 97%.

Setups/Changeovers

There are setups all around us, some of which you may recognize immediately. Setups occur on the racetrack, such as pit stops; on major league football fields, that is, changeover from defense to offense or to special teams; on baseball fields, changeover between teams up to bat and taking the field; all around the home, such as preparing to participate in a game or getting ready to go on a trip; and in your own office, like loading paper in the Xerox® machine. The amount of time it takes to set up or change over part of a line, an entire line, an area, or a piece of equipment drives us into thinking we must run large batches of products. Mixed model environments like machine shops, running small lots and high mix, like paint lines, and injection molding lines, take too long to make each piece one at a time. This concept is one of the main drivers of our batch thinking. The longer the setup or changeover time, the more inventories needed to buffer the changeover. Long changeovers usually drive us toward batching larger and larger lot sizes. We must reduce setup times before moving to OPF for these areas. It is important to note long setup times do not just occur in die changes on presses. A setup can occur simply by unloading and loading a part in a machine. The concept of internal time extrapolates to any device or machine that is down waiting for us to unload and load it. Focus should be on separating internal and external setup times,

Figure 3.11 Grinder operation.

converting as much internal time to external setup as possible, and streamlining the setup process as much as possible. Setups can be improved! Small lot production requires short setups and setup time reduction results applying Lean tools, over time of 50%–90% and more is common.

Batch to Lean Results: One of the secrets of Lean is that we are never done. The journey requires iteration after iteration. At a company called Diamond Chain in Indiana, their team continually went after their press setup yielding an 83% reduction in internal clock setup time and 66% in labor time. This freed up 16.6 hours or more a week, depending on the number of setups, of capacity for the press. The following story illustrates:

At one factory outside Chicago, the operations Vice President (VP) asked me to look at their grinder operation (see Figure 3.11). The VP stated they had done everything they could think of to increase capacity and lean out the operation including having one operator running two machines. There were 26 machines in total, and they were having problems with machine downtime because there was no time to do preventive maintenance. The customer was very upset they were not meeting their delivery requirements so there was already a requisition written and approved to purchase three more machines at a cost of over $2 million. When we videoed several of the grinding cells, it became apparent that several things were missing from the cells:

1. First was an understanding of planned versus actual production or a day-by-hour chart. There was no way to determine if the cell was on schedule or behind the production plan.
2. Each operator was keeping a statistical process control (SPC) chart for each grinding machine. This was necessary in case offset adjustments were needed to the machine (although, some machines had probes and were self-adjusting). However, we found the operators updated

their SPC chart when the machine had stopped. So, the actual machine cycle time was now the cycle time of the machine plus the machine's idle time waiting for the operator to unload, load, and cycle (start) the machine. We explained the unloading and loading of the machine should be looked at as a traditional setup. But we aren't trained to think this way.

3. The operators were not measured by the actual work they produced but were measured against the output each supervisor felt the operators could produce from experience. The supervisor in essence reduced the standard hours for production by including all the problems and downtime currently inherent in the operation. We refer to this as "demonstrated capacity." This downgrading of the standard hid what the cell could produce.

4. Also missing were standard work and line balancing. While it was considered more efficient when each operator ran two machines, no one figured out or trained the operators how to run two machines. They just moved the machines, stuck the operator in the, and told them to run it.

As a result, we found when watching the video, and following the product (part), the machines would complete a part and then wait 30 to sometimes 45 seconds for the operator to get around to unloading and loading (setting up) each machine. This is because 50% of time the operator was recording SPC data and the rest of the time they were just not focused on the job at hand. Since there was no expectation of output (i.e., day-by-hour chart) the operators had no targets to meet. The real total cycle time for unloading, loading, and cycling the machine was 60 seconds.

This means they should have been able to average a 30 second cycle time per part between the two machines. This translates into a plan on the day-by-hour chart of 60 parts per hour for each machine or 120 parts per hour for each cell of two machines. To achieve this result, we reviewed the videos with each operator and showed them the internal downtime on the machine due to their idle time during the changeover from one part to the next on the grinder. This helped them to understand it was necessary to have the next part in their hand ready and waiting, to load in the machine as soon as it stopped, and the internal time was reduced to a few seconds.

Batch to Lean Results: We created standard work allowing them to both inspect their parts per requirements and still be ready to change the part over immediately. We increased the capacity of the area by over 45% and freed up three machines that could then be used for total productive maintenance (TPM) and external tool changeovers. External changeover means it allowed us to use an idle machine for setting up the next job. In the past, they would have shut down the entire cell to change over the grinder since the operator did the changeover. The other machine would not be run until the setup was completed. We also eliminated the need to purchase the extra three machines and cancelled the open requisition for $2 million. Within a couple of weeks, the company was caught up with their customer delivery requirements. This whole process was conducted in the evenings during a five-day Lean seminar at the company. We spent only three to four hours using the Lean tools in this book to arrive at the improvement (this time included involving and training one of the cell operators; the next week all the operators in the area were trained in the new standard work).

Travel Distance

Whenever we introduce travel distance into an operation, no matter how small, we drive batching. This is evident in why we only go to the supermarket once a week. If we are going shopping, we are going to purchase all the food items we think we will need for the week. How often would we go to the store and purchase only one day's worth of groceries?

At a wedding, when waiting in line at the bar, we tend to double up on our order, so we don't have to wait in line again. It is ironic this tendency to double up on our orders makes the line take longer, driving others to double order thus continually slowing down the line even more. It also causes our drinks to become diluted, therefore adversely changing the product. Applying this to the simple replenishment of materials, the travel distance drives us to fill the bins on the line as much as possible to avoid refilling them so often. In the office, people will stash loads of office supplies, so they don't have to keep visiting the cabinet. Nurses, for instance, stash things they really need all over the hospital floor.

The longer the distance, the more pieces we want to carry between places. For example, we may carry multiple parts from one work center or stockroom to another on a cart versus carrying them one at a time. Another example closer to home is a firewood delivery. The firewood is often dumped on the driveway, and the homeowner uses a wheelbarrow to move the firewood usually to the backyard. The homeowner would never carry the firewood, one log at a time, unless there was no access to a wheelbarrow, or the pile was very small.

Exercise: Take four pens or pencils and place them at the end of 4×6 table. Then ask for a volunteer to move the items to the other side of the table. You will find they will grab all four and move them as a batch. Ask them why they did not move them one at a time. They will look at you like you are crazy and then answer because I had to walk all the way to the other side. Why in the world would I take one at a time?

Batch to Lean Results[6]: In a hospital ED process (Figure 3.12), by cutting down travel time for the provider, we reduced the wait time to see the provider by 80% and reduced the waiting room time from 10 hours to 0. In the winter "snow-bird" season, 16% of people left before seeing the doctor; now, it is less than 1%.

Equipment

Some equipment is designed to operate batch. We have seen machine shop tools used to perform an operation on a batch of parts, change tools, and do the next operation on the same batch of parts. There are some machines designed to work as many as 25 parts at a time. Here, we collect parts, in lot delay status (we are waiting for the rest of the lot to be completed), until we receive 25 parts that allow the operator to run the parts through the machine. Many times, this is driven by an actual, or perceived, lengthy run time for the machine. Once the machine run is complete, we must manage 25 parts all at once and we need space to accommodate the material handling now associated with all these parts. At one company, they had spent extra money to design test equipment that could handle up to 20 parts at a time versus one at a time. It took up a lot more space than an OPF tester and resulted in significant batching and parts waiting to be tested on the machine. They had all this space utilized as a parts hotel and were looking at thousands of dollars to convert the machine back to single-piece flow. Once the analysis was done, we found we needed one to four parts testing at any one time depending on the cycle time of the line.

Machines that Batch

At one plant, they had a milling machine that batched parts. The machine selects a tool from the machine tool carousel and performs an operation on the tombstone for up to six or eight pieces at a time. The machine then selects the next tool and performs the next operation on all the pieces, etc.

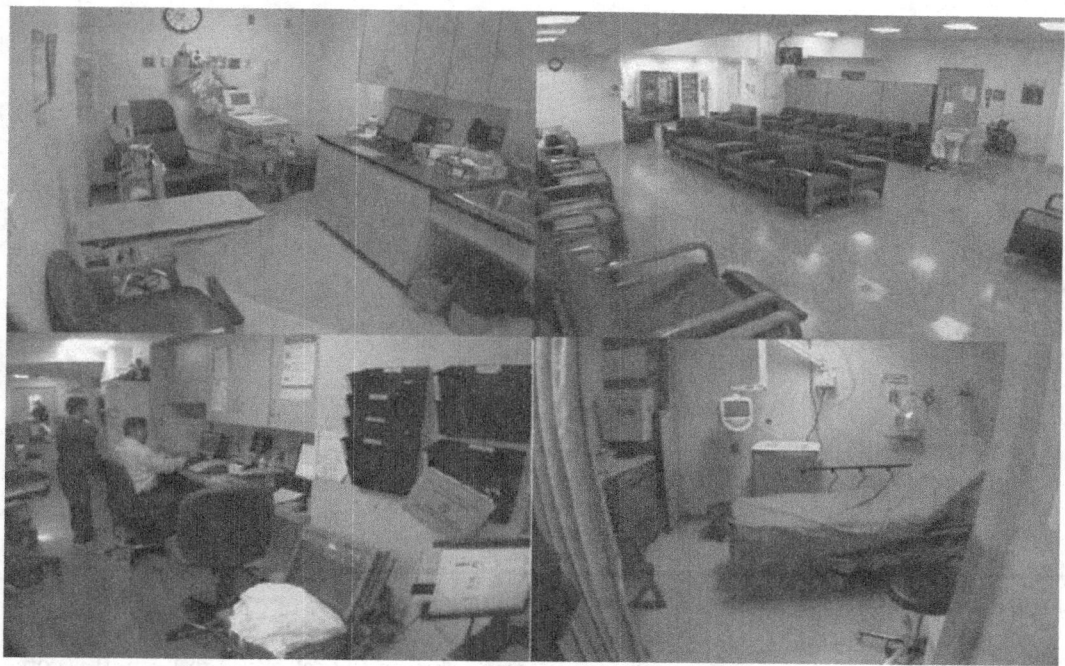

ED results

(Emergency rooms see approximately 58,000 patients a year across 7 campuses)
- Average door-to-provider time dropped from 3.8 to 2.3 hours, a 40% improvement in just 11 weeks.
- Two years of additional improvements have further reduced that to 1.6 hours—a 58% improvement over the pre-Lean state. Now less than 50 minutes and near 30 minutes at some campuses.
- The average length of stay for inpatients fell from 15.4 to 11 hours, a 29 % gain. Two years of additional improvements have since reduced that to 7.9 hours—a 49% improvement.
- The number of patients who left without seeing a doctor fell from 16% (February 2005) to as low as .7%.
- 2012—Now ED wait time (to see a provider is less than 45 minutes at all campuses and averages in many cases 10–20 minutes or less. There is no longer anyone waiting in the waiting room.

Figure 3.12   Emergency room results door to doctor in 10 minutes.

The net result is a piece that is not complete until the entire batch of six to eight pieces is completed. If one piece is found defective, they all will most likely be defective. In addition, extra inspection occurs before and after the machining operation because the operators don't trust the machine.

The food-service industry utilizes many batch pieces of food-service equipment such as ovens and mixers. However, many of the chain pizza restaurants utilize continuous cooking ovens and not large batch ovens. Take notice of the flow ovens in use the next time you visit a pizza restaurant. Office equipment used to be batched (i.e., copier machines with sorters on the side), but now, most scan in the paperwork and then make complete or collated sets. Another example we encounter every day is the elevator (batch) versus the escalator (single and continuous flow).

Batch to Lean Results Robotic Cell Making Sprockets for Motorcycles (Figure 3.13): Lean tools were applied to the equipment as well as the labor. Cycle times on the equipment were reduced from 37% to 50%, and one of the two robots was freed up and used in another cell.

Robotic cell before Lean

Operators	4.5
Output (includes OT)	759
WIP	1255
DL (minute/unit)	3.55
Lathe cycle time (seconds)	70
Enshu cycle time (seconds)	74.5

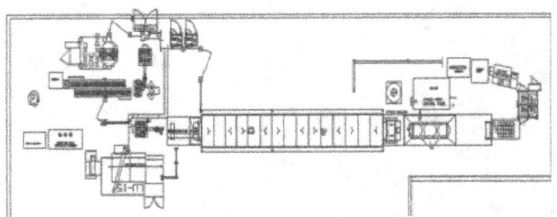

Phase I actual results

Operators	3	−33%
Output (no OT)	859	+13%
WIP	80	−94%
DL (minute/unit)	1.67	−53%
Lathe 1 cycle time	35	−50%
Lathe 2 cycle time	47	−37%

53% Increase in productivity
Decreased operator walking distance by 2,250 ft per shift

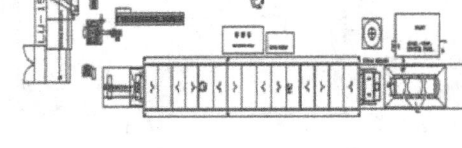

Figure 3.13   Before and after results of robotic operation.

In addition, there was no longer a need for the second shift in the cell. Prior to Lean, this company located outside Chicago was supposed to have a one-week Kanban supply of parts for their customer, a major motorcycle manufacturer, and could never keep it full even running two shifts. Now the Kanban is full, and the cell only must run a couple days for one shift to keep the Kanban full. In the time they freed up, they are now making other customer products in the cell during the first shift.

Processes

Some processes are naturally batch-type processes like foundries that make steel or aluminum. These processes are not unlike (Table 3.2) those you can observe in home cooking and restaurants. Making cookies at home is a good example of a batch process. We may make one batch, a double batch, or triple batch of cookies. After we combine the ingredients, we put the dough onto several trays and place the trays in the oven. It is not until most have been baked and they are cool enough to taste that we can suddenly discover we forgot a key ingredient. Forgetting chocolate chips or baking soda could result in scrapping the entire batch. We find similar processes

Table 3.2   Changeovers at a pouring station for a foundry

This Company, a Foundry, Utilized Batch Processing for Their Castings			
Old Avg (minute)	New Actual (minute)	Variance (minute)	Potential Savings to the Bottom Line
6.227	2.500	3.727	$2,376,053.97

Source: BIG Archives.
They cut their changeover times down for a three-shift operation by 3.727 minutes per changeover, yielding a $2.3 million annual savings, due to the increased capacity.

in powdered metal, FDA, or biotechnology processes. Many biotechnology companies have kitchens where they will produce buffer solutions to save time in mixing final solutions. Some work processes are batch such as central receiving areas or where there may be the need to do off-line operations.

Idle Time

Idle time drives batching. If someone is idle on their job, they look for tasks to do that typically reinforce batch practices and will potentially do unnecessary work or overproduction. Humans in general prefer keeping busy and do not like to be idle. Most employees, if left alone, will continue working at their station. If a person is running at a faster cycle time than the person they are feeding, they will continue to make parts and bury the next person downstream, rather than sit idle. This is where the concept of the in-line process Kanban or WIP caps was developed. To not bury the person, we are feeding, we told the operators to only build until the Kanban square was full, whether it was one piece or up to the WIP cap. Generally, we have seen operators ignore the WIP cap and observed the operators continue to build until there is no room for any more parts. This is especially apparent in sit-down station-balanced lines; thus, sit-down lines embrace and help create batching.

Batch to Lean Results (Figure 3.14): At a company called Cleveland Motion Controls in Ladson SC prior to the purchase by Lincoln Electric, operators in the machining department used to stand idle and watch machines for up to three minutes at a time. They thought they were world class because each operator was running two machines. The parts then went to the washing department, marking department, and packing department. After Lean, we moved washing, marking, and packing into the machine cells. We changed the process from laser marking (very expensive) to a scribe-type marker, which was cheap and had a small footprint. We eventually eliminated the need for the washing, marking, and packing departments' ten people and no one was laid off (handled through attrition). The supervisor of the departments was promoted to the health, safety, and facilities management position. The productivity improvement was over 200%. In another machine department area, through video analysis, we were able to increase from one person to one or two machines to one person to six machines by implementing a strict standard work process. This was a 200% improvement in productivity and freed up two to three operators for each of the two shifts.

Space

Space in the work environment is extremely important to manage, as too little or too much can lead to batching. Let's examine when we have too much space. In this case, we tend to batch because we have surplus floor space to store the extra inventory. We have found that providing more space than needed encourages batching and at a minimum embraces the accumulation of items not needed, that is, junk. At one company, we had operators complain incessantly for over a week that we did not provide enough space in the layout. When we pointed out they didn't need any more space, the employees went to HR and complained. We met with HR (who did not understand Lean at the time) and were ordered to provide an additional table. We met with the line employees to advise them of this, and they were so happy they had won and gotten their extra table. We put the table in the work area that night. The next morning, there was so much junk on the table, in terms of tools and extra parts, the line was out of balance, and the operators were complaining they had less room to work and demanded another table. HR representatives visited

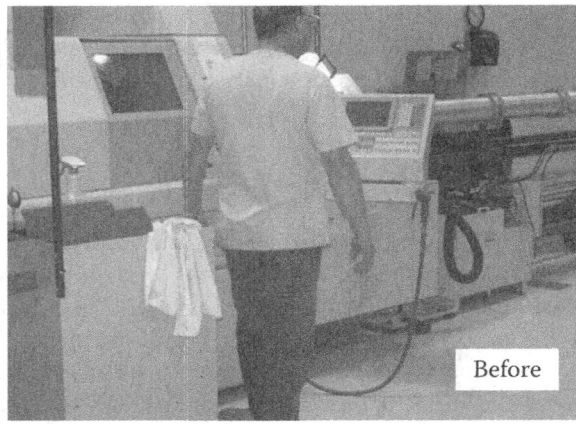

Figure 3.14 Before and after—Waiting and watching converted to a finished product cell including washing, marking, and packing-with no increase in labor. After implementing at all machines we eliminated the washing, marking and packing departments. No one was laid off.

the line and observed the new table fraught with junk. They agreed with us and said we could remove the table.

Too little space can create batching as well. When we don't have enough space, we tend to batch in the space we have simply because we don't have room to flow the process. This is because there is not enough room to lay out the parts and tools in the proper order, thus forcing the operators to batch one or two operations at a time prior to setting up to do the other operations.

Lesson Learned: This is one reason why layouts are so important. A poor layout will drive waste.

Batch to Lean Results Prior to Lean, everyone at a company located in South Baltimore which made micro dryers for drying plastics for injection molding machines, back in the late 1990s complained about the lack of space. (Figure 3.15): They had installed eight mezzanines (some with smiley faces) to store all the WIP. They used to shut down four days a year (once a quarter) to physically count the entire inventory. Much of it was over one or even two years old. This company decided to improve their lines prior to a sales meeting. The team members painted the area on their own with no one asking and then worked with the Lean team to transform the area in less than

Baseline metrics (1/98)		Metrics (5/98)		Metrics (9/99)		Includes:
Operators	13	7	−46%	6	−54%	Overhead reduction
Units per day (includes OT)	2.3	5	+117%	5	+117%	Water spider
Labor hours per unit	52	9.3	−82%	8	−85%	Supervisor
WIP (pieces)*	29	13	−55%	13	−55%	In line welder
WIP dollars	$45k	$26k	−42%	$26k	−42%	Parts not stocked
Floor space (ft^2)	3275	2456	−25%	2456	−25%	
Throughput time (working days)	20	3	−85%	3	−85%	
Cycle time (est. batch minute)	240	80	−67%	80	−67%	

85% increase in productivity—9× return on consulting fees
All Lean implementation costs paid back well within first year
Teams pick up activities normally associated with overhead

Figure 3.15   Before versus after—Plastics dryer line.

eight weeks. The welding department was split up, and welding was added to the front of the line with Kanbans set up to sheet metal and paint. All the raw material was moved to the floor, freeing up 25% of the space in the stockroom. Eventually, we were able to consolidate another building's production into the space freed up in the stockroom. We eliminated all but one mezzanine. The company was able to sell the building and still had room to grow.

Batch to Lean Results: At a client in Europe with severe space limitations but with requirements to produce more due to customer demand. Applying Lean principles and reorienting the product in the facility resulted in a savings of 55% in terms of space and an increase of 50% in productivity, reduction in use of cranes to move the product to the next cell, etc. We must have the ability to expand our thinking by looking for waste in a different way and at a much higher level of detail (Figure 3.16).

Variation

Variation in processes drives batch production. It is not unusual to hear "We used to have an assembly line." When asked what happened to it, employees normally say the product mix kept growing and they did not know how to handle it anymore. Test problems often are the result of process variations. As test problems occur, the parts begin to pile up at test stations and the production lines slowly disappear. Variation is often the cause to blame when assembly lines are abandoned. We have run into cases where the variation was so bad it was difficult to even set up a Lean line until some of

Figure 3.16 Space for growth.

the variation was designed out. We have been successful in implementing and balancing lines with high variation using some of the line balancing techniques that we will describe later in this book. We have found that many companies are forced to batch due to significant variation in their manufacturing processes. Listed in the following are other types of variation:

1. Variation shows up due to poor engineering practices where the old craft mentality surfaces. This mentality is apparent when an operator must develop a certain "feel" based on their experience to make the part work. Sometimes, this means hitting it with a hammer, and other times, it shows up when the product must be shimmed. This leads to trial-and-error-type builds. We see it where engineering has designed in tweaking or in-line manual tests, and it is especially apparent in very small lots—high-mix product lines. The variation also occurs in high-technology manufacturing with large amounts of touch labor.

   Walk through Toyota Motor Corp.'s Camry and Avalon plant in Georgetown, Ky., and you will see some clever manufacturing ideas. But one thing you won't see is a rubber mallet—at least, not a legal one. Last year, Georgetown banished the rubber mallet. Why? Because in this age of high-octane innovation, Toyota's work force concluded; if you need a rubber mallet to pound something into place, you must be doing something wrong. It sounds radical. But this is the beauty of the Lean manufacturing philosophy.[7]

2. We also see variation with part shortages caused by MRP systems, vendor deliveries, or parts lost in the stockroom. In addition, inadequate vendor part packaging, container sizes, and minimum lot requirements can cause batching.

3. Having operators responsible for obtaining their own materials causes variation as the operators often need to search for parts prior to starting a work order. Another example is when operators are forced to perform material handling activities, such as removing bearings from small plastic bags and unwrapping parts placed in boxes full of peanuts, to have parts for use on the line.

Baseline metrics–station balanced

Operators	3
Units per day per person	12
Paid minutes per unit	120
Throughput time (working days)	5.5
Cycle time (minute—est. batch)	41.9
Overtime #hours estimate per week	15
Space (ft^2)	728
Travel distance (ft)	257
WIP #	324

Actual after Lean metrics

Operators	2	.3%
Units per day	35	65%
Paid minutes per unit	27.42	77%
Throughput time	.5	89%
Cycle time (minute)	12.2	70%
Overtime #hours	0	100%
Space (ft^2)	728	0%
Travel distance (ft)	52.4	77%
WIP #	65	80%

Note: The supervisor's desk and all the raw materials were added into the cell where the space was freed up.

77% increase in productivity

Figure 3.17 Web tension line—Before and after.

Lesson Learned: One must overcome these barriers to allow OPF as the more efficient process with long-term sustainability. Failure to overcome these barriers will result in the "I told you Lean wouldn't work here" scenario.

Batch to Lean Results: This company was in jeopardy of losing all the business for this product line due to delinquent deliveries. It was a very difficult product to produce with multiple stages involving epoxies and various cure times at different temperatures. In the past, the only way they could handle it was by batching. The employees, many of whom had been producing the product since its inception, were extremely skeptical when introduced to OPF (Figure 3.17). We heard "This will never work for this product." There is too much variation in the types, cures, epoxies, etc. There was an additional cure later in the process as well. When we applied the Lean tools, we reduced the throughput time from 5.5 to 0.6 days. We increased the product value added from 1.6% to 16%. We reduced the total labor time (TLT) by 77%.

Converting from Batch to Lean Is Not Easy

At a major printing company in Maryland, their VP of Operations had been introduced to Lean at a seminar and instantly became a zealot. He went back to his company preaching the ideals of Lean and their need to undergo a Lean Transformation. His first step was to cut lot sizes. As he made this decision, he encountered a significant amount of pushback as none of his peers had been through this training. They told him repeatedly that cutting lot sizes would jeopardize the schedule because their turnover times were too large. In fact, they told him they needed to increase their batch sizes! Stubbornly with the thought that "I'll show all the concrete heads" he instituted the changes. Within a week, the company was losing ground fast and already delinquent to customers. Within a month, the company was so far behind he was terminated. All his peers were then saying, "I told you this Lean stuff wouldn't work here!"

Lesson Learned: You must reduce setup times prior to reducing lot sizes. The bull in a china shop approach to Lean can result in unintended consequences and result in a career-ending move (CEM). Remember, the first rule of a change agent is to survive. You must have a good thorough understanding of Lean prior to trying to implement it in real time. A good first step to Lean is reducing setup times and then lot sizes. Where multiple parts are required for an assembly or final product a good first step in the batching environment is to start making smaller lots of "sets" of parts, i.e., if there is part A and part B and you currently run 100 piece lots of each, reduce the lot size to 50 of each or 25 of each type and supply them to the final assembly line as a set of parts. Again, this assumes the setup times have been reduced to support the lot size reduction.

Batch to Lean Results: An accounts payable process used to be batched several times a day (Table 3.3). The clerk would constantly (doing a three-way match) check the receivers, packing list, and invoices. During the project, we discovered the invoices were generally ten days behind the receivers. So, we created a standard WIP queue of ten days. Now, when the receivers were checked against the invoices, they were always there. We changed the three-way match to a two-way match (eliminated the packing list) and then relocated the personnel. The AP clerk was co-located in purchasing and the AR clerk was moved to customer service. No one was laid off; however, one of the clerks retired (in her 70s) and the AP supervisor's job was eliminated since there was no one left to manage.

Table 3.3 Accounts Payable Lean Office Implementation

Accounts Payable Process, 81.7% Productivity Improvement		
AP Lean Implementation		
Baseline Metrics—3 Way Match Process	Actual after Lean Metrics—Pay by Invoice Process (%)	
Operators	2.33	<0.5	78.5
Units per day avg	93	93	0
Mins per unit	14.2	2.6	81.7
Throughput time (working days)	11	11	0
Cycle time (minute)	6.45	2.6	59.7
Overtime #hours per day	2.5	0	100
Space (ft²)	286	64	77.6
Travel distance (ft)	590	0	100
WIP #	1048	930	11.3
81.7% increase in productivity			

Source: BIG Archives.

When Batching, If One Is Bad, They Are All Normally Bad

At Company X, they believed in mass batch production. Their best customer needed 1,000 parts right away, a large and significantly profitable order for the company. The president of Company X and the president of the customer were good friends. They golfed together often that always put more pressure on the factory to get the parts out right away. Operations, knowing the importance of the customer, put two full-time production control people on the order for two days to track, expedite, and report on the order's progress at each production step and make sure the parts never sat before or after any operation. The parts were made in record time, and everyone was happy.

The last stop for the order was the final test and inspection. Inspection found a tolerance stack up issue with one of the subassemblies in the completed parts. It was determined a washer within the subassembly did not meet the flatness specification. Somehow the washer made it through incoming inspection where flatness was a key characteristic for the part and should have been caught at inspection. The inspector who signed off the paperwork, of course, insisted he performed the check. So, the hunt went on to try to find someone to blame when the report had to be made back to the president.

At this point, every completed part in the lot was bad and had to be disassembled to retrieve the subassembly, and then the subassembly reworked to replace the bad washer. However, they soon realized every other subassembly already built and waiting in the stockroom for final assembly had the incorrect washer as well. Since they had pre-built and stocked all the subassemblies, they were not sure if they all had the bad washer or not, so they had to go through and 100% inspect all the subassemblies to see if they contained the bad washer. After 100% inspection, they didn't find one part that met the spec. They then checked all the washers left in stock and found out they were bad as well. It turns out the supplier also batched all their parts! Since they couldn't recover, the manufacturing manager had to explain to the president what happened. The president was furious and told the manufacturing manager "heads will roll over this." The manufacturing manager proceeded to fire the inspector, and that weekend, the president ended up playing golf without a complete foursome.

Lesson Learned: Batching (like Lean) is a system. With every system come advantages and disadvantages. Companies that batch share the same systemic problems with other companies that batch. When we assess a batching company, we can normally predict where they are having problems (i.e., poor delivery, cash flow issues, two to three sigma quality, expediting). The senior leadership generally becomes very highly paid expediters in batch systems and is always trying to make the end-of-the-month numbers. This is difficult because they are always pulling in orders from future months causing more and more chaos in production. In these systems, we are always looking for someone to blame when there is a problem. Adding inspection is never a good corrective action and should never be the only corrective action when a problem is found. One-Piece Flow is very counterintuitive to most individuals; however, flow works better than batch. Once you initially "Lean out" an area and reduce or eliminate batching, the following will occur:

■ Reduction in floor space.
■ Productivity increases, overtime hours decrease, and eventually, overhead labor is reduced.
■ Team members become very visible on the line, as there is nowhere to hide, leading to more efficient (and easier) supervision of the Lean lines.
■ Supervisors have additional time to encourage ideas, cross-train employees, and work on improvements. This is a paradigm shift from a reactive to a proactive management approach.
■ Problems and process or product variations become much more visually apparent.
■ Results can occur quickly within a specific area or process.

In many cases, even though we think we know, we really don't have a good understanding of what it means to batch paper or parts. A key part of our Lean foundation is to understand what constitutes batching, why we batch, and why we think batching is better. If you think your line is Lean, take the test in the following.

Lean Indicator Quiz

1. Do you have any employee idle time in your line?
2. Do you only have one operator to one machine (or maybe two machines)?
3. Do the operators have to watch the machine in case it breaks?
4. Do you have excess material on or between the lines?
5. Do you use a day-by-hour chart?
6. Do you use a report each day or week or month to analyze your problems?
7. Do you spend all day in your office or in meetings?
8. Do you have a suggestion box, in place?
9. Do you have standard WIP (i.e., sequence of operations with cycle times for each step and WIP locations identified)?
10. Do you have a pull system in place?
11. Does each employee know how they are contributing to the strategic plan goals?
12. When an employee asks you a question, do you immediately give them the answer?
13. Do you have in-between process Kanbans within the line with WIP cap calculations?
14. Is your safety stock separate from your line stock?
15. Can you pick up a tool in your factory and know what line and to which station it belongs?
16. Do you have the end-of-the-month make the numbers crunch?
17. Do you still have issue parts from a stockroom and then kit them to the line?
18. Does your company preach they will live or die by the enterprise resource planning (ERP) or MRP system?
19. Do you have more than four voluntary suggestions per person per month with a 95% implementation rate?
20. Do you measure your Lean journey maturity by the number of kaizen events each year? Do you have more than one kaizen event per month?

Answers/Scoring

The answers listed as follows warrant a score of zero (0) points. If you answered correctly, you receive 1 point. If you scored all 20 correct, then you can consider yourself well down the Lean maturity path, but as we all know, there is always a better way, and the journey is never ending.

Answers

Answer	Score	Answer	Score	Answer	Score	Answer	Score
1 = Yes	0	6 = Yes	0	11 = No	0	16 = Yes	0
2 = Yes	0	7 = Yes	0	12 = Yes	0	17 = Yes	0

3 = Yes	0	8 = Yes	0	13 = Yes	0	18 = Yes	0
4 = Yes	0	9 = No	0	14 = No	0	19 = No	0
5 = No	0	10 = No	0	15 = No	0	20 = Yes	0

Types of Batching
Pure Batch

Pure batching is working with a lot or group of parts and doing each task to each part as a group. For example, consider mailing holiday cards. We write notes on all the cards, then we put all the cards in envelopes, then we address each card, and then we stamp each card. We can't mail our cards until they all are completed. Most restaurants batch by table. They ask each person what they want to drink; then they come back and pour water for each person while the bar is making up the drinks in a batch; then they take everyone's order; then they bring the drinks; and then they bring the salads, main course, and lastly, dessert and coffee. Since everyone's main course is not done at the same time, someone's dish will inevitably end up under a warmer or sometimes not and it gets cold. Batching always creates systemic batching-type problems.

Segmented Batch

Segmented batching is processing a batch of products one piece at a time, for example, running only one type of model down the line at a time and then converting the line over to run another model type. For example, this would entail building all Camry's on the same line in the morning using OPF, then building all Corollas on the same line in the afternoon using OPF. In a machine shop, it would be equivalent to running one part type for a day or several days to minimize setup times. This may be an interim strategy for companies that aren't ready or will never pursue or have a need to pursue truly mixed model production.

Bartenders do segmented batch. If they get a drink order with six separate drinks and three are the same, they will batch the three drinks (each step) and then proceed to make the rest of the drinks OPF, and then they are all served as a final batch. Here, the process or system inherent in restaurants and bars where everyone is served at once drives batching. In restaurants, how often is one meal colder than another? You can normally tell if your dish was microwaved or sat under heat lamps waiting for the bottleneck order.

Cashier Line: Segmented Batch

This style is apparent in most retail stores. Picture everyone in line for each cashier (Figure 3.18[8]). Suddenly, the person in front of you doesn't have the bar code or a radio-frequency identification (RFID) tag on their product. The cashier hits their andon light or pages a manager or anyone on the floor for a price check. Meanwhile, you are stuck behind this person waiting. How often do you pick the wrong line?

A more efficient model is to have one line feed all the cashier stations. This model is in use at the service line in Best Buy®, T.J. Maxx®, Home Goods®, Marshalls®, and in some organizations such as banks and Disney World®. This does hide the waste of the slower cashier but allows

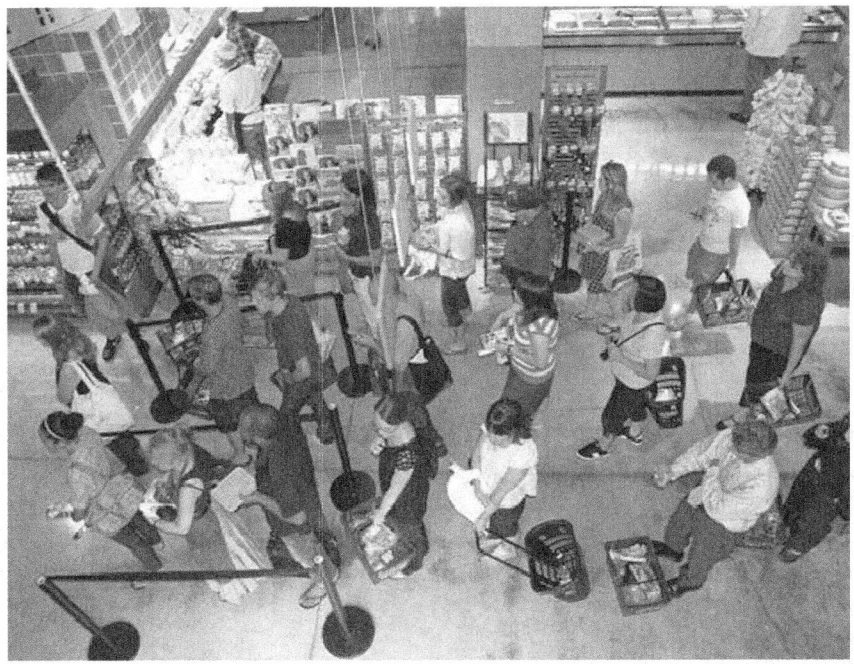

Figure 3.18   Batch queue.

customers to keep moving without trapping one of them in the event there is a problem at one of the cashier stations.

Period Batch

Period batching[9] is working on a batch of things or tasks for a specified time. An example of this might be in the machine shop where work is performed on one type of part on the second shift and then other parts on the first shift. In a biotechnology company, it is typical for work to be done on one type of solution for eight hours and then switched over, and work is performed on another type for eight hours. Traffic lights are like a period batch. They batch traffic for a certain amount of time.

Location Batch: Kanbans

This is a new type of batching category we have created due to the physical location of the products produced. For example, a product is forged in building 1, then sent to building 2 for machining, then sent to building 3 for heat treatment, and finally, to building 4 to be assembled. Another example is whenever we outsource or subcontract to another location, they are forced to batch up their products prior to shipping them. Even at Toyota, their subassemblies are built at other supplier plants. For example, Dana Corporation would make the chassis and then ship it to Toyota in 2-hour intervals. In essence, Kanbans are a result of the location batch designation as they are used to link processes or companies together. In a move to minimize some of this type of batching, many companies are moving their manufacturing cells or, in some cases, entire product lines right into or outside of the customer's plant. Ancon Gear, for example, moved their gear cell used for the position transmitter inside their customer's plant. This strategy yields the results listed below:

Supplier

- Creates barrier to entry for competition
- The new location can supply products to other customers as well
- Provides a working model that can be used for other customers
- Improves communication
- Possible opportunity to supply other products to the same customer

Customer

- Lowers shipping costs
- Reduces expediting fees (overhead costs)
- Reduces inventory carrying costs
- Reduces space needed to store inventory
- Improves communication

Evils of Batching

What type of problems does batching cause? Before reading further, how many can you list? Our list includes these hidden costs and impacts on the following:

- Quality—Problems aren't found until the batch is completed forcing the whole lot to be scrapped or reworked.
- Waste of longer lead times delaying product or service to customers.
- Space—Batching creates the perception of the need for more space that is driven by all the stored inventory collected during and between processes.
- Tracking information—Batching forces us to create cost accounting standards, labor collection processes, and tools to track the standard cost of the batches as they move through the factory. These tools were brought to manufacturing and other industries by Frederick Taylor (who learned it from benchmarking the railroads in the early 1900s) and can be an impediment to Lean thinking.
- Resources—Batching results in more production and inventory control people to schedule, expedite, and track the product as it moves through the factory.
- Respect for people—Batching leads to repetitive motion problems and requires sit-down operations that result in increased health issues. We often hear the objection that Lean makes us robots, when, in fact, it is the reverse. Go and observe a person batching. They are sitting down performing one operation repeatedly to hundreds of pieces, normally an ergonomic nightmare, and compare that to standing and walking over multiple operations per piece and then ask yourself in which case are people being treated more like robots.
- Delivery—Batching slows down product velocity and throughput time resulting in longer lead times and repair times for our customers.

- Customer satisfaction—Batching results in poor customer satisfaction due to missed schedules with 80%–90% on-time delivery (OTD) to customer promised dates (if they even measure it) and less to customer request date.
- Cash—Batching companies normally run three to four and normally at most six to eight inventory turns tying up precious company cash. Batching leads to non-continuous cash flows, as products are shipped and invoiced in batches. The result could lead to cash shortages and additional financing costs.

Lesson Learned: Batching hides problems and drives overproduction both in number of pieces and building prior to when it is needed. Wherever there is excess inventory, there is a problem hiding behind it.

Batching Is a Root Cause of the Eight Wastes and Drives Overproduction

In Lean, we have a saying:

> When you work on something you don't need, you can't work on something you do need!

This is extremely important. While this saying sounds simple, it is the premise behind all overproduction, and it is violated all the time. A common example of overproduction in manufacturing is building subassemblies off-line or pulling in shipments from next month to this month to make the revenue targets or building one year's worth of parts and then shipping them as needed. Whenever we build more than what we need or build it before it is needed, we are overproducing. It is the most difficult waste to overcome in any manufacturing organization because all our results focused metrics drive the waste of overproduction.

Think of the behavior this batching drives. The practice of bringing in batches of product before they are needed ultimately requires more labor and space to handle all the extra demand throughout the system. We must call the suppliers, rearrange their schedules, pay expediting charges, work overtime, and rush the jobs through creating scrap and rework, all to make the end-of-the-month numbers. Batching production can result in the following, depending on what is being produced:

Lesson Learned: A product, information, or person in a batch process spends most of its time (greater than 80%) in waiting (storage) and typically less than 1% in value-added processes. Queues in the process result in longer throughput times, requiring more inventory, space, staff, and in hospitals larger waiting rooms to fill the demand. This also creates unhappy customers. Batching doesn't really save us anything and only costs us in the long run; therefore, batching is not truly efficient.

Batch to Lean Results: This company made chemical detection equipment for the military and was having difficulty paying their bills. Prior to Lean, it took almost eight operators to make one unit per day (Figure 3.19). After Lean, we cut the number to two operators, and eventually, one operator who could get two units per day by themselves. Lean helped this company avoid bankruptcy, secure more contracts to increase their product offerings, and eventually expand into a new facility.

Before	
Operators	7.5
Units per day (includes OT)	1
DL per unit (hour)	60
WIP	50
Throughput time (hour)	149
Cycle time (hour) est.	8

After actual		
Operators	2	−73%
Units per day (includes OT)	1	0%
DL per unit (hour)	16	−73%
WIP	2	−96%
Throughput time (hour)	6.5	−96%
Cycle time (hour)	6.5	−18%

17% savings using VMI, 55 transactions to 5

73% increase in productivity = $423,000 contract savings

13×return on consultant fees

Figure 3.19 Before and after.

Batching Is a Hard Habit to Break

Our experience is that batching is so ingrained in all our minds it is a very difficult habit to break. Based on the research, it is generally accepted that on average, it takes up to 66 days and sometimes as many as 254 days to break a habit[10] (Figure 3.20).

Batching Excuses

How often do we hear the following?

- "You guys are crazy! What do you mean you want me to do these one at a time?"
- "I would have to pick up this tool each time."
- "I retire in a year. Do you really have to start this initiative now? Why don't you wait until I'm gone?"
- "If I do these steps one at a time, it will take forever."
- "There is no way you could do this OPF the way we are set up now. It just won't work."
- "Every time we turn around, we get another engineering change or specification sales says we can meet but we can't even test for it! Don't you understand, we must batch this."
- "I thought you wanted me to do this efficiently."
- "There is no way OFP could be faster than how I am doing it now."
- "I don't care if you think it takes longer; this is the way I am going to do it! If you want, you can do it OPF."
- "The parts never pass the tester, so if we implement one-piece flow, we will be down, and everyone will be idle. By batching, we can all keep making products (inventory)."
- "I would have to walk over there each time to set it down."

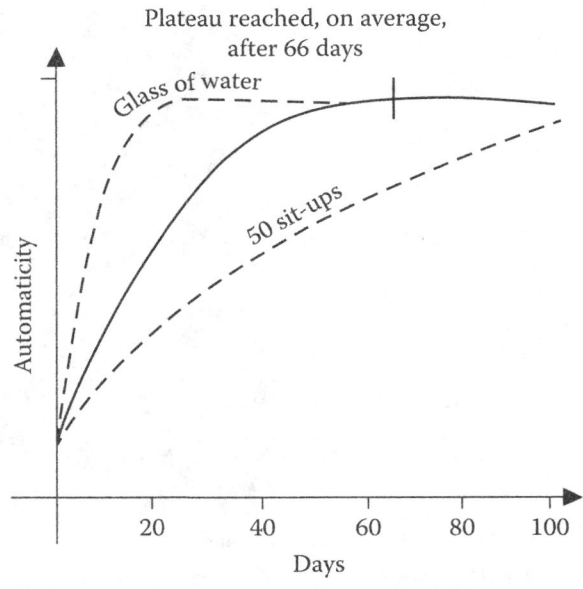

Figure 3.20 Breaking habits.

- "I don't have room to lay all this out in a line. By the time I do, I could be done."
- "If I am doing this operation on one, isn't it more efficient just to do it on the rest? This way, I have better quality and won't miss a step."
- "We always do it this way."
- "OPF won't work. You just want to make us all robots!"

The fact that these basic, fundamental responses are so ingrained in our thought patterns is the main reason why developing a Lean culture is so difficult and ultimately the reason why so many companies fail.

Sometimes Batching Is a "Trust" Issue

At Company X, we watched curiously as an operator proceeded to disassemble a batch of product prior to and instead of continuing the assembly operation. When we asked him why he was tearing the parts down, he said it had been produced by someone else and he did not trust them. This was a 250-piece lot of production! He was averaging two to three minutes to take each one apart and rebuild it again prior to moving forward with the rest of the operations! No one in management even knew this was going on. We found it occurred repeatedly as people moved around from cell to cell. Does this happen at your company?

One-Piece/Person Flow (OPF)

One-piece/person flow (OPF) is processing or servicing each thing, paper, or person one at a time. OPF is always faster, in comparison to processing things, information, or people in batches. Sometimes one must change the process to support one-piece flow and overcome the reasons we may be forced to batch. Converting from batch to OPF reduces cycle times by reducing non-value-added steps and delays in the process and hence reducing the inventory needed within the process and normally increasing the quality. As we implement OPF, it highlights waste and variation showing clearly what is value added versus non-value added at each step in the process.

Envelope Example

By reducing steps in the process, we also reduce the opportunity for defects in the process.

Consider the common example of folding and stuffing 100 envelopes in a batch mode:

Step 1: Fold the letters. The first letter is picked up off the stack of copies and folded. Once it is folded, it needs to be stored or placed somewhere, which requires space, and space cost money! The next letter is then picked up, folded, and placed on top of the first folded letter. In the process of folding the letters, some may fall off the pile or off the table, requiring the process to stop or impact quality. We may have to recount the stack of letters to validate how many we folded. The process continues until all the letters are folded. Individual tasks for step 1 are as follows: reach for a letter, grasp and pick up the letter, fold the letter, move the letter to the table, put down the letter, and recount or fix (re-fold), if necessary.

Step 2: Stuff the envelopes. The first folded letter is picked up and stuffed into the envelope. We then remove the adhesive strip and seal the envelope. The envelope is now placed down in a new location, which requires even more space! Once again, space costs money. (When this concept is expanded to consider the entire inventory in an area or system, it results in the need for some type of computerized inventory tracking system.) Individual tasks for step 2 are as follows: reach for the letter, grasp and pick up the letter, move the letter, reach for the envelope, grasp, and pick up the envelope, move the envelope into position, stuff the letter in the envelope, seal the envelope, move the envelope back to the table, and put down the envelope on the table in a new location.

Step 3: Placing stamps and mailing labels. Each envelope is then picked up again and a stamp and mailing label are placed on the front of the envelope. Once again, they are placed on the table in a third location, requiring additional space! Individual tasks for step 3 are as follows: reach for the envelope, grasp and pick up the envelope, move the envelope, reach for the labels, grasp, and pick up a label, move a label into position, apply the label to envelope, repeat the process for the stamp, move the letter to the table, and finally, put down the envelope in a third location.

There was a total of 22 individual tasks across all three steps. If each of the three major steps (i.e., fold, stuff, place labels) took one minute for each piece, the entire batch would be completed in 300 minutes (100 envelopes × 3 tasks × one minute each = 300 minutes); however, the first envelope would be completed and ready to be mailed at 201 minutes, but we wouldn't normally see it until the entire batch of 300 was completed. This does not include the time it took to pick up and put down each letter and the envelope every time.

Lesson Learned: In fact, it is this time that makes OPF more efficient than batching.

Exercise 1: Try this envelope exercise yourself. It can be done with three people batching and then three people doing OPF. It can also be done with just one person batching and the same person doing OPF. Whenever we try this exercise, people are amazed OPF is always quicker.

Exercise 2: This exercise is very simple as well. Cut out about 50 strips (or use sticky notes) if three people are participating. Run the exercise for 4–5 minutes.

First, have each person print their first and last name on the strip of paper in ten-piece batches. After the first ten are completed, pass them to the next person and start on the next ten. Continue this batch process until the time is up. Once the time is up, record on a flip chart the following:

- When was the first piece completed?
- How many strips of paper were completed with all the names?
- How much WIP was left in the system?
- How many defects, that is, unreadable names or spelled wrong?
- How many strips of paper would have had to be checked and maybe scrapped if a defect was found in the first batch?

Then run the exercise again using OPF. Compare the same information at the end. What did you discover?

Errors and Defects

Now let's explore quality. First, with batching, when do we find the defect? The answer is normally once the batch is completed or in the last step. Six Sigma teaches us each step is an opportunity for a defect. There were 22 total steps in this process. It can be postulated that each of these steps is an opportunity for defects to occur. For example, can something or someone (like in a hospital) get damaged during transportation? Patient falls are one of the biggest problems in a hospital. Can things get damaged in storage? Have you ever seen an equipment get damaged in storage in a factory, an operating room, hallways, or equipment storage area? How about at home?

One-Piece Flow Example

Let's revisit the envelope example. If we revise our process to OPF, it will look like the following:

1. Reach for the letter.
2. Pick up the letter.
3. Move the letter.
4. Fold the letter.
5. Reach for the envelope.
6. Pick up the envelope.
7. While holding the envelope, stuff with the letter already in your other hand.
8. Seal the envelope.
9. Reach for a mailing label.
10. Put the address label on the envelope.
11. Reach for and pick up a stamp.
12. Place the stamp on the envelope.
13. Move the envelope.
14. Put the envelope down.

When do we get our first piece? The answer should be 3 minutes, that is, fold, stuff, and label. Using single-piece or OPF, the process went from 22 steps to 14 steps or a 36% reduction

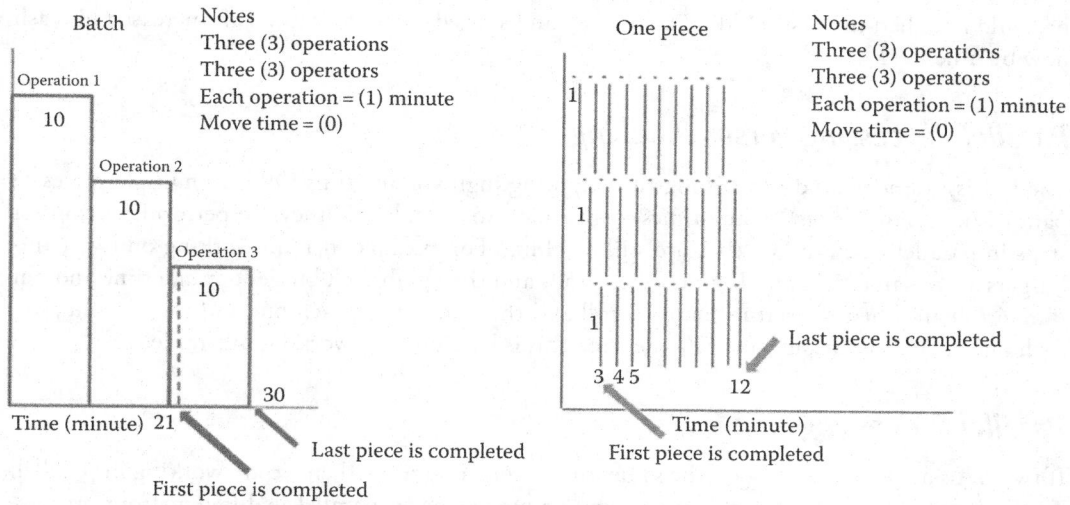

Figure 3.21 Batch versus flow example.

in individual tasks! So, batching doesn't really save us anything; it only costs us in the long run. Therefore, batching is not truly efficient (Figure 3.21).

With OPF, the first envelope was completed in 3 minutes compared to 201 minutes when batching. The entire process was completed at 300 minutes that is equal to the batch processing; however, we don't see the first piece in the batch model until the entire batch is completed. In our OPF scenario, if the number of resources performing the work was increased to three staff members, then all the work would have been completed in 102 minutes (3 minutes + 99 minutes). The first piece would have been completed in 3 minutes, with the remaining envelopes being completed with a cycle time of every minute versus the 300 minutes in the batching environment.

In addition, eight steps were reduced, thus reducing eight opportunities for defects times 100 pieces, for a total reduction of 800 defect opportunities. While Lean may not always yield an increase in quality, it will certainly not cause degradation. However, it is not unusual to get an increase in quality, and many times, it is unexpected. In addition, if a defect does occur in our OPF scenario, we find it right away, and our rework is minimal and limited to one piece, instead of at the end of a batch where the entire batch may be defective.

One-Piece Flow and New Construction

An office building construction project involving four new two-story office buildings was underway in Sparks MD back in the mid-2000s. The traditional way to approach the project would have been to do the foundation for each building, and then the first floor for each building, then the second floor, and then the roof, etc. This developer, however, employed the OPF methodology. After the first foundation was poured, he started on the first floor of the first building. Then he started on the second floor of the first building. He then began the roof of the first building and in parallel started the foundation for the second building. If, for example, we say each step took a week. In the old method, he would not have finished the foundations for four weeks and would then start the second floors. However, this way, his first building was complete in four weeks, and he could start renting it out right away. In the old method, it would have taken 13 weeks before he could have had the first building completed and started receiving cash. This increased his cash flow by nine weeks!

Parallel Processing versus Batching

The key is to understand in the long run anything high volume runs OPF or multiple pieces in parallel (i.e., traffic lanes). Many times, companies mistakenly feel they are performing work or steps in parallel when in fact they are still batching. For example, if I am working on two hamburgers at the same time and I put out both rolls and then grab each burger one at a time and put it on a roll and then put lettuce on each roll and then tomato on each one and then ketchup on each one and then mustard on each one, etc. This is batching not working in parallel.

Parallel Processing

If two of us are each working on the same unit at the same time, then we are working in parallel. Traffic lanes run in parallel. Manufacturing or processing in parallel is different from processing in a batch. Running in parallel means we can run multiple products at the exact same time through the process or operation. Many high-volume food and beverage production lines run this way. For example, if ten donuts are loaded at the same time across the conveyor line and all are fried in hot oil, then coated with icing, then cooled, etc., there is a batch of ten donuts being processed at the same time. We call this segmented batch or small lot flow. This is one reason why we refer to Lean as OPF or small lot production. Small lot can also refer to companies that have customers who require very small order quantities. So, the company is frequently changing over from one order to the next. The Lean production system was created to address exactly this type of production. An example would be building subassemblies in parallel to meet up with a final assembly unit. However, if we end up with more than one piece waiting for the final assembly, we consider this batching.

Note: On a side note, how often do you get on a 50 mile per hour road only to have to stop at every red light? If you are reading this book and just happen to work in a traffic management job, please time the stop lights to keep the flow going! So much time is wasted in the United States due to our inefficient transportation systems. In Europe, except for some highly populated downtown areas, there are traffic circles at almost every intersection so cars can continue to flow, saving time, and precious fuel. High-speed rail systems cut the travel time in some cases by 80% versus the highway. Another example of parallel processing is as follows:

When boarding a Southwest plane in Burbank, or an Alitalia flight from Turin, we could board both ends of the plane at once using stairs because they didn't have the jet ramps in place. However, people were so programed to load from the front of the plane, only some boarded through the back of the plane. Sometimes, our current single systems (and thinking) get in the way of more efficient loading operations with multiple jet ramps. Another example of this "thinking" is found in bathtubs and showers. Where are the controls located for the showers? In almost every case, we must get wet to turn on the shower. What if the controls were located adjacent to the shower? (see Figure 3.22).

Lesson Learned: To eliminate batching, we must first be able to identify batching for what it is, determine the root cause leading to the desire to batch, and then work to eliminate the need for it. While we don't have the technology available to prove this, we would hypothesize the batching paradigm is embedded in our minds. It is apparent just through basic observation. Give anyone five things to work on at once, with multiple operations, and everyone will start batching.

Figure 3.22   Shower—Where should the controls be located?

It's what we do. It's in our makeup. Working to overcome this innate human trait to embrace batching is a major stumbling block for most companies.

Engineering Changes in a Batch System

Batching and Engineering Changes

At company in Michigan, the design group was engineering some updates to our new wheel dryer products. We were revising some sheet metal panels to improve the ease of assembly and commonality across units, so good improvements to the product, right? The boss sent a concerned (somewhat agitated) email asking why we had ordered so many more parts before the change was completed. I had to break the news we had 70 panel parts in stock and due to the engineering design change cycle time, it would be months before we could implement the change.

Lesson Learned: All phases of the enterprise are impacted when the firm embraces batching. This just confirms the inflexibility and cost that comes with believing hoarding inventory is good. Engineering is a very difficult department to initially work with implementing Lean techniques. They normally feel Lean does not apply to them. What they don't realize is that truly Lean companies understand Lean starts with Engineering Design.

Hidden Gems

When we brought up the Lean line at a company in Southern California, I asked the production manager if she realized more output compared to when she was batching. She said she didn't really see much difference. I was very disappointed. Then she said, but you know what? We only ran it with two people. I asked her how many people she normally uses, and she said between three and four people!

Lesson Learned: A product or person in a batch system spends most of its time (greater than 80%) in storage or waiting and typically less than 1% in a value-added process. Queues in the process result in longer throughput times requiring more inventory, rooms, or waiting space to fill the demand.

Why Do We Encourage Everyone to Check Out at the Same Time?

We were staying in a hotel in Columbia, SC, when a bellhop saw me waiting for the elevator around 11:00 am—checkout time! Much to the chagrin of his front desk supervisor, he said to me, "You know, if they would just stagger the checkout times, the waits for the elevator wouldn't be so long." I told the person he was correct and saw the front desk supervisor look at him with an angry smirk!

Many companies and departments have similar strategies as the hotels. They schedule processes to occur at the same time each day, week, or month. For example, we run our MRP/ERP system once a day, or we only print checks in accounts payable once a week. Whenever we batch up processes or systems, we automatically invite all the problems associated with batching.

Gray Area between Batch and Flow: Group Technology[11]

Group technology is the process of identifying the processes and characteristics for each part and then dividing products into families or similar/like groups or services based on those process steps or product characteristics or profiles. The next step is to create a cell composed of machines or process steps that will support the family or parts. The next step is to process them through the cell using OPF or small lots, noting every part may not hit every process step or machine.

Group technology falls in the middle between batching and OPF and generally leads to segmented batch processing. An example is having cells set up that work on a family of parts using the same tooling with a limited number of parts and tools; thus, we can run the cell with no setup time impact. Take note that over time, this matrix must be updated, especially in small-volume high-mix machine shops, as machines and customer requirements change over time. The first sign is when a part in a family must leave the cell to run on another machine in another cell. This is known as cross-cell processing and results in batching the parts up to transfer them to the outside cell. The more cross-cell parts required, the sooner one needs to revisit the families and update them. There will always be parts that don't fit any family, and normally, a model shop cell is set up to handle such misfit parts, noting some parts will always go across cells no matter what families are created.

Batch to Lean Results: Even on very quick operations and machines, Lean tools facilitate the continuous improvement process. This company in Chicago uses high-volume secure serializing machines (Figure 3.23). Even though their operators were only spending 8.75 seconds in labor time on each card using the Lean tools, we were able to reduce the time to three seconds.

- Reduced operator time from 8.75 to 3 seconds resulting in 30% increase in productivity
- Increased productivity on machines by over 50%
- Reduced cycle time in pack and ship from 2 minutes to 33 seconds or 72.5% increase in productivity

Figure 3.23 Improved one piece flow results by reducing excess motions.

True Mixed Model Sequencing

True mixed model sequencing is working true OPF regardless of the type of product. An example in the automotive industry is when any model type can be produced, one behind the other, on the same line. This requires the line to be level loaded. Level loading is the concept of averaging out the demand for daily production. For instance, suppose we make 10,000 Coronas working 20 days a month with a breakdown of 5,000 sedans, 2,500 hardtops, and 2,500 wagons. This means we must divide the total per month by the number of working days. So, 5,000 sedans divided by 20 working days would equal to 250 sedans per day. Applying the same logic to the other models would result in 125 hardtops and 125 wagons made daily. Once we have the daily production calculated, we must determine the sequence for building on the production line. The line could be arranged on the production line as follows: one sedan, one hardtop, then a sedan, then a wagon, and so on.[12] This example shows how the production line at Toyota is finely tuned as each day, they are planning for the next several days, the next several weeks, as well as production a few months out.

Lesson Learned: We need to establish level-loaded pull systems and advanced planning to better manage the day-to-day flow through.

Homework: See for Yourself

Exercise 1: Lay out 20 pieces of paper, 20 envelopes, and 20 labels on a table. Then ask someone to stuff and label the envelopes. How do they do it? Most will batch, which means they fold all the papers first, then stuff the envelopes, and then put the labels on each one.

Exercise 2: Ask someone to make tuna fish salad using three cans of tuna. How do they do it? Most will take the lids off each can, then scoop the tuna into a bowl, then wash out the cans, then put in the mayonnaise, and then keep adding spices (tweaking) and tasting until it is just right. This is trial-and-error processing. The only exception would be if they have a lot of experience or a recipe that gives them the quantity of each ingredient.

Exercise 3: Have someone make up ten peanut butter and jelly sandwiches. How do they do it?

Exercise 4: Unlace both of your shoes. Then lace the first two grommets on each shoe, then the second, etc. Time how long it takes to complete each one. Then lace each in a OPF. Which way is quicker?

Exercise 5: Pick a process, any batch assembly process, that has about five minutes of labor time and is running with one or more persons or run the letter process described earlier for yourself. Calculate the average cycle time by dividing the total time for the batch by the number of pieces produced. Then set the process up (as a pilot) for OPF. Get every part or piece of paper in exactly the right order, make sure there are no reasons forcing you to batch, and then assemble the item using OPF. Record the cycle time and compare it to the batch process. What were your results? What differences did you observe with each system?

Chapter Questions

1. Is OPF better than batching? Why?
2. What are the problems that come with a batch system?
3. What are the eight reasons that force us to batch?
4. What is a segmented batch?
5. What is the difference between batching and working in parallel?
6. Why is Lean so hard to implement?
7. Think of examples where you batch at home or at work. Why do you batch? What would it take to flow?
8. What is a mixed model? When would you use a mixed model? Discuss why a mixed model might be selected.
9. What is parallel processing and what are the advantages, if any? Describe an example in a manufacturing environment and an example in an office environment.
10. If batching is bad, why is it so hard to stop? What are the barriers of resistance that support batching?
11. What did you learn from this chapter?

Notes

1. Dwight D. Eisenhower, http://www.brainyquote.com/quotes/authors/d/dwight_d_eisenhower.html.
2. From Middle English bache (or bacche), Old English bæcce (something baked), bacan (to bake). Compare German Gebäck and Dutch baksel.
3. Personal correspondence with Craig Fankhauser, 12/3/12 Toledo Metal Spinning, http://www.toledometalspinning.com.
4. http://asq.org/quality-progress/2008/08/global-quality/in-the-know.html, Govindarajan Ramu.
5. Charlie Brown is a cartoon character created by Charles Shulz. The sentence references the last line in the script after Linus' 1-minute New Testament speech.
6. For more information, read Leveraging Lean in Healthcare, Protzman, Mayzell, Kerpchar ©2011, CRC Press.

7. Manufacturing: If you give a man a mallet .... Toyota plant bans a tool and the reason it was needed—by Lindsay Chappell Automotive News/August 05, 2002.
8. http://commons.wikimedia.org/wiki/File:Waiting_in_line_at_a_food_store.JPG.
9. Jan Riezebos, Design of a Period Batch Control Planning System for Cellular Manufacturing (The Netherlands: Print Partners), 2001.
10. Jeremy Dean is the author of PsyBlog and Making Habits, Breaking Habits, http://www.spring.org.uk/2009/09/how-long-to-form-a-habit.php—When the researchers examined the different habits, many of the participants showed a curved relationship between practice and automaticity of the depicted (solid line). On average, a plateau in automaticity was reached after 66 days. In other words, it had become as much of a habit as it was going to become. This graph shows early practice was rewarded with greater increases in automaticity and gains tailed off as participants reached their maximum automaticity for that behavior. Although the average was 66 days, there was marked variation in how long habits took to form, anywhere from 18 days up to 254 days in the habits of this study. As you'd imagine, drinking a daily glass of water became automatic very quickly but doing 50 sit-ups before breakfast required more dedication (dotted lines). The researchers also noted that missing a single day did not reduce the chance of forming a habit. A subgroup took much longer than the others to form their habits, perhaps suggesting some people are habit resistant. Other types of habits may well take much longer.
11. John L. Burbidge, Group Technology (London, UK: Mechanical Engineering) 1975.
12. Taiichi Ohno, Toyota Production System (New York: Productivity Press), 1988.

Additional Readings

Burbidge, J.L. 1975. The Introduction of Group Technology. London, UK: Heinemann.
Collins, J.C. 2001. Good to Great. New York: Harper Business Press.
Monden, Y. 2012. Toyota Production System, 4th edn. Hoboken NJ: Institute of Industrial Engineering.
Ohno, T. 1988. Toyota Production System. Portland, OR: Productivity Press.
Ralph, S. 1993. Flight of the Buffalo. New York: Warner Books.
Riezebos, J. 2001. Design of a Period Batch Control Planning System for Cellular Mfg. Print Partners.
Sewell, C. 1990. Customers for Life. New York: Pocketbooks.
Shingo, S. 1988. Non-Stock Production. Cambridge, MA: Productivity Press.
Shingo, S. 1989. A Study of the TPS from an Industrial Engineering Viewpoint. Portland, OR: Productivity Press.
Shingo, S. 1992. The Shingo Production Management System. Cambridge, MA: Productivity Press.

Chapter 4

Leveraging the BASICS Lean®
Business Delivery System for
Continuous Improvement

Accepting constructive feedback is like being a trusty old knife. It can always be sharpened.[1]Welcome the feedback and always strive for the sharper blade of continuous improvement.

What Is the BASICS Lean® Business Delivery (BLBDS) System?

The goal of the Lean enterprise is to supply the best value to the customer at the right time, with the highest quality at the lowest cost. This means creating a culture of continuous improvement and an environment where everyone in the organization participates in eliminating waste and streamlining processes to supply the best value to the customer. Best value means meeting or exceeding the customer's expectations for price, both product specification quality and customer desired quality,[2] delivery, and service. Any company's primary mission is not solely to satisfy its customers and exceed the customers' expectations and promote customer loyalty. In doing so, it is important to remember the company must make a profit so it can stay in business.

A true Lean system, sometimes referred to as operational excellence, integrates or is simply an extension of all our past initiatives, including the assembly line, quality circles, total quality (TQM) management, Deming's 14 points, just in time (JIT), Six Sigma, Lean, Kanbans, point kaizens, and training within industry, to name a few. When we work with companies, we implement what we call the BASICS Lean® Business Delivery System (BLBDS). Many times, this gets renamed as the company's production system. Each word is important in this term in that it is not myopic and applies to all business processes from concept to delivery to receipt of cash.

DOI: 10.4324/9781003185772-4

BASICS Lean® Business Delivery System Has Its Roots in the United States

Lean is typically called a Japanese system of production. Most people think of the Toyota Production System (TPS). Yet, many people are surprised to find out the TPS model has its roots in the United States. It is based on an American system which Toyota has been working on perfecting. In its simplest form it is based on the following five parts, which we will explore throughout the book:

1. Henry Ford's assembly line but modified for high-mix low-volume production
2. The American supermarket replenishment system (JIT)
3. Total company wide quality control
4. Setup reduction
5. Participative management

While Henry Ford came up with the concept of single-piece flow, it was Charles Sorenson[3] who determined how to implement the assembly line process. Sorenson was the production manager who worked for Henry Ford. Sorenson later figured out how to produce one B24 airplane per hour from a greenfield plant in Willow Run during World War II (WWII). Production from dirt to flying took only two years.

Most of what we know as Lean today can be attributed to Henry Ford who also introduced concepts like job rotation, machines to do boring or dangerous work, the concept of continuous improvement (kaizen), and the idea there is an advantage to constantly working to reduce your pricing while increasing wages, the creation of a suggestion system, and much more.[4] Setup reduction can be traced back to the early 1900s; however, many of the Lean concepts we have today originated much earlier, some say even with the Egyptians or Romans. TQM, the scientific method known as PDCA, and participative management were taught to the Japanese by the Civil Communications Section (CCS) in 1948 and 1949 as part of a four days a week for half day—eight-week training course in American management and followed up with visits by Deming and Juran.

We feel it is important to realize Toyota didn't create Lean and it is not a Japanese system. Toyota took what they learned from the US automotive industry and American supermarket and adapted and improved upon it. Toyota should get credit for developing and implementing the concept of jidoka and marrying the JIT concept with the assembly line and of course for developing and sustaining the system over the last 70 years or more. It is sad most companies around the world forgot what we taught the Japanese and only remnants of what used to be the CCS Management System survives outside Japan today.[5]

BASICS Lean® Business Delivery System Vision

The vision for a BLBDS is to create a learning organization without waste fueled by daily continuous improvement. Imagine any business process today with zero waste. Waste exists in all areas of an organization and at all levels. Lean initially started as a process improvement methodology for manufacturing, but an LBDS is not just a manufacturing shop floor initiative. Lean is now used for all business models and, if Lean principles are implemented properly, they will prompt changes from all parts of the organization, including IT, finance, accounting, purchasing, marketing, contracts, sales, human resource (HR), and engineering. Eliminating waste (muda) can be applied to anything that is a process for delivering a physical product, a service, informational or cyber-based product to the customer.

BASICS Lean® Business Delivery System Components (BLBDS)

The BLBDS at a high level is depicted in the model pictured in Figure 4.1:

- On the left side is the BLBDS, which comprises all the processes required from order entry to shipping, invoicing the customer, handling returns, and ultimately recycling. Lean tools can be applied to anything which is a process. This side can be further divided to consider both the task (scientific management) and people (respect for humanity) pieces of implementation.
- On the right side is what we call the marketing and growth piece. The goal is to grow the business at the same rate we are improving the business.

While Lean is an enabler for growth but does not guarantee growth. Lean is applied in organizations to take advantage of being able to do more, with the same or less resources. Organizations must proactively have a plan for sales for their business to grow. Growth must be part of the overall Lean initiative to succeed. When a company can produce its products with less waste than its competition, it has a distinct advantage. The increased profits can be invested in research and development, capital equipment, higher wages, or passed on to customers to undercut the competitor's price.

Organizations must understand waste negatively impacts all our jobs and the health of the business. Remember, once the organization achieves a competitive advantage through Lean, it must communicate its benefits and key differentiators to the consumer to recognize its full growth potential. Utilizing Hoshin planning, management can make sure everyone is aligned toward the true north, where each employee has input to and knows how they are going to help meet the organization's goals. "True north" is a term used to define a company's vision and values, ensuring all are aligned with their organizational goals.

Lean Is a Journey

Depending on the improvement needed and waste identified, a multiyear program is necessary to establish and determine sequential initiatives that will drive the desired results. Remember, the

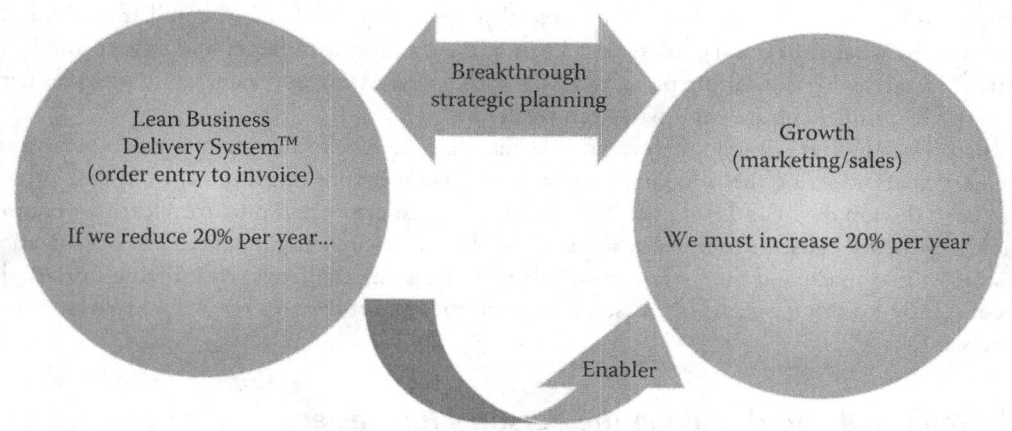

Figure 4.1   Lean business delivery system overview—Lean is an enabler but doesn't guarantee growth.

business delivery system consists of many interrelated parts; many x's (or causes) will impact a big Y (goal). For example, there are many little x's that drive a manufacturing process and result in on-time delivery (a big Y). The team members must be available, must start on time, return from breaks on time, and each must understand what his/her role is, or what we call their standard work. There may need to be several Lean projects to effectively tackle a particular value stream. An overarching goal of Lean thinking is to get everyone in your organization focused on identifying and improving the process.

The difference between Toyota and American companies is Toyota makes thousands of improvements every month because every employee is working together with his/her team leaders, group leaders, and managers. Occasionally, one might get a big return on investment (ROI) improvement but is not the focus. In the United States, we tend to only focus on the largest ROI projects first and miss the opportunity to get everyone involved in implementing all the little ideas that add up to big improvements in the process. When we think of many little ones, the picture that comes to mind is many participants versus large ROI projects driven by a few. Lean is an enterprise approach that involves everyone.

Lesson Learned: You will know you are further down the Lean culture path when building a culture of ongoing continuous improvement every day outweighs the insistence on implementing only those perceived large ROI projects first. Thousands of small improvements turn into large overall returns. Sometimes, a project with a lower ROI can lead to a project with a higher ROI. Many times, jumping to the highest ROI project is not the best strategy.

As organizations embark on their Lean journey, they need to understand every department within the enterprise can benefit from becoming Lean. If every area is not actively engaged in the pursuit of waste elimination (or becoming Lean), you have not crossed the cultural chasm of Lean thinking.

One main reason why so many companies fail in this cultural transformation is that organizations tend to implement pieces of the Lean system or much of the Lean system in a small area, but seldom do they get the whole system in place in one small area much less the whole company. Lean must embrace the entire organization and Lean thinking is a major systemic cultural change. If it stays in the realm of multiple point kaizen events or random spot projects, it will run out of steam when resources and budgets get tight. To be truly successful, an organization must be leadership-driven, with Lean implemented through the line organization.

It is a very challenging and difficult journey that ultimately requires understanding and commitment to be successful. The book *The Leadership Road Map*[6] explains in detail from a CEO's point of view what is necessary to create a Lean culture and how to begin and sustain the Lean journey. It starts with the culture piece, that is, creating your vision and values, and provides templates or blueprints to create your own Lean roadmap.

Lesson Learned: It is imperative everyone be relentless in the elimination of waste by analyzing all components affecting the value stream. A culture of continuous improvement must be created from both the top down and from the bottom up. We must create and nurture a learning organization, which will cause us to unlearn some of the things we currently practice. The organization must be willing to expand the toolkit to be able to address any challenge, by utilizing Lean tools. By constantly lowering operating costs, we increase the opportunity to reward and improve our processes.

It Is Really All about Making the Person's Job Easier

Think about it, who really makes the money in a company? The answer is the person on the shop floor or office frontline closest to the customer. Does it make sense to have the frustrated people interacting with the customers all the time? How often have you heard a customer service or sales-person from a company complain and whine to you about their environment or boss?

Not Working Harder but Working Smarter

Employees don't normally buy into this principle. Sometimes it should be reworded to say not working harder but just working all day. In batch environments, employees are normally stressed out, go through periods where they are very busy, and do the best job they can with what tools and materials they are given but are not really working much of the time. Why do we say this? Because when you analyze the work content you will find most of their time is doing non-value-added activities, searching for this or that, getting up from their chairs to walk over to a shelf to get parts, or to the flammable cabinet to get epoxy, notifying their supervisors of problems, or sometimes just waiting to figure out what to work on next. It's not that we are lazy, we're not, it's just that the work is not generally laid out properly to be efficient.

BASICS® Model for Continuous Improvement

We discussed earlier there are a variety of problem-solving models utilized, plan–do–check–act (PDCA), define, measure, analyze, improve, control (DMAIC), etc. We will introduce a new model called BASICS®, which we think is a great tool for implementing Lean systems. The BASICS® model was constructed to provide a practical guide to approaching a Lean implementation. The main objective was to present an easy-to-use roadmap in which the terminology helps guide the users on what should be occurring as you move through the roadmap. The roadmap is broken down into six phases or process steps (Figure 4.2):

- B for baseline
- A for assess
- S for suggest solutions
- I for implement
- C for check results
- S for sustain

Within each step, there are overarching categories to assist implementers to understand what needs to be considered, at what step during an implementation and what activities to focus on. The categories under each BASICS® phase are as follows. The BASICS Lean® system implementation approach is based 50% on the principles of scientific management, developed primarily by Frank Gilbreth and taught by Dr. Shigeo Shingo, and 50% on change management discussed throughout the book. This approach is utilized to convert processes from batch to one-piece flow.

Process-Focused Metrics

In Lean, we utilize process-focused metrics versus results-oriented metrics. These metrics include value-added percentage, number of operators, total labor time (direct and indirect), first pass yield, safety, product travel distance, operator travel distance, work-in-process (WIP) inventory, through-put time, cycle time, setup time, and productivity. We generally use the metric of paid minutes per unit or units produced per person per shift or per hour as a metric to measure productivity. It should be noted we don't discriminate between direct and indirect labor. Any labor required to

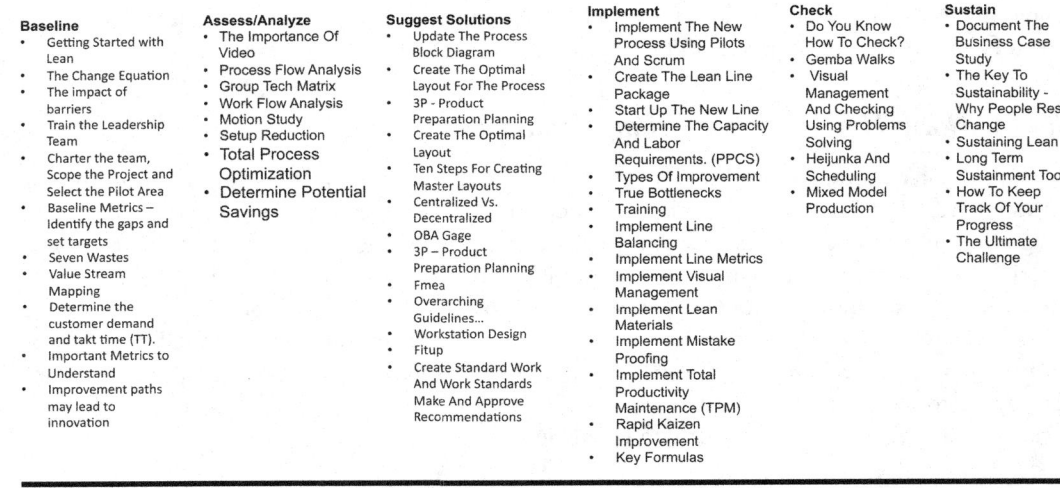

Figure 4.2 BASICS® Lean implementation methodology.

produce a part, including indirect labor, should be accounted for when calculating productivity. Initially we generally limit this labor to operations as it is difficult to capture the balance of the value stream, especially if it is divided or flexed over many functional areas, cells, or product lines.

Summary

When leveraging this model, please be mindful of the following:

1. BASICS® acronym was selected as it is easy to remember, each letter is representative of what is occurring during that phase, that is, B = baseline, A = assess, etc.
2. Think of BASICS® as a large toolbox for ongoing continuous improvement.
3. It is purposefully designed to align with other models like PDCA and DMAIC.
4. It is more descriptive of the steps required versus the P in PDCA, which is very global and does not really guide the user to the activities needed during the plan step.
5. The activities in each phase are represented as when they will most likely occur or are initiated.
6. The activities/tasks listed are for consideration, you must determine which tools are critical for your initiative depending on size or complexity.
7. The model is a dynamic guide, and the activities and overarching categories are meant to remind you to consider all aspects of the deployment. For example, you probably would not have a successful implementation if you included only task tools and did not include any people tools or communication plan.

The underlying Lean strategy for BASICS® is to refocus, realign, and revise the process:

■ Refocus
  – To add value
  – To serving the real customer

- Realign
  - The organization
- Revise the process
  - Flow, flow, flow
  - Link work in and between cells
  - Eliminate waste and non-value adding activity
  - Physical layouts
  - Decision-making, problem-solving
  - Process improvement

Chapter Questions

1. List and describe two fundamental principles when developing a single-piece flow line.
2. Describe the BASICS® Model.
3. What is the BASICS Lean® Business Delivery System?
4. Explain the high-level BASICS Lean® Business Delivery System model.
5. Why do we say Lean is a journey?
6. How does the BASICS® model compare to PDCA or DMAIC?
7. Is Lean about working smarter and not harder?
8. Why do people always think they are working harder when implementing Lean?
9. What is the difference between one-piece flow and batching?
10. What did you learn from this chapter?

Notes

1 Inspired by the National Geographic Channel Show Preppers that aired on December 9, 2012.
2 Yoshio Kondo, translated by J. H. Loftus, Company Wide Quality Control (Zenshateki Hinshitsu Kanri) (JUSE Press) Professor Yoshio.
3 Charles Sorenson, My 40 Years with Ford (New York: Norton), 1956.
4 William Levinson, Henry Ford's Lean Vision (New York: Productivity Press), 2002.
5 Kenneth Hopper and William Hopper, The Puritan Gift: Reclaiming the American Dream Amidst Global Financial Chaos (New York: I.B. Tauris), 2009.
6 Dwane Baumgardner, former CEO of Donnelly Corporation, and Russ Scaffede, senior vice president of Global Manufacturing, Donnelly Corporation, past general manager/vice president of Toyota Motor Manufacturing Power Train, and consultant.

Additional Readings

See those noted in the chapter, in addition:

Baghai, M., Coley, S., and White, D. 1999. The Alchemy of Growth. London, UK: Orion Publishing.
Camp, R. 1989. Benchmarking. New York: Quality Press.
Dees, B. 1997. The Allied Occupation and Japan's Economic Miracle. Surrey, British Columbia, Canada: Japan Library.
Hammer, M. 2003. The Agenda. New York: Crown Business.
Harrington, E. 1911. The 12 Principles of Efficiency. New York: Engineering Magazine Co.
Harrison, A.F. and Bramson, R.M. 2002. The Art of Thinking. New York: Berkley Publishing.

Harvard Business Review 1994. Strategies for Growth. Boston, MA: Harvard Review Press.

Hino, S. 2006. Inside the Mind of Toyota. New York: Productivity Press.

Kenichi, O. 1982. Mind of the Strategist. New York: McGraw Hill.

Leimann, D. 1996. The Achievers. Great Quotations Inc.

McGuire, K. 1984. Impressions from Our Most Worthy Competitor. Falls Church, VA: APICS.

Productivity Press 2002. Kanban for the Shop Floor. Portland, OR: Productivity Press.

Schonberger, R.J. 2008. Best Practices in Lean Six Sigma Process Improvement. Hoboken, NJ: John Wiley & Sons.

Stack, J. 1992. The Great Game of Business. New York: Doubleday.

Chapter 5

Getting Ready to Implement the BASICS Lean® Business System

Everything is made of atoms, so anything is possible.

Sam Jaffa

Senior Manager Operations, Ciena Corp.

Phase I: Pre-implementation—Planning for Success

The first question before reading further is, "Are you genuinely committed to establishing a truly Lean organization?" The chapters in this section are intended for reference and planning and include, in detail, key components to consider as you begin your implementation. We have geared the themes to the level of the Lean practitioner (LP) during a point or system kaizen event). Kaizen is the Japanese term for improvement, or change for the better, and it has since come to refer to the philosophy or practices which focus upon the continuous improvement of processes.

Everyone involved must realize this is an extremely difficult undertaking and requires much perseverance to be successful. If it did not, every company, government agency, and healthcare institution would be Lean by now! The effort must be part of the long-term strategic plan and needs to be budgeted for both capital and expense. The most successful Lean efforts are thought out at the highest level with the board of directors understanding and buying in. Successful Lean organizations can be thought of as learning organizations, thinking organizations, or organizations of innovation through people.

A truly Lean organization involves more than just implementing a certain amount of point kaizen events per year or leaning out part of some product lines or office areas. A truly Lean organization embodies the people piece or Lean culture, which generates and implements ideas from the frontline employees or team members. The Lean organization thinks and acts about how they

DOI: 10.4324/9781003185772-5

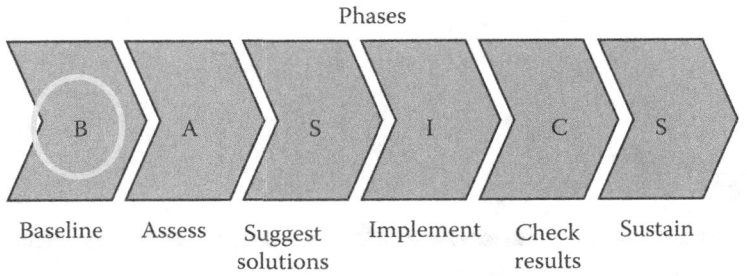

Phases

Figure 5.1 BASICS® model—Baseline the process.

can continually create value. Pre-implementation is a key component in a Lean project. Regardless of the implementation model selected, it is most important to set the initiative up for success. Pre-implementation sets the stage for you to be able to understand your current state or as is process.

Everything Starts with the Customer: Customer Value-Added Proposition and Voice of the Customer

The BASICS Lean® Business Delivery System (Figure 5.1) begins with understanding customer expectations. Let's start with a basic example of going out to a restaurant. What kind of demands or expectations do you have when you walk into a restaurant? Most of us expect good food and great service within some anticipated time frame, which may vary with the type of restaurant. We expect the server to be attentive to our needs and, if we go there frequently, recognize us, and address us by our name. We expect the staff to wash their hands, deliver our food within a timely manner to our order specifications in the quantity promised on the menu, and serve our food at the appropriate temperature. We expect the meal to be fresh, prepared in a clean and orderly environment, and prepared correctly or in essence done right the first time. The restaurant needs to understand their value proposition. Do their customers want the following?

- Good fast food
- Great food, with excellent yet slower service
- Plain food but with a great view

It is critical to understand what your customers want, what they value most, and what they are willing to pay for that value. We call this the customer value-added proposition. Most of us just expect good value for our money. Sometimes, we are willing to pay a little more if we know we are receiving superior service. We are increasingly becoming a society with the expectation of perfect execution combined with phenomenal speed. We are experiencing shifts in many industries where their products are becoming more of a commodity.

Lesson Learned: If the customers demand speed, one needs to understand that improving the speed of the delivery process may only result in a temporary increase in customer satisfaction. As customers, we get used to speed very quickly. We take the speedier process for granted, and we raise the bar for our expectations. We see this in hospital emergency rooms. For instance, in hospitals, reducing the door-to-doctor time will immediately increase customer satisfaction; however, if in the next visit, the same or better time is not experienced, it will more likely result in decreased customer satisfaction.

Easy to Do Business with (ETDBW)

The term ETDBW[1] means an organization is easy to do business with. The book The Agenda inspires this discussion. ETDBW means the business accepts orders or requests for service when and by whatever means is most convenient for the customer. It means the orders or services are provided in the customer's terminology. It means the organization makes it painless for a customer to check the status of an order or result. Businesses need to eliminate the endless series of futile phone calls to uninterested and uninformed functionaries, who have been trained only to refer the caller to someone else equally uninformed or hang up because they exceeded their response time metrics.

The business sends a simple bill expressed in comprehensible terms—in other words, a bill someone other than a cryptanalyst can decipher. Companies have a greater responsibility to communicate with their customers in simple language, for the services and instructions they provide. Is your company or healthcare enterprise ETDBW? If I miss or change a flight with Southwest Airlines, I still receive a complete credit for the flight. I can rearrange flights easily online with no penalties versus the hundred-dollar change fees, baggage fees, and miscellaneous charges from other airlines. I always try to fly Southwest Airlines but recently had to fly on another airline into one of their hubs to catch my flight home. This airline uses the hub model versus Southwest's point-to-point model. Jim Womack refers to this hub model as "huge self-sorting people movers"[2] in his book Lean Thinking. What is truly amazing is to see this "system" at work.

These "hubs" now have shopping malls and eateries for all the people with connecting flights who are stuck in the airport and really do not want to be there. Even if the other airlines wanted to change their business model, it would be much more difficult now with major investments in this system. Once the centralized model (hub system) is in place, that is, things start growing in and around it, and the stores, food plazas, massage therapists, etc. now are well established in airports. The more entrenched the model becomes, the harder it is to change. Too many jobs now depend on it, which is like how government agencies seem to work.

Lesson Learned: This happens in business as well. As soon as a wall is constructed:

■ Things end up getting attached to it
■ Things run inside of it
■ Things are put up against it

All of these are now making it more difficult to take the wall down. When companies invest a tremendous amount of money in batch and queue equipment, we are told we cannot do Lean until they write off the equipment, which has those long depreciation schedules.

The Seven Flows[3]

All problems can be solved by looking at and understanding the 7 flows.

Chihiro Nakao

In the book, Lean Thinking, authors James Womack and Daniel Jones, outlined lean thinking in terms of focusing on clearly specifying value, lining up all the value-creating activities along a value stream, and making value flow smoothly at the pull of the customer in pursuit of perfection. Following these deceptively simple concepts, many of us struggle on the path to becoming Lean as we constantly get stuck in the muck of waste, status quo, and egocentric leadership. Let us look at just the concept of flow. Sounds easy enough to understand, right? Most of us know what is meant by flow and what is not flow. Flow is going down the highway at full speed with little or no traffic, whereas getting stuck in a bumper-to-bumper traffic jam is not flow. But how do we make value flow smoothly?

Many years ago, I was taught by one of my Japanese sensei, Nakao-san, the seven flows in manufacturing:

1. The flow of raw material
2. The flow of work-in-process
3. The flow of finished goods
4. The flow of operators
5. The flow of machines
6. The flow of information
7. The flow of engineering

We must first observe each of these flows to gain a full understanding. In our observation, we will take notes and sketch out the seven flows as we see them. It is very important not to skip this step and sketch out the seven flows regardless of our artistic skills. Why do you think it is important for us to sketch them? As we are sketching the seven flows, what are some of the things we should be observing? To help us think more about flow, here are just a few things to look for while in Gemba.

Baseline: Data Collection/Training/Planning

The following is a list of the project steps/tasks we follow as we engage in a company's system kaizen (or large scale known as Kaikaku) Lean implementation. The steps outline a series of actions, which comprise components to achieve a well-thought-out Lean implementation. Not everyone has to be performed ahead of time, there is flexibility in this model, and sometimes, we perform a pilot implementation and come back and complete the steps.

However, at some point, we need to accomplish these steps to be successful and get the most benefit from the implementation. We explain each step (action) in detail throughout this chapter. This list does not necessarily have to be implemented in this order; denoted next to the task is the most aligned phase(s) of the BASICS® model:

1. Conduct a company-wide baseline assessment and conduct an informal debrief. Follow up with a formal proposal and statement of work (baseline or prior).
2. Put a list of data requirements together (baseline or prior).
3. Gather voice of the customer (VOC) data, feedback, and requirements (baseline).
4. Review and revise or create the company's vision statement, target condition, and company values by which it will make decisions (baseline).
5. Conduct leadership and organization-wide training—depending on how the organization is deploying Lean (baseline through sustain).
6. Select the pilot or pilot within a pilot line (baseline).
7. Outline the team:
   a. Assign the executive steering team.

b. Create the team and charter the team, define deliverables and scope, determine, and notify prospective team members, discuss what we look for in the team members, and create a team charter document; define the executive steering team, key stakeholders, and scope of the project; and beware of the scope creep (baseline).

8. Set up a training/war room facility close to the floor—with the equipment list for the team to meet (baseline).

9. Develop key plans.
   a. Communication plan
   b. Training plan
   c. Resource plan
   d. Change management plan
   e. Contract for change (baseline)

10. Create a Lean implementation roadmap focused on both tools and culture with hard dates and specific, measurable milestones (baseline) and obtain approval from the board of directors (if applicable).

11. Hold required rollout meetings and propose an implementation plan (baseline).

12. Have leadership agree to a no-layoff strategy concerning any improvements implemented (does not necessarily refer to layoffs necessitated due to business conditions which should always be a very last resort [i.e., after voluntary leaves, retirements, temporary shared cuts across all employees, including senior executives]. Engage human resources [HRs] for potential retraining and redeployment strategy) (baseline through sustain).

13. Conduct a Lean overview training session for the Lean implementation team and key stakeholders (baseline and may move into other phases).

14. Document the site in video and digital pictures (baseline through sustain).

15. Begin the implementation rollout.

Outlined in the following are the key steps or actions required to plan your Lean initiative.

Conduct a Company-Wide Baseline Assessment and an Informal Debrief and Follow Up with a Formal Proposal and Statement of Work (Baseline or Prior)

What Do We Look for during a Baseline Assessment?

Plant Tour

There are two schools of thought here. One is to observe and take in as much information (which we call data) as possible. The other is to berate the person taking you around pointing out obvious wastes, lack of visuals, idle time, monuments, and other problems. We can do either but prefer not to judge at this point but just to observe, listen and sometimes answer questions, or turn the questions into learning opportunities for those asking. The first thing we observe is who is conducting the tour. If it is a lower level person, it can potentially reveal the following:

- The plant manager does not think the tour is important.
- The plant manager does not feel confident enough to take us around the plant.
- Lean is not important to the plant manager.

The plant manager is just too busy (which is data).

You see, if the plant manager was far down the Lean maturity path, he or she would have welcomed the chance for outsiders to highlight problems and opportunities to improve and insisted they provide a list of problems/opportunities either immediately after or upon return to their companies.

Lesson Learned: We can tell one's level of Lean maturity just by the questions they ask us (or if they ask us) or sometimes how they ask and how they describe things during the tour. It is important to just listen and collect as much data as possible during the tour.

Observations

The questions we ask vary based upon who is taking us around. If the plant manager is leading the tour, we ask more detailed questions to determine the extent to which he or she is familiar with the plant floor and office areas. We may also ask some strategic questions and about plant metrics. If a lower level person is taking us around, we ask questions geared toward the level of the person, their role, and perceived level of knowledge.

Batch and Queue

The first part of the assessment is to observe whether there is any flow, if work cells are in place, if visual controls exist, and how much inventory is lying around. In one glance, one can determine if the company is batch and queue (see Figure 5.2). If they told us they have some Lean experience, we ask to see what they have done in Lean to date and how long they have been working on it.

Some companies start Lean by working on the culture piece in which case they may have some visual controls, or employee teams, which might have done some point kaizen events. Having the tour guide show what they have done helps to assess their level of Lean knowledge. During the tour, you can start looking for what might be a good pilot line on which to begin your Lean implementation. We also inquire about on-time deliveries (OTD), quality, material requirements planning (MRP) system, parts shortages, kitting, Kanbans, vendor-managed inventory (VMI), various cycle times, etc.

Some Lean Observations

If there is a Lean line in place or they conducted a point kaizen event, we walk through their accomplishments, how it was done, over what time frame, and who participated. We ask them to walk us through the process or typical kaizen event. If it is a manufacturing plant, we visit the line to see if people are idle and if there is any excess material on the line. We observe if people are sitting or standing and if they are batching and how the line is balanced. We look for production planning information and see if any standard work exists. We ask questions like the following:

- How do you know if the line is on schedule to plan? Often, they tell us there is a log, or they record it in the computer. More likely, they keep little information, if any, and the validity is questionable.
- We also ask people how they are measured. What metrics are they accountable for? What happens if they meet or do not meet them?
- We ask about setup times.

Figure 5.2 Batch and queue production.

- Do you have an MRP system, and do you have a stock room and kit parts?
- We look at everything from utilities to workstation design.
- We look at the bathrooms, which tell us a surprising amount about a company.
- Who are your top five customers and how do you receive feedback from the customers?
- What are your top goals in your strategic plan?
- We ask about their supply chain management, Kanbans, long-term agreements (LTAs), and VMI.
- How do you encourage suggestions from the frontline personnel, and what is your suggestion and implementation rate per month per employee?
- How and when (frequency) is information communicated?
- How many people know this job?—If only one, what do you do when they are absent?

For Some Companies, Lean Is All About the "Show"

When coming from outside the organization to assist with Lean, we find that the company takes us to what they perceive to be the best areas. The recently swept freshly painted area sometimes is full of various display boards staged beside the line. At first glance, it looks great. To the non-Lean observer, one would think they are far down the Lean path. At a company in upstate New York, they told us they were working on Lean the last 10–12 years and showed us U-shaped cells that, of course, ran counterclockwise. However, one needs to look for what is hidden behind the show,

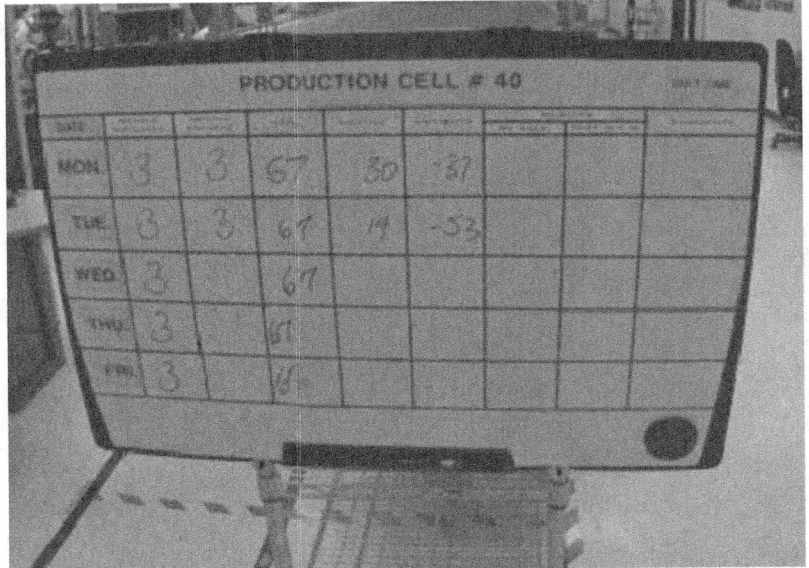

Figure 5.3 Production cell board capturing batch results and is not actionable.

what is on the display boards, when it was last updated, what visual management systems exist if any, and what is the sustainability and standardization used to tie standard work into the company's procedures. Observe the personnel's continuous improvement training and site certification models. Scrutinize suggestion systems and employee involvement. When you look at the pictures, you notice things as follows:

■ Everyone is sitting down.
■ A lot of inventory is everywhere.
■ Kits are staged on racks.
■ Several kits are at each operator station.
■ Everyone is batching.
■ Two operators work together to build their own kits, one does the early operations and another more experienced does the later operations.
■ There is no line balancing.

The production boards look great but are capturing batch results (see Figure 5.3). Notice that the first two days are negative, and suddenly on the last day, they are back on schedule. Patrick Adams has since written a book on this topic called Avoiding the Continuous Appearance Trap.[4]

General Questions: What to Ask the "Employees" When Touring

The following are some pointed questions to ask while touring:

1. Who are your top five customers? Do you hear their complaints or suggestions?
2. How many shifts are worked? When are the breaks?
3. Do you use an MRP system?

4. Do you have Kanbans?
5. How do you know if you are doing a good job?
6. How do they rate your performance? Do you have a development plan?
7. Do you have standards you have to meet?
8. Are you valued as an employee?
9. How many ideas did you suggest in the last month?
10. How many or what percentage of the suggestions were implemented?
11. What would you do if you were the site leader or general manager for the day?
12. Do you have paperwork or computer problems?
13. How much training does the company provide and in what?
14. Does the company keep continuous improvement metrics? Is there a proof of interactions of improvement?
15. What are the three to five top goals the company is working on?
16. Is what you are working on tied to those goals?
17. Is what you are doing value added?
18. How do you know what the next steps are to build the product?
19. Have you received Lean training? What Lean books have you read?
20. Do you see/speak to your supervisor often?
21. Do you have stand-up meetings with your supervisor?
22. How do you feel about your job in terms of providing value to customers?
23. What frustrated you today?
24. Does your leadership ask how they can help you?
25. What are your average setup times?

We may skip some of these questions once we initially view the factory. We ask the leadership team the following:

- Why are they or why do they want to implement Lean?
- Do they have a compelling need to change?
- Who owns it?
- What books have they read?

If they have a Lean person there, we ask them the following:

- What books have they read?
- What is their vision for Lean?
- What is the company's Lean vision?
- What does a Lean line look like?
- How are you measured?
- Does top management support or lead Lean?
- What is your primary vehicle to implement Lean?
- How many kaizen events did you conduct last year?
- Are you a Lean expert or master?

Depending on their answers, we inquire as to their biggest obstacles and get their opinion on what they would do or how they would approach the leadership to overcome the barriers. One must be careful how to utilize this data. It is easy to jump too fast or to the wrong conclusions. Listed in the following are key attributes you should exhibit when performing an area assessment.

Who and What to Ask?

Try to ask the same questions at all levels of the organization and then compare the responses.

The key is to listen, listen, and listen. This is an information-gathering exercise. The information conveyed during the tour is part of collecting the data. Until you have enough data, it is difficult to know what to do with it. It is surprising how eventually over a couple of hours of tours/interviews we start to find conflicting information. Take notes, pictures, or video, if possible, to provide specifics later of what you saw or heard. Record your interviews in a small notebook, tablet computer, or clipboard as you are walking around to show or discuss later.

Don't Talk or Give Your Opinions

It is important not to interject an opinion or critique until the tour is completed and you assemble for the debriefing, unless they ask you questions during the tour. If they ask you questions, sometimes it can be turned into a learning opportunity. Depending on the question, consider asking them what they think the answer might be. It is also important during the assessment to keep your opinions to yourself until the debrief meeting. It is too easy to make invalid assumptions during the tour until you have had a chance to take it all in. The overarching goal is to find out the true needs and reasons why they even have you there looking around.

Informal Debrief

After the tour, take a half hour or so, put together your notes, and meet with the entire leadership team to discuss your findings, after which, there is generally a discussion on the next steps and where to start. In most cases, the tour reveals a potential pilot area and the need to obtain more data. Sometimes the debriefing can be turned into a short Lean overview training session. People's styles also play a role here. At a machine shop in southern Maryland, I was asked what I thought immediately after the plant tour. I said, "do you really want to know what I think?" He said, "yes. I spoke. 'I think it's a mess.' He said 'I completely agree with you.'"

Put a List of Data Requirements Together (Optional: Data May Be Collected during the Assessment) (Baseline)

Taking the time to compile a list of data can save a significant amount of pre-work as well as give you an idea of how the company is managing their operations. If the data are limited or significant gaps exist, it may indicate that more time is required for the LP to truly understand your current state. Outlined in the following is a recommended list of data elements to obtain:

- Any existing industrial and process engineering data (standards, process sheets, etc.).
- Existing quality data (defects per unit, control charts, first-time yields, etc.).
- Baseline data: Production output rate, hours per unit, number of direct and indirect folks associated with the line, cost per case, first-pass yield (FPY), any cycle time data available,

inventory dollars and turns, takt time (TT), product material, and labor cost breakdown. Turn the data into days' worth of inventory.
- Indented bill of material with historical and projected usage, quantity per, supplier, cost, description, unit of measure, lead time, etc.
- If there is a machine shop, it is important to collect the list of parts with routing information, electronically, which should include which parts cross what machines with standard and actual setup and run times, description, quantity per, etc.
- A copy of the layout preferably in some type of CAD format.
- It is extremely helpful to identify and for the team to have access to the person(s) responsible and with access to OSHA, FDA, government, security, safety, and other regulatory standards.
- Need the ability to transport video cameras in and out of the area or site. Most sites have a camera pass procedure, may need to review the policy of capturing pictures and video, and have employees sign consents (if needed).
- Need the ability to make copies of videos and digital pictures and take them with you when you leave to use as examples for other training, noncompetitive, implementations.
- Need the ability to film all processes required as necessary on demand and have access to people filmed for reviewing the videos.
- Conduct a company-wide baseline assessment and informal debrief. Follow up with the formal proposal and statement of work.

When a company begins a Lean initiative, it generally starts with a brief meeting and a walk-through of the factory and office areas for an initial informal assessment. This preliminary assessment provides a starting point to ask questions that will benchmark where the company is in their Lean maturity path (beginning, middle, or advanced). By just looking around and letting the factory talk to you, one can determine how far down the path they are with respect to tools. From a lean tool's perspective, one can look at how much of the product piece they have, how much of the operator piece they have, and where they are on their setup processes. By talking with the team members on the floor, one can determine where they are from a culture standpoint. We will explain more about this later.

Gather Voice of the Customer Data, Feedback, and Requirements (Baseline)

Customer Feedback (VOC)

VOC feedback is critical as everything in Lean starts with the customer. Do you know what your customer really wants? First, we need to implement the Lean Six Sigma and total quality (TQ) tools with the customer in mind. Without the customer, we have no business. Would you want to waste time in an area if it did not ultimately influence your customer in a positive way? Our goal should be to provide the customer with the highest quality product for the lowest cost, safely and in the shortest time possible, and with the most efficient use of our company's and natural resources (see Figure 5.4).

In business, organizations often lose sight of the primary customer. One must also remember we have internal customers as well. We must never lose sight, when designing our processes, to ensure we focus primarily on our external customers. Sometimes, designing for just the internal

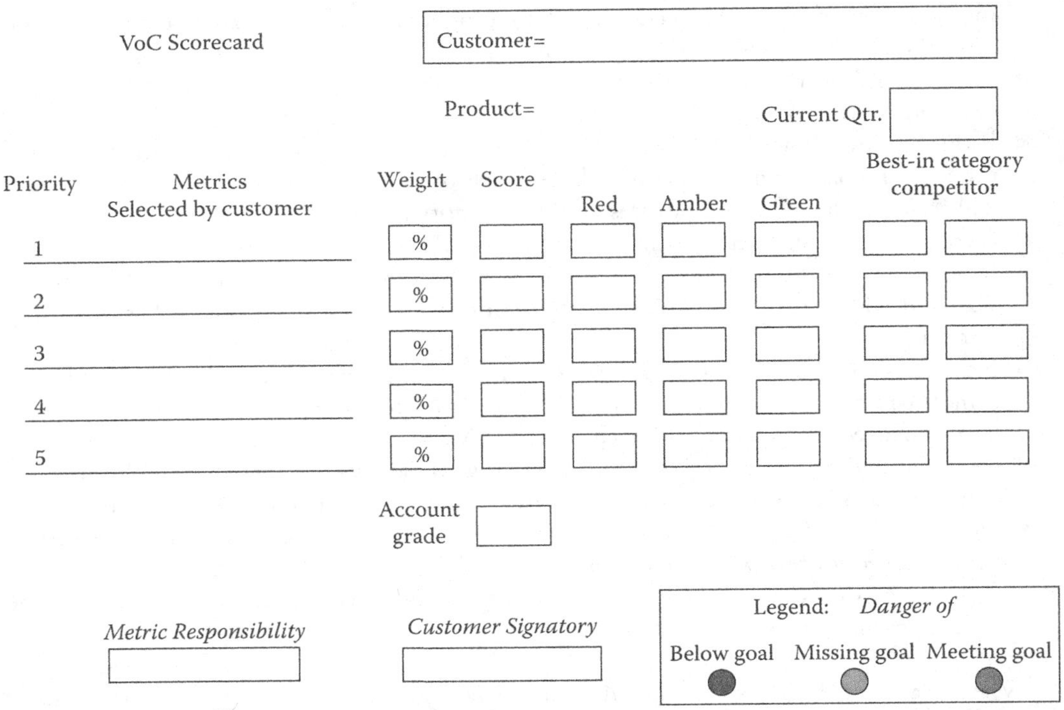

VoC Scorecard

Customer=

Product=   Current Qtr.

Priority	Metrics Selected by customer	Weight	Score	Red	Amber	Green	Best-in category competitor	
1		%						
2		%						
3		%						
4		%						
5		%						

Account grade

Metric Responsibility

Customer Signatory

Legend: *Danger of*

Below goal   Missing goal   Meeting goal

Figure 5.4   Voice of customer scorecard.

customers hurts the external customers. This is the case in many hospital systems. They tend to forget the patient is the ultimate customer.

Lesson Learned: We use BASICS® tools, as needed, to secure the necessary customer and stakeholder feedback, to solve the problem at hand, or to expose the waste necessary to identify the root cause. In other words, use the tools needed to solve the problem—no more or no less.

We must train ourselves to really listen to what the customer is telling us and not twist it in our minds. There is an American television show called Shark Tank,[5] where four wealthy investors (and savvy businesspeople) look for opportunities to invest in new companies. On one show, a young woman came in pitching her new business to the sharks. Unfortunately, every time they asked her a question regarding her financial numbers, she did not know. They critiqued her (provided feedback) saying that the fact she did not have her numbers prepared or the fact that she did not even understand her numbers was horrible. They proceeded to explain to her that this should be a lesson to other inventors watching the program to make sure they know their numbers prior to pitching their ideas to an investor. However, what she heard was something totally different. During her exit interview on camera, she stated that she was very upset that they (the sharks) called her business horrible, which is not what was said by the sharks. She was closed-minded to the feedback and missed an opportunity to go back and prepare herself for the next investor presentation and was left convinced her business was not horrible.

Lesson Learned: Be open to feedback, welcome it, and don't be defensive or twist what was said into something you are more comfortable hearing. You need to listen to what was said, not what you think or want to think they said. Learn to critically see, evaluate, and accept the immutable reality of the current state.

Voice of the Customer Surveys/Interviews

We must solicit feedback directly from our customer to determine their real needs. (see Figure 5.5) There are many ways to obtain VOC, such as holding focus groups, leveraging subject matter experts, and conducting customer surveys. The customer survey can be done face to face, via e-mail, via Internet (i.e., Survey Monkey[6]), by phone, etc. The goal is to understand the big Y or desired outcome of your customer and understand what is required (the x's or little y's necessary) to meet the big Y. It is also important to feel the pain points your customer feels and understand your customer's ultimate expectations or what they deem valuable. There is nothing like experiencing the process yourself to feel what the customer goes through.

It is important when developing surveys to establish some type of objective, measurable criteria, and solicit open-ended feedback with questions written in such a way to lead to unbiased answers. The measurable feedback of a customer satisfaction will allow us to see if we are improving. The answers we get to subjective questions provide significant value and insight into what customers are really thinking. It is important not to violate the survey rules and use a 3- to 7-point scale[7]; this will allow for some stratification.

Author's Note: The executive's experience may not be the reality. At many companies, we have witnessed the all-important phone call from the president or one of the senior leadership team, to notify the department director, one of their own, is coming to the plant, which sets up the all-important VIP visit protocol. Everyone in the process scrambles to make sure everyone knows who the VIP is and when they are coming. It is not unusual for the referring leader to visit or accompany the VIP through the process. Often, this is the president's or senior leader's only exposure to how the processes really run. It is also the only time the staff may ever see them. However, the senior leader does not see how the normal process runs; they only see the VIP process. Therefore, the leader gets a warped, unrealistic view of the process.

Lesson Learned: If you are the executive in any organization and you must call to set up a VIP visit, your process needs much improvement. Otherwise, why would you call ahead to arrange the VIP visit? Shouldn't all our customers get the VIP treatment?

Figure 5.5 Ashes of problem customers.

Customer Perceived Results from Implementing Lean Manufacturing

Price

- Allows for reduction in price while maintaining or improving margins.
- Strengthens the competitive position of the supplier in the marketplace.
- Sets the stage for long-term contracts and relationships.

Quality

- Builds the customers' confidence in our ability to build a quality product, by consistently delivering quality products on time.
- Reduces the customers' time and frustration dealing with warranty and rework, because of reduced variation and defects in the product.
- Reduces customer on-site source inspection.

Delivery

- Reduces the manufacturing throughput time.
- Increased responsiveness to product design changes.
- Flexibility to handle short-term changes in volume and mix.
- On-time delivery of product at customer-demanded rate.
- Leaning transactional or service processes can decrease throughput time and provide better service response time to customers.

Get Aligned to the Vision

The first step the company must do is to develop the framework for their Lean culture starting with a Lean vision statement (see Figure 5.6). Do not underestimate the importance of this step. This is one of the main parts of organizational alignment. Generally, the CEO and senior leadership team must conduct this part of the Lean process and review it periodically.

Set the Target Condition

Once you have your baseline information, it is important to set the target condition (or goal(s)) within a designated time frame. This will provide a framework against which to measure your progress. This should be realistic. It is not unusual to divide Lean implementations into phases to make it easier to execute. The objectives should include periodic reviews by the senior leadership team. The goals should encompass people, the desired behaviors, and tasks. The Lean roadmap plans should encompass a one-year, and three- or five-year Lean plan divided into phases. It should be updated each year as part of the strategic plan. While we can't measure behaviors, we can work to nudge the behaviors toward the desired stories. Sensemaking is a good tool for this.[8]

What Specific Outcome Is Required?

It is imperative we begin each initiative by understanding what the customer values and desires are.[9]

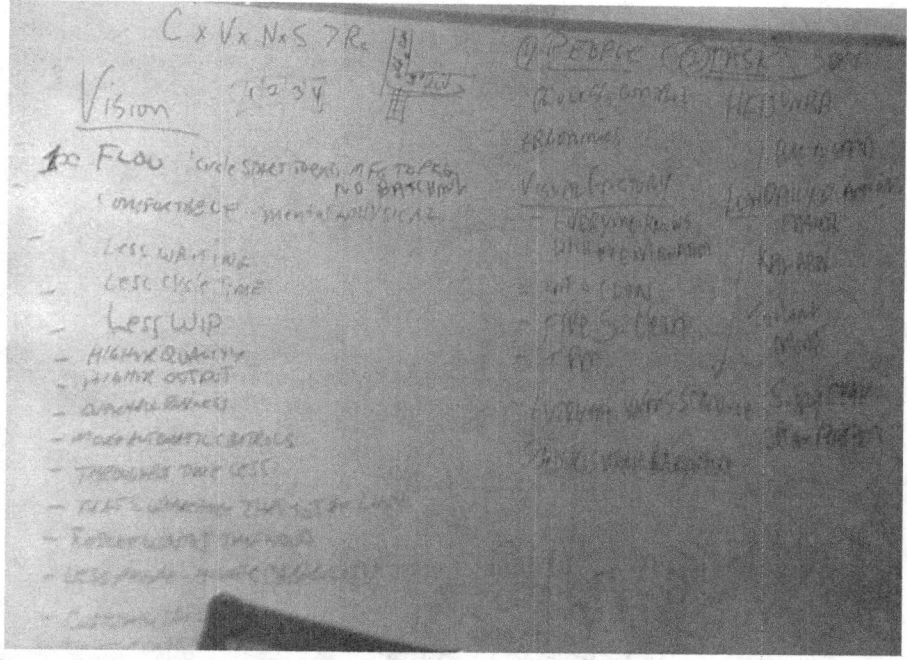

Figure 5.6   The change equation transformed into a Lean vision.

$$\text{Customer value} = \text{Function} \div \text{Cost}$$

Too often, when we go into companies, the staff tells us the customer expectations, but when we probe a bit, we find the expectations communicated were not those of the customer. They were what the staff thought the customer wanted. It is important to understand what makes a good customer experience through the customer's lens, not the lens of the staff. One must clearly define the customer's expectations to ensure the organization does the right things to meet those expectations. Go and see the customer to get clarification if unsure and then use the PDCA process to understand the root cause and work to continuously improve meeting those expectations. (Figure 5.7).

Check with the Customer!

At a company outside Chicago, they were expending significant labor to meet what inspection had interpreted as a critical dimension on the print. Inspection typically reviewed 100% of the parts and sent the bad ones back to the work center to be reworked until they thought the parts were acceptable to the print. The company went to visit their customer, a major producer of tractors and farm equipment. The customer showed them where they used their parts in the process. The first step in the customer's process was to grind down the part where it was being 100% inspected and reworked!

Lesson Learned: Find out what is important to your customer. Do not be afraid to ask them. Ongoing communication is the real key to increasing customer satisfaction. The lack of

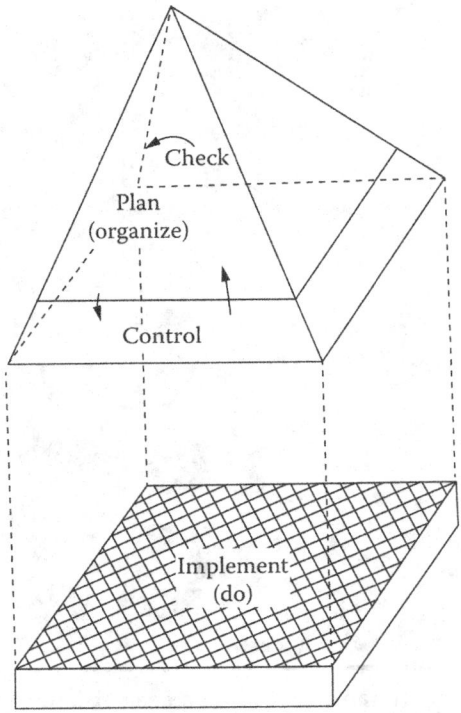

Figure 5.7   Use PDCA to help improve your customer's expectations.

communication creates voids and leads to anxiety-driven customers who do not know what to expect and fear the unknown. Do not base your inspection criteria on what someone thinks or interprets based on the customer spec or ISO 9000 or other documents. Check with your customer!

Conduct Leadership and Organization-Wide Training (Baseline)

Leadership training and certification is critical to any continuous improvement program (see Figure 5.8). Leadership needs to role model and drive the necessary behaviors. Leaders should be provided and required to read several books to obtain a background in Lean and attend an initial one- to two-day Lean overview session, followed next by conducting those training sessions themselves. We recommend leaders not only support but lead and participate in system and/or point kaizen events (also see training plan section in the following text). This step is critical to ensure the Lean journey is successful.

Select the Pilot or Pilot within a Pilot Line (Baseline)

The initial pilot is critical to the successful implementation of any program. The pilot area must meet the following criteria:

- Be representative of most areas in the company.
- Be strategically the key to the business.

Figure 5.8   Leadership training.

- An environment where the implementation has the best chance of success and sustaining.
- The supervisor and staff are willing to make the necessary changes and lead the area with the new changes in place.
- People in the pilot area have a positive attitude toward change.
- Have a way to measure before and after results and set targets for implementation.
- It should test the new tools being utilized.
- Solutions should be transferred to other lines.
- The implementation team should have members from the pilot area and include persons from both the next area and persons from a previous area (i.e., potentially the internal customer) to be worked on in addition to those subject matter experts you are working to develop, that is, Lean core team or kaizen promotion office (KPO).

Create the Team

Create the team, charter the team, define deliverables and scope, determine, notify prospective team members, discuss what we look for in team members, and create a team charter document; define the executive steering team, key stakeholders, and scope of the project; and always beware of scope creep.[10]

Assign Executive Sponsor or Steering Team

Since we all hate creating yet another committee, we recommend making the senior leadership team the Lean steering team. We also recommend one of the board members be designated as an executive sponsor for the overall Lean program. We recommend this not to be a new or separate committee. If Lean is going to be our culture, then Lean becomes the way we do business. Therefore, implementing Lean should become the job/mission of the CEO, the board, and the senior leadership team. For ongoing Lean projects, it helps to assign a different executive to sponsor each team (where it makes sense). At a smaller plant level, we would probably skip this step, as the plant manager would be the executive sponsor of each team.

Key Stakeholder's Analysis

The stakeholder's analysis (see Table 5.1) lists each person that is part of, dependent on, or has ownership over the process, including internal and external customers. In general, it should include anyone who can influence the initiative in a positive or negative way. This helps the team gain an understanding of who is in the critical path to influence the changes proposed as part of the Lean initiative. The list of the members should be categorized and assigned priorities in some way. We recommend creating a decision matrix, by using some or all the variables in the following text, to determine the highest priority stakeholders. The potential list of stakeholders for any project will always exceed both the time available for analysis and the capability of the mapping tool to display all the results. As you run into the challenges, update this analysis periodically throughout the implementation. The key is to focus on the few vital stakeholders who are currently important and to use the tool to visualize this critical subset of the total community:

■ Power (high, medium, low)
■ Support (positive, neutral, negative)
■ Influence (high or low)
■ Need (strong, medium, weak)

Scope of the Project

The project scope starts out with a high-level problem statement and includes the following:

■ The factors critical to quality (CTQ)
■ The baseline or current state of what is going to be addressed and targets if known
■ The potential impact on key corporate strategies
■ What's included in the scope (input and output boundaries)
■ An outline of what is out of scope
■ The target customers
■ The risks

The project scope also contains and details the following:

1. Input boundary: This is the starting point of the process to be improved.
2. Output boundary: This is the ending point of the process to be improved.
3. Major subprocesses: These are the major steps within the process.
4. Internal customers: List anyone or department that will be impacted by changes you may make to the targeted process.
5. External customers: List any external customers, potentially impacted by changes made to the targeted process.
6. Related activities: List any other processes affected by changes made to the targeted process.

This document forces the leadership and the team to think through the project requirements prior to starting the implementation. You can also use it for any sublevel project kickoff.

Table 5.1 Stakeholder Analysis Example

Stakeholder Analysis

Key Stakeholder Name	Role	Strongly Against	Moderately Against	Neutral	Moderately Supportive	Strongly Supportive	Action
Person 1	Champion				×	√	Need more participation with the team
Person 2	Director ED		×	√			Invite to team daily check-in (huddle), weekly check-in between director and charge nurse
Person 3	Process Owner					×√	
Person 4	CNs			×	√		
Person 5	ERN				√	×	
Person 6	CNs			×	√		
Person 7	CNs				√	×	
Person 8	CNs			×	√		

Current level of commitment denoted with × and minimum level of commitment to successful achieve change √.

Source: BIG Archives.

Sample Charter Document Definitions

1. Problem statement/opportunity: Enter a clear statement of the problem or process to be improved.
2. Strategic goals: Enter the goal of the kaizen and how it relates to the vision, strategic goal, or the end customer need.
3. Principal owner of the process: Enter the name of the major stakeholder for the targeted improvement project.
4. Objectives: List any major objectives for the kaizen or advantages expected from the improvements targeted.
5. Targeted metrics: Enter the specific metrics targeted on the point kaizen event or Lean system implementation summary sheet.
6. Team members: Enter the names of the champion, team leader, team members and their function, and the facilitator.
7. Scope: Enter the input and output boundaries as well as what is not in scope.
8. Budget: List any budget available if applicable for necessary tools and purchased or modified equipment.
9. Potential benefit: List any non-monetary or intangible benefits expected from improvements to the process.
10. Exit criteria: List specifically the deliverables required to consider this phase complete. Any changes or open actions transfer to the team leader.
11. Empowerment level for the team: Note the team empowerment level. Is the team empowered to recommend solutions to the champion prior to implementing or are they empowered to make the changes? Note if there are any health safety and environmental or other departments or certification boards that require approvals prior to implementation.
12. Steering group/review council: List what group the team is going to report out to and at what frequency.

Pilot Team

The pilot team should include the supervisor and selected hourly team members from the pilot line. They will be responsible to sustain the line and continue to improve it once the LP team moves to the next line or next project.

Lesson Learned: If you do not include the supervisor, even if they do not want to participate, the chance of success and sustaining diminishes to close to zero! The supervisor must be involved in and understand the changes.

Even Supervisors Need Training

We tried to implement Lean at Bendix on a product line where the supervisor refused to be involved in the process. When the time came to run the line, we tried to coach the supervisor to drive the right behaviors and enforce the standard work. He constantly disagreed with all our suggestions.

> He became very frustrated and said, "If you think you are so good why don't you run the line?" We said, "Fine, we would be happy to run the line and we would like you to join us."

After seeing the output double over normal production with half the former team members, he became somewhat humbled and concerned for his job. He began to think, if someone who had never built these products before could run the line better than he had, he could be considered expendable. So, he asked for the line back. We said we will be happy to turn it back over to you once you can demonstrate and live and drive the right behaviors to capture the hearts and minds of the team members. It took two to three weeks for him to understand how the line should run and how to coach the team members in following standard work and soliciting and helping to implement ideas. It is interesting to note this was in a union environment.

Lesson Learned: As part of our implementations, we now run the line for one to three weeks prior to handing it back to the supervisor. This holds true whether he has participated on the team or not, and it has worked out quite well as a best practice for us. We need time to train the supervisor in the new Lean methods.

Attributes of Lean Pilot Team Members

The pilot team members need to be very open-minded and have a tough skin. It sometimes helps to put the informal leaders on this team. Sometimes, the initial pilot team members take some verbal abuse jokingly or seriously from some of their peers inside or outside of work. Leadership needs to positively frame the team participation. What's in it for them? It should be an honor to be chosen for this team. How often do individuals from the floor get the opportunity to work on developing their own new line process? They will acquire marketable skills, which will benefit them as they move into supervisory or management positions within the company. The team should have a cross-functional makeup with a minimum of one to two people that work in the area: a supervisor or team leader and a design, process, manufacturing, or production engineer. Black belt skills are optional as criteria for team members. The purpose is to train this team in the application of Lean concepts and tools. They will be responsible to baseline, analyze, and implement the changes necessary for the pilot line. These pilot team members and supervisor will be responsible to sustain and continuously improve the line.

All team members should be 100% dedicated full time during the project timeline. The pilot team members return to their jobs or participate in subsequent implementations as desired. Other individuals who cannot be dedicated can be part time or utilized on an as-needed basis. Each team member needs to sustain the initial changes, create the new standard work, and continue ongoing continuous improvement. If the supervisor is not on the team full time, they must allocate the necessary time to meet with the team and be involved in the decision-making to secure his/her buy-in to every change no matter how large or small. The supervisor must ultimately own and be held accountable to implement and sustain the changes. It is a normal practice in a factory environment for the Lean team to run the line and hand back to the supervisor. If financial metrics are used, consider including a member of finance on the team full time, or worst-case part time, to validate results.

Lesson Learned: The Lean core team members or KPO members are jointly accountable for the success of Lean implementations. The line organization must ultimately own the implementations and be held accountable as part of their performance reviews and bonus systems to sustain the changes.

Go Forward Person(s) (Optional)

This person(s) is going to be leading or be a team member on the next implementation line or project. One should consider selecting team leaders and members that might be part of the organization's succession plan.

List of Skills and Characteristics of Project Team Leaders and Team Members

Team Leader

- Can lead a team and manage to a project deadline
- Is familiar with the business
- Is open to change
- Has the respect of both the senior leadership and the organization as a whole?
- Is technologically curious, imaginative, and insightful
- Has good common sense
- Is not afraid to ask why (dumb question), admit error, create structure where no structure exist, and identify good talent
- Computer skills: Has good working knowledge of Microsoft Excel and Project
- Is not afraid of confrontation
- Has good communication skills
- Has good presentation skills
- Has good interpersonal skills
- Has detailed process knowledge
- Is respected within the team
- Has grown up in the system—promoted from within
- Is dedicated and committed—does whatever it takes to get the job done with respect to that effort and time commitments
- Is a critical thinker

Team Members

- Have good communication skills
- Have good interpersonal skills
- Provide 110% effort
- Conduct constructive critical evaluation of their own work
- Have a good/positive attitude
- Are open to change
- Computer skills: A good working knowledge of Microsoft Excel and Project preferred but not required. (Note: We do everything on pencil and paper or whiteboards first, nothing must be done on a computer. Many times, we just take pictures of the papers or whiteboards to preserve them.)
- Willing to work long hours if necessary
- Are team players

Lean Practitioner Levels

The LP team is to become subject matter experts and your future LPs. They will be dedicated full time for the next couple of years and will become the trainers in your organization. They should spend as much time as possible with the consultant to transfer knowledge and become self-sustaining. We have five levels that are as follows:

1. Foundations level—Lean overview knowledge of the BASICS® System and must pass the foundations level exam

2. Apprentice level—Six months to one year learning how to implement the BASICS® model for assembly, machining, and continuous flow environments—must pass an Apprentice exam
3. Journeyman level—One to three years with coaching and mentoring—can implement the BASICS® model and Leadership Development Path Model in all environments—must pass Journeyman's exam
4. Masters level—Three to ten years—can implement the BASICS® model and Leadership Development Path Model and train others
5. Sensei level—Ten years—recognized by their peers

The LP core team should be composed of two to three persons (of the six to eight total pilot team members). They should be high-potential, informal organization leaders who will ensure success. It normally works best if these people are in the management level or above to have credibility within the overall organization.

They should be selected very carefully during the pre-implementation phase, as they will be developing highly desirable skills that will increase their outside marketability. They should be dedicated 100% full time for several years.

However, we have experimented with this person having joint roles like advance manufacturing engineering manager/director and LP champion. This has been successful, but this person must have 75%–80% of their time to dedicate toward this effort, and they must be 100% dedicated while the consultant is training them. The company can rotate this position over time returning the Lean team member to a staff or preferably line position. Prior to selection, leadership should consider the person's development plan during and after the implementation. The LP team will be responsible to design and implement the changes resulting from the analysis of the product, operator, and setup/change over within the area scoped by the management in accordance with the Lean principles throughout the rest of the organization.

Set Up a Training/War Room Facility Close to the Floor: With Equipment List for the Team to Meet (Baseline)

It is critical the team members have dedicated space to assemble, over the entire length of the project, with the proper equipment to work, brainstorm, analyze, and train. Reserve meeting and training facilities in advance. Provide Internet access, power strips, computer projectors or monitors, whiteboards, flip charts, markers, yellow stickies, and bowls filled with candy with ample ability to accommodate the number of members or teams. The war room or obeya room should provide a visual storyboard of the project as it progresses.

Develop Key Plans: Communication Plan, Training Plan, Resource Plan, Change Management Plan, Contract for Change (Baseline)

Communication Plan

The communication plan (see Table 5.2) is a critical part of Lean implementation. It should be created initially and actively worked throughout the entire Lean initiative to ensure a successful

Table 5.2 Communication Plan Example

Communication Plan

Company X Proposed Communication Plan for Lean Implementation — 10-13-09

Meeting	Purpose	Owner	Key Tasks	Frequency	Duration	Delivery Via	Date	Location	Attendees/Distribution
Kick-off meetings									
Lean kick-off meeting	To discuss scope, charter document, and overview of process	Jim	Set date and create agenda for meeting	Once	TBD	Verbal	TBD	TBD	All hands
Rollout notice letter	Top management letter to explain what we are doing and why. Create sense of urgency. No layoffs due to Lean	Joe	Waiting on corporate	Once	In process	Letter	TBD	NA	All hands
Ongoing communication									
Newsletter	Communicate progress of Lean teams, Lean training	Hr	Solicit teams each week for updates, gm/vp corner, Lean training	Weekly	Ongoing	E-mail or handouts?	Start this week	TBD	All hands
Switch group meeting	Communicate progress of Lean teams, Lean training	Jim	Solicit teams	Weekly	10 minutes	Verbal	Thursdays at 3:10 p.m.	In switch area	Switch group
Fab switch group meeting	Communicate progress of Lean teams, Lean training	Jim	Solicit teams	Weekly	11 minutes	Verbal	TBD	In fab area	Switch fab group

Table 5.2 (Continued) Communication Plan Example

Communication Plan

Company X Proposed Communication Plan for Lean Implementation—10-13-09

Meeting	Purpose	Owner	Key Tasks	Frequency	Duration	Delivery Via	Date	Location	Attendees/ Distribution
Bulletin boards	Lean progress pictures and training	Jason	Solicit teams	Weekly	N/A	Visual	Ongoing	Five Locations throughout plant	All hands
Lean update	Communicate upper management support and drive	Joe/Jim D	Monthly	Ongoing	E-mail or letter?	Ongoing	All plants in division	All hands	
Lean question box	Surface questions or concerns from staff and address in newsletter	Hr	Need location and setup, should communicate during initial kick-offs and note in newsletters	Review daily	Ongoing	Written	TBD	In house	All hands
Distribute applicable Lean articles	Education	Bill H		TBD	Length of project	Written or e-mail		In house	TBD
Idea board	To visually display improvements and begin culture of CI	FF Mgrs	Implement boards include in daily meetings	Daily	Ongoing	Verbal		FF	Team members

(Continued)

Table 5.2 (*Continued*) Communication Plan Example

Communication Plan

Company X Proposed Communication Plan for Lean Implementation— 10-13-09

Meeting	Purpose	Owner	Key Tasks	Frequency	Duration	Delivery Via	Date	Location	Attendees/ Distribution
Payroll inserts	Communicate high- visibility information	HR	Develop messages	Use sparingly	Ongoing	Paycheck			
Wallet cards	Handy source of vision, values, goals, problem- solving models, etc.	DO	Develop messages	As needed	Ongoing	Physical			
VOC Quality Surveys Complaints	Communicate VOC to employees	Marketing	Communicate survey results, failures and complaints, and good feedback to floor	Quarterly or as received	Ongoing	Do stand-up meetings FF meetings newsletters			
Daily focused factory meetings Qdips Failure boards/ stations	Review past day activity and coming days' activities. Solicit participation from team in all areas. Have areas running in top condition	FF Mgrs	Need daily preparation, follow up on all qdip tasks, invite necessary people to meeting, pick meeting roles	Daily	Ongoing	Stand-up meetings			

Table 5.2 (Continued)   Communication Plan Example

Communication Plan

Company X Proposed Communication Plan for Lean Implementation — 10-13-09

Meeting	Purpose	Owner	Key Tasks	Frequency	Duration	Delivery Via	Date	Location	Attendees/ Distribution
Daily Lean team update meetings include HR, quality, HS&E weekly	Review past day activity and coming days' activities. Look at status of big picture items/ committees	DO	Lean team leaders need to be prepared with daily update. Need to update action item list	Daily	Ongoing	Meetings in do office or war room			
Management scripting of changes	Align managers with responses to employee questions or concerns	DO	Update scripting as necessary	As needed	Ongoing	Stand- up meetings			
Escalation process									
Events									
Dumpster days									
Cookouts									

Source: BIG Archives.

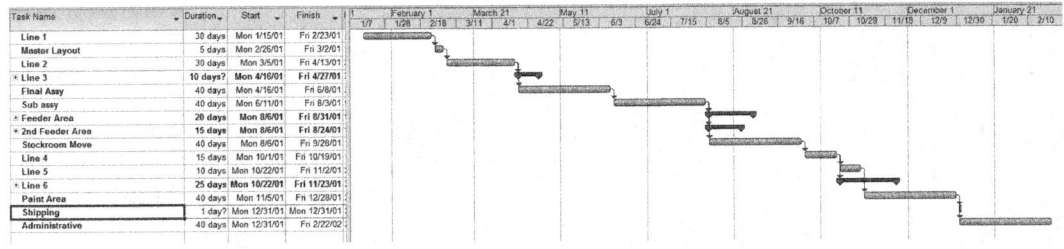

Task Name	Duration	Start	Finish
Line 1	30 days	Mon 1/15/01	Fri 2/23/01
Master Layout	5 days	Mon 2/26/01	Fri 3/2/01
Line 2	30 days	Mon 3/5/01	Fri 4/13/01
Line 3	10 days?	Mon 4/16/01	Fri 4/27/01
Final Assy	40 days	Mon 4/16/01	Fri 6/8/01
Sub assy	40 days	Mon 6/11/01	Fri 8/3/01
Feeder Area	20 days	Mon 8/6/01	Fri 8/31/01
2nd Feeder Area	15 days	Mon 8/6/01	Fri 8/24/01
Stockroom Move	40 days	Mon 8/6/01	Fri 9/28/01
Line 4	15 days	Mon 10/1/01	Fri 10/19/01
Line 5	10 days	Mon 10/22/01	Fri 11/2/01
Line 6	25 days	Mon 10/22/01	Fri 11/23/01
Paint Area	40 days	Mon 11/5/01	Fri 12/28/01
Shipping	1 day?	Mon 12/31/01	Mon 12/31/01
Administrative	40 days	Mon 12/31/01	Fri 2/22/02

Figure 5.9 Lean model site high level implementation plan.

transition post pilot. Too often, the communication to the area staff, stakeholders, and organization takes a backseat to other activities on the project task list. It is culturally important to have the appropriate level of communication related to the activities to help disseminate Lean across the organization. Figure 5.9 shows an example of a Lean model site implementation. This plan can be developed and used at any level for any project.

Graphic Arts/Publications: Newsletter

Many companies will start a newsletter as part of the communication plan or include the Lean initiative in their existing newsletter. Publish an introductory article just prior to the start of the continuous improvement program.

Lesson Learned: We have found it best not to roll Lean out as a new program but as a continuation of past improvement activities. Therefore, people do not feel it is a new flavor of the month program. Frame it as taking the company to the next level.

Training Plan

The training plan (see Table 5.3) should encompass training at all levels for all aspects of the implementation to be carried out in the initial phase. It should incorporate levels of training from basic Lean concept training (for area employees and stakeholders) to broader and deeper Lean tool training as needed (LP team members) depending on the level of participation within the project. It should also include the seminar or shop floor classes and content along with the topics and approximate timing. These plans normally start out very high level and broad and get expanded into more detailed plans. Use them at any level for any project and revise as necessary to ensure inclusiveness.

There are many models in which to train and deploy an understanding of Lean concepts and tools. The more practical exposure, the better it is. The best training opportunities are the ones in which individuals can not only learn the background and concepts but also get to experience the application of tools firsthand. Training plans can vary depending on how the organization is deploying Lean. Lean training can range from an exposure training of 2–4 hours to 1 day to provide a brief overview of the concepts of Lean, tools, implementation, and results to an extensive multiday (three to five) training that provides a deeper dive into the concepts, tools, culture, and hands-on exercise to allow trainees to gain a full understanding of the concepts and impact of Lean. Generally, the upper management begins with a 4- to 8-hour Lean training to gain a shared vision of the potential of a Lean journey. Training for the area

Table 5.3   Training Plan Example

Training Plan

Surgery PI Project Proposed Training Plan

Meeting	Type	Purpose	Who Will Deliver Training	Frequency	Date	Location	Attendees/Distribution
OR PI team	On the Job	Educate on the Lean tools and principles	OPI	As required	Starting at beginning of project	War room	
Steering committee		Educate on the Lean tools and principles	OPI	One time	Phase II TBD	TBD	Steering committee members that would be interested
Surgery managerial staff	1 day or 2 day spread out	Educate on the Lean tools and principles	OPI	Could be spread out	Phase II TBD	TBD	
Nursing staff	2-hour overview	Show them WIIFM	OPI	One time	Phase II TBD	TBD	PACU, perioperative, preadmission testing, SPD, materials
Surgery support staff	2-hour overview	Show them WIIFM	OPI	One time	Phase II TBD	TBD	PACU, perioperative, preadmission testing, SPD, materials
Physicians	1-hour executive overview	Show them WIIFM	OPI	One time	Phase II TBD	TBD	Any that would like to participate

Source: BIG Archives.

undergoing the Lean implementation could be approached in a variety of ways. Generally, we find Lean deployed in three ways:

- Lean deployment with organizational commitment
- Grassroots driven
- Middle management driven (or one plant or part of a plant out of a multisite division)

Option 1: Scalable training model—it is generally driven at the senior level where there is an organizational commitment to Lean:

- Management training: 8- to 16-hour training of Lean, concepts, strategic advantage, cultural transformation—includes the executive leaders, the upper management, and if possible, all leaders as they may be stakeholders in areas not initially engaged in Lean (this sets the vision from the CEO and board and provides limited exposure to start the learning).
- Team members and key stakeholders training: Aimed at any area engaging in the implementation as well as the cross-functionally impacted areas of the deployment. It is recommended that these individuals have a three- to five-day Lean training that is broader and deeper. The training should include area executives, leaders, supervisors, and designated staff who will be engaged in Lean implementation as they begin the journey within the organization. Additional three- to five-day training should be offered as full deployment of Lean occurs across the organization. This type of multiday training can be critical to breaking down the silos and should be leveraged to bring in stakeholders who might be critical in breaking down the barriers across the value stream. Having leaders and staff from functionally dependent departments learn the concepts and gain an understanding together can help begin the cultural transformation necessary for a successful Lean journey. The Lean team members would continue to have hands-on tool training throughout the project.
- Frontline staff training: 2- to 4-hour multiple training sessions for staff impacted by the Lean initiative, so there is a common language and understanding of waste, tools, and the reasons behind what they are experiencing as changes occur in their areas.

Option 2: Grassroots model—it is often used if there has not been the top-down organizational support.

If a grassroots initiative of Lean is occurring (i.e., not being driven by the CEO or senior executive team), an area may opt to begin with a practical training, as they have limited time and resources. This is generally recommended only for initial engagement of Lean implementation in one focused area. It might look like this:

- A 4-hour background on Lean to area managers and staff
- A limited overview on use of tools and concepts that will be applied
- A real-time detailed training for participants prior to applying tool and concepts in their work area
- A debriefing after tool and concept application to reinforce learning
- A one-to-one and a half-day Lean overview for senior leaders (board members if possible)

Pros: These provide a practical hands-on approach, rapid deployment, and limited planning; a see one, do one model.

Cons: These are geared for smaller grassroots Lean approach and do not promote transformational Lean deployment and organizational understanding of Lean.

Option 3: The middle management has been engaged in Lean in another organization and understands the value of deploying in his or her area:

- A one-to-one and a half-day Lean overview for senior leaders (board members if possible)
- An 8-hour background on Lean to area managers and staff
- A real-time detailed training for participants prior to applying tool and concepts in their work area
- A debriefing after tool and concept application to reinforce learning

Resource Plan

This plan defines the resources required to implement Phase I of your rollout. It should include and specify full-time and part-time resources and the percentage of dedicated versus part time. This is a very important document and somewhat of an initial feasibility study. It should include how to back up and distribute the workload of those dedicated full time to the implementation. Again, it can be used at any level for any project. It is important to have clarity among supervisory staff for the team members selected for the project to ensure the team members are allocated the appropriate time to commit to the Lean initiative.

Communication/Change Management Plan

This plan is designed to force you to think as to what barriers lay ahead from a change management perspective. You can leverage your stakeholder's analysis by identifying any potential key individuals that could negatively influence the effort. It should include a list of potential concrete heads and how you plan on dealing with them. It is basically a failure modes and effects analysis (FMEA) for change during the implementation. In short, it is a tool used to analyze a process to see:

- What could go wrong
- The likelihood of it going wrong
- The severity if it does go wrong
- Creating a risk mitigation plan in case it does go wrong

A simple example of FMEA is to ask yourself, "How many tires does a car have?" Did you answer four? If so, in most cases, you are wrong as just about every car has a spare or fifth tire. This fifth tire is part of the risk mitigation plan. What is the likelihood of getting a flat tire? How often do you see someone on the side of an interstate changing a tire? How often have you had a flat tire? How severe is it if you get one? Our plan is to carry a spare and the equipment to change the tire or carry a can of Fix a Flat® to mitigate the risk. Part of this plan could include a benchmarking trip(s) and book assignments to help foster the change. The change management plan should be continually updated and revised as needed throughout the initiative. Change management is a critical component of the adoption of Lean concepts and the Lean implementation cycle (Figure 5.10).

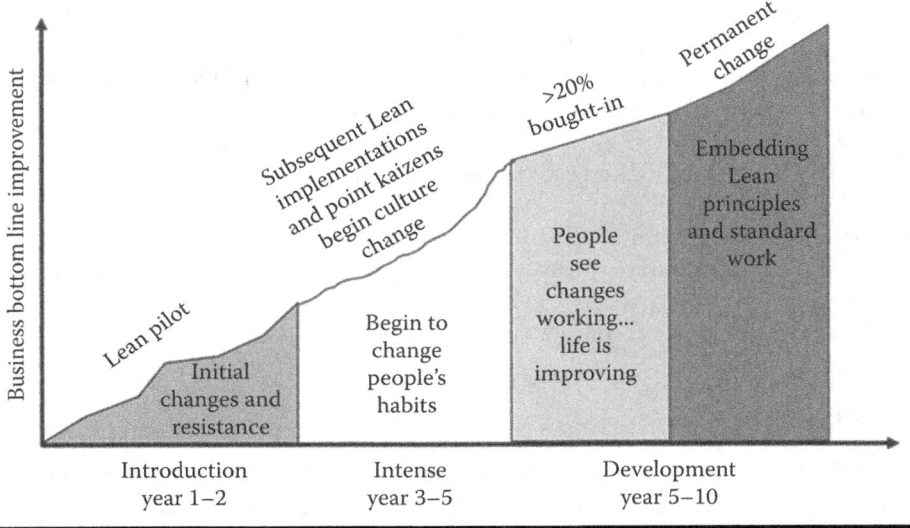

Figure 5.10 Lean implementation transformation cycle.

Contract for Change

This document has been extremely useful from a culture standpoint to ensure everyone is on the same page and having them literally sign and date the contract for change document. It should contain the vision, goals and objectives, an escalation plan, methodology, and commitment. It can be used at any level for any project. It is critical to have an escalation process in place to help the improvement teams or supervisors remove barriers to improvement. Many times, people are afraid to complain to their bosses or their bosses may be the problem. Failure to have this process in place will force these issues to be hidden and not come to the surface. The escalation process should proceed all the way to the CEO. Several times, we have had to go to the CEO during Lean implementations to make the final call. Create a Lean implementation roadmap focused on both tools and culture with hard dates and specific, measurable milestones (see Figure 5.11).

High-Level Implementation Plan

This is the plan outlining the high-level steps. We suggest that once a pilot implementation is conducted, the senior leadership get together and form a steering committee to plot out their roadmap with deliverable milestones. This should be a three- to five-year plan. It should contain a communication plan and a training plan for the site. A good book for this is Leadership Road Map[11] by Russ Scaffede (see Figure 5.12).

Implementing Six Sigma Before Lean: Beware

We have found many companies engaged in Six Sigma efforts prior to learning about Lean. This can lead to difficulties when trying to implement Lean. In some organizations, a competition between green or black belts and so-called Lean specialists or Lean masters develops, when, in fact, a synergy of the tools and concepts should be leveraged to gain a better result.

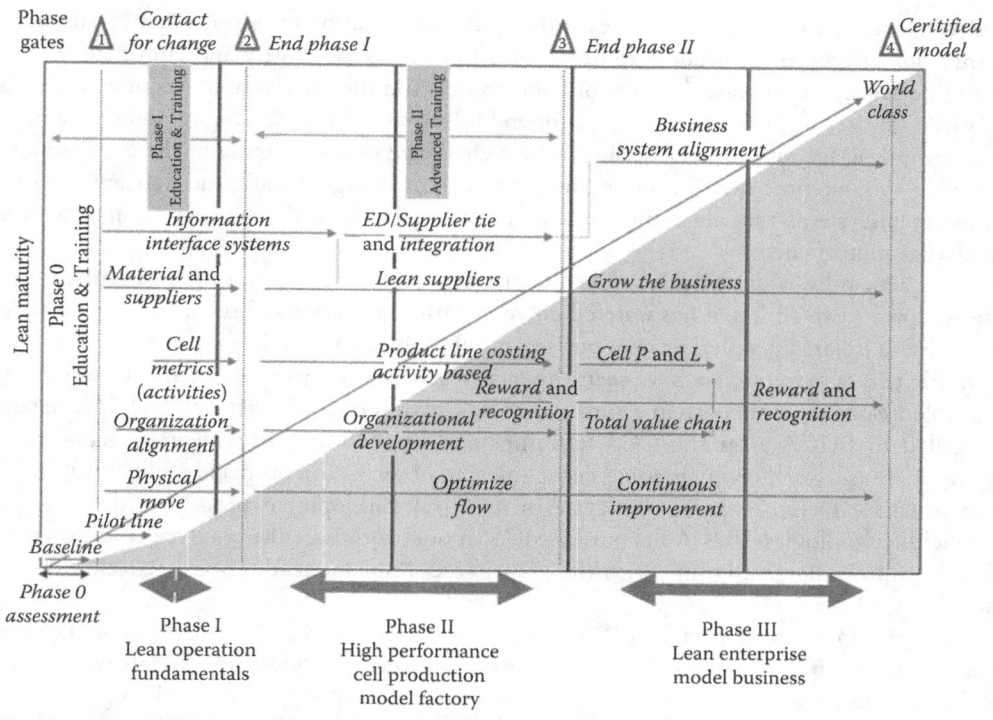

Figure 5.11 AlliedSignal Lean roadmap.

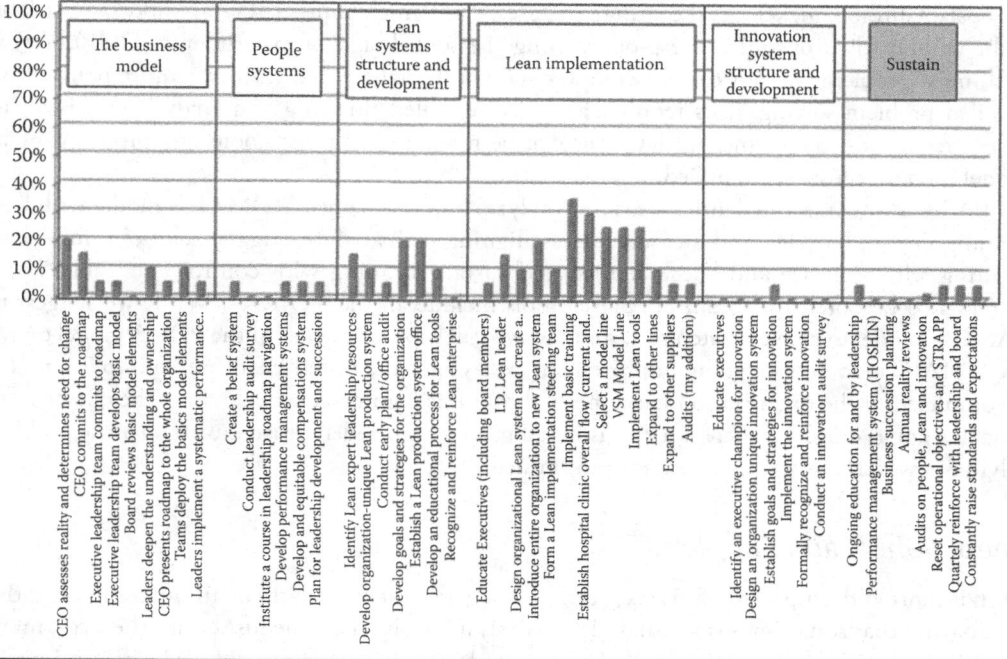

Figure 5.12 The leadership roadmap detail.

Because there are unstable processes with significant variation or non-normal variation, most organizations find it more prudent to begin with Lean tools to identify and eliminate waste and streamline processes. As waste is taken out of a process and the process becomes more predictable and variation rises to the surface, we recommend following up with Six Sigma tools to refine and strive toward perfection. Otherwise, it can be a challenge to utilize some of the Six Sigma tools on widely variable processes; however, there are many Six Sigma tools and concepts related to measurement systems that augment the Lean tools in relation to data collection, interpretation, and change management.

In an article by Mike Micklewright, he claims, "Six Sigma training is wasteful …. It has watered down Lean efforts, it has watered down variation reduction efforts, it has created bureaucracies, it has isolated people," so he is putting his black belt up for sale![12]

While this is extreme, we have seen this occur at some companies. We must keep in mind all problem-solving models stem from Shewhart's plan–do–study–act (PDSA). The Japanese changed it to PDCA after the CCS teachings and Dr. Shingo changed it to plan–control–do–check. It is also known in some companies as observe–orient–decide–act (OODA). The Department of Defense applies the cycle in its spiral development process of designing new battlefield technologies. PDCA fits our BASICS® model with baseline, analyze, and control and suggests improvements aligning with the plan phase, implement (do) phase, check phase, and sustain (act) phase.

On page 253 of the Toyota Way,[13] author Jeffrey K. Liker writes, "… Toyota does not have a Six Sigma program. Six Sigma is based on complex statistical analysis tools. People want to know how Toyota achieves such high levels of quality without the quality tools of Six Sigma. You can find an example of every Six Sigma tool somewhere in Toyota at some time. Some more complex problems may require use of more sophisticated quality tools Examples might be heat treating, food and drug ingredients formulation and mixing it into a product to standardize and optimize the costs, Chrome, nickel metal coating processes, etc. Which requires several important variables to be combined to optimize the process using the tool design of experiments (DOE). Yet, we find, most problems do not call for complex statistical analysis, but instead require painstaking, detailed problem-solving. This requires a level of detailed thinking and analysis that is all too absent from most companies in day tools can be made to fit in just about any problem-solving model if common sense is applied."

BASICS® fits into the define, measure, analyze, improve, control (DMAIC) model with baseline aligning with design and measure, assess aligning with analyze, suggest solutions, implement aligning with improve and check results, and sustain aligning with control (see Table 5.4). It should also be noted that Lean Six Sigma tools include all the TQ tools. While we suggest the BASICS® model to convert batch to Lean flow, we still support the use of the PDCA model or even the DMAIC model for ongoing improvement cycles once the initial Lean system implementation is completed, if the organization has a method that it is comfortable deploying. The choice of the model is not as critical if there is a consistent, logical, organized approach to an ongoing problem-solving in which every employee has been trained.

Keep It Short and Simple[14]

Keep it short and simple (KISS) is the Lean way of getting it done without all the complex statistical analysis that sometimes is an analysis paralysis to resolve a simple just do it. The Lean manufacturing practice of 80% complete is OK for implementation; we can always kaizen to improve the 20% of the rest later.

Table 5.4 BASIC Model Interaction with Other Problem Solving Models

BASICS Model Interaction with Other Problem-Solving Models				
PDCA	8D Automotive Model	AlliedSignal 9-Step Model	DMAIC	BASICS Model
Plan	Form team	ID opportunities	Define	Baseline
Grasp the current situation Background and current condition	Describe the problem	Form team		Analyze
Containment plan needed?	Contain the problem	Analyze current process	Measure	Suggest solutions
Set goals/target condition		Define desired outcomes for improved process	Analyze	
ID root cause	ID root cause	ID root cause and proposed solutions		
Identify gaps, devise counter measures and create implementation and follow-up plan, obtain approval	Formulate corrective action	Prioritize, plan, and test solutions		
Do	Correct the problem and confirm the effects	Refine and implement solutions	Implement/ Improve	Implement the plan
Check		Measure progress and hold gains	Control	Check
Act	Preventive action			Sustain—update standard work, remove containment, Yokoten/ reflection
	Congratulate the team	Acknowledge team and communicate results		

Source: BIG Archives.

Dedicated Versus Non-Dedicated Teams

We have found dedicated teams to be a best practice for companies starting with Lean. The teams can change from project to project. However, if you are bringing in a consultant, it is extremely important to have people designated for the consultant to transfer knowledge. One of the goals should be to have the knowledge and resources to phase out the consultant over time. These designees should be selected carefully so as not to invest a lot of time and money in training and experience only to have the person take it to another company or worst case—competitor. We have found part-time teams generally don't work well. The day-to-day business always wins out and Lean gets put on the back burner.

Part of this strategy should be to make the line organization responsible for the rollout from the beginning. This means the person to which the consultant will be transferring knowledge will be the plant manager or production manager along with a manager from the transactional (office) side, that is, the controller or engineering manager. They are now responsible to put the teams together and are responsible for the results of the continuous improvement journey.

Experience Counts—Especially in Lean

At a home healthcare organization in Maryland, the leadership decided they wanted to implement Lean across the company. They hired two people out of college that had Lean courses and gave them the objective to transform the enterprise. After a few months of meeting with some of the offices (which were scattered throughout the State), they decided to centralize all the major office systems, change the reward systems, and pay scales, eliminate 30% or more of the positions, and do everything on the computer. During one of their observation sessions, they noticed the personnel ran the entire office off a couple of whiteboards. The system was very visual and kept everyone focused on staffing the nursing shifts for their clients. The Lean person said it was taking way too much time to update the visual boards and said it was not Lean. He wanted everything done on the computer. Now, reports are printed out daily that go to the office manager, who has no time to look at them, and their percent of staffed shifts has gone down, and no one knows what's going on because it is in the computer and no longer visible.

Lesson Learned: While reading Lean books is extremely important, you can't become an LP solely by reading books or expect to be an LP straight out of college with maybe one intern-type implementation under your belt. One must have a thorough knowledge, understanding, and grounding in the principles, and then implement and practice and make mistakes and learn. It takes years of practice! However, we see this all the time. Very well-meaning, college-educated, and book-smart individuals are put in charge of Lean journeys but have no experience in how to handle the change or how to analyze the processes.

There are those few that really do get it and are patient and understand the big bang for the Lean buck will come over time (a five-year commitment that never ends). In my opinion, these highly successful managers are patient with the progress, but impatient with the results. These managers decline to sit in the nosebleed sections and instead want to be part of the action and get their hands dirty. They realize by getting more and more personally involved and getting more of their employee base involved, their culture will ultimately transition to one that generates ideas yielding ongoing continuous improvement. These are the management people who pull for more and more Lean resources. This does not mean adding Lean resources; it means they understand how to take the resources they have in any given area and transition those resources into real-time Lean leaders.

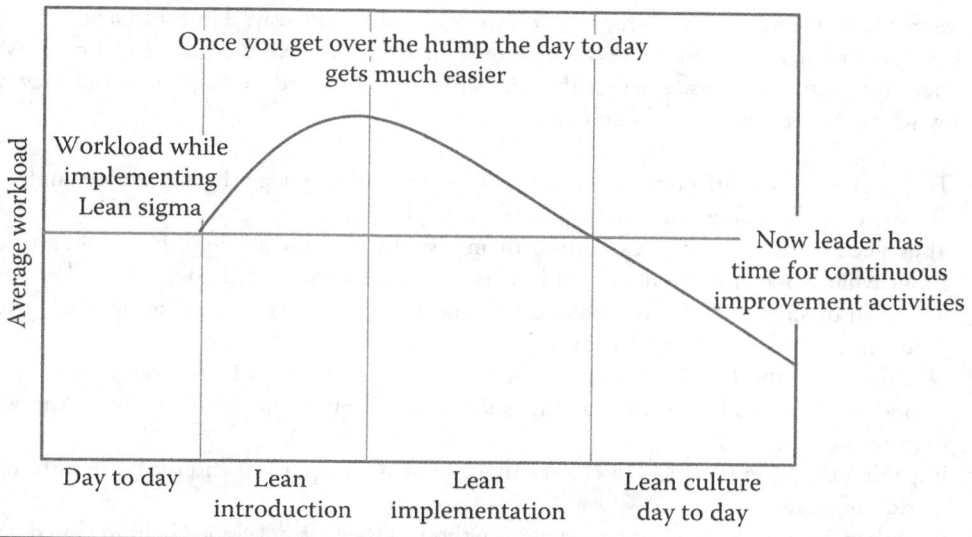

Figure 5.13   Lean implementation workload cycle.

Lesson Learned : In the beginning Lean is more work for the supervisors and managers as we have to implement the changes while keeping the operations going. However, over time, everyone's job gets easier as standard work, visual controls and daily management are implemented. Thus, our old day to day job is transformed into working & living Lean, developing and engaging our people, and driving continuous improvement! (see Figure 5.13)

Five Keys for Successful Implementations

Once resources in each area fully understand and speak the language of Lean, an endless stream of incremental improvement will start to take place. These leaders understand their current processes are outdated and must be changed. Taking the A and B players, from the line organization, and dedicating them to the project significantly increases the chances for a successful Lean journey. In a recent Association for Manufacturing Excellence (AME) article, they identify (five) key variables that predict a successful Lean transformation[15]:

1. The development of teams as the supporting structures for Lean
2. The calculation and communication of metrics
3. The communication among organization members, particularly across organizational barriers
4. The communication to employees regarding their specific role in the Lean transformation
5. The acknowledgment and celebration of successes toward the Lean transformation

We will cover each of these in detail:

Development of Teams as the Supporting Structure for Lean

Within the Lean structure, teams are important because the whole process must work together to build the required value for the customer. If there are no team structures in the area targeted for improvement, everyone may work for the customer in a different way. Time and again, we hear each shift does their work their own way and constant confusion exists as to the end goal. When implementing Lean, all teams, whether they are shifts or cells, need to be aligned and they need to know why they are being asked to change:

a. Teams or groups of affected employees need a common language they all understand.
b. They need to be trained in common Lean principles and tools.
c. They need to design the work around them visually so there are high levels of agreement about what work must be done and how it should be done (standard work), either person to person or shift to shift. This should be done as a group so they can immediately expose problems and resolve them as a team.
d. Not involving the frontline team in the process of continuous improvement will lead to second guessing and resistance at various levels and even alienate them from the whole improvement process.
e. Engaging the team is critical in change management (acceptance) and the cultural transformation of Lean.
f. Apprehension will exist when trying new methods if they are developed behind closed doors. If all employees are not involved, the project leader will miss valuable inputs to improve the process. There are many hidden factory (and office) items we need to capture and document to standardize the way our processes work. Whether you agree with this or not, there are huge amounts of workarounds being performed by employees every single day to get their jobs done. These workarounds exist because current (old) processes haven't been changed. New ideas have sprung up out of necessity to get the job done quicker and, in many cases, better and more efficiently. We have seen evidence of employees being told to do it the current way or else, reducing productivity by 50% or more in some cases!
g. In a Lean environment, teams need the autonomy to manage and improve their processes (they need to do this under the guidance and support of management); this is how they grow and how we start turning the culture and begin the cycle of problem-solving and continuous improvement at the frontline level.

Calculation and Communication of Metrics

Area metrics should be developed and owned by the people that own the process. These metrics should be easy to update by the process owners themselves. Management must support these metrics, and they must assist in deciding who will review them (see Figure 5.14). These metrics must point in a steady and consistent direction toward the ideal state you want to achieve. Metrics mandated and pushed down to the floor suffer from a basic misunderstanding from those running the processes. Not having them involved in the formation and calculations will hamper their growth and understanding of the achievement desired. Employees engaging in the development of area metrics help them understand the line of sight to what they are doing on the front line and how it connects to the strategic goals of the organization.

Communication among Organization Members, Particularly across Organizational Barriers

In a Lean environment, "process focus takes priority over functional focus." Communication must take place across functional boundaries. How can you effectively do this if you do not

Figure 5.14 Lean communications board.

involve them in the Lean process? It's bad enough in the organizations we have been exposed to that we have the silo syndrome all over different areas. Breaking down the functional walls creates smooth transitions in the Lean process, and the people are aware of what is going to happen, and they are not surprised when it does happen. Communication in a Lean environment must be vertical and horizontal and two-way. Just having a Lean leader or Lean project manager who is an excellent communicator won't get the job done. Lean project leaders must convey all elements of the Lean project to the team and upwardly as well. Employees involved in the Lean change need to see that the individuals at the top of the organization are also changing the way they think before they will do the same, thus leading by example. Bottom-up communication is equally important; it provides the reality of what the new changes are doing to the process and how it is really affecting people. Not having this bottom-up communication will create resentment and the feeling these changes are dictated and we don't value the employees' opinions.

Communication to Employees Regarding Their Specific Role in the Lean Transformation

What is my role as an employee in this new Lean environment? This is the main question employees ask when they are not involved in the process to implement Lean. Lack of getting employee commitment was found to be one of the top barriers to implementing and sustaining continuous improvement or Lean. Roles will and must change as the organization progresses toward Lean maturity. A key to the success of Lean is making sure employees have a good understanding of their new role.

*Acknowledgment and Celebration of Successes
toward the Lean Transformation*

Defining the milestones and celebrating the result is the key linchpin in the success of Lean. It is highly critical that once the Lean implementation is up and running, accountability and auditing of the process takes place. Putting a Lean project in place and not rewarding those whose working lives you are changing could be a big mistake. Many times, we are asking all employees both vertically and horizontally to become multiskilled and to be multitask oriented. Reward and recognition play critical roles in the successful sustaining of Lean.

Hold Required Rollout Meetings and Propose an Implementation Plan

Actively planning what meetings need to occur is important to the overall success of the initiative. It is helpful to review what you are trying to accomplish and follow the five Ws approach:

- **Why** are you having the meeting?
- **Who** are the key participants and who needs to attend?
- **What** type of meeting are you holding? Is it for problem-solving communication? What are you trying to accomplish by meeting (message, decision, go/no go, etc.)? Are they for updates, related to certain milestones, or for decisions that need to be made?
- **Where** is the location of the meeting?
- **When** to hold the meeting(s):
- Are they once or reoccurring?
- What is the timing of the meetings?

Types of Meetings

Listed in the following are different types of meeting to consider when rolling out your Lean journey, point kaizen event, or Lean system implementation.

Union Leadership Meetings Where Applicable

Joint Management/Union Leadership Meeting (if Applicable)

When: This is done prior to videoing.

Attendees: These include the director/manager of operations, director/manager of HRs, and union leadership.

Purpose: This is to provide Lean manufacturing overview, brief sequence of events, and expectations.

Operations: All Employee Staff Meeting

When: This is done prior to starting the implementation.

Attendees: These include the operations director and staff.

Purpose: This is to present a brief overview of what will be transpiring, and a review of the lessons learned from other sites.

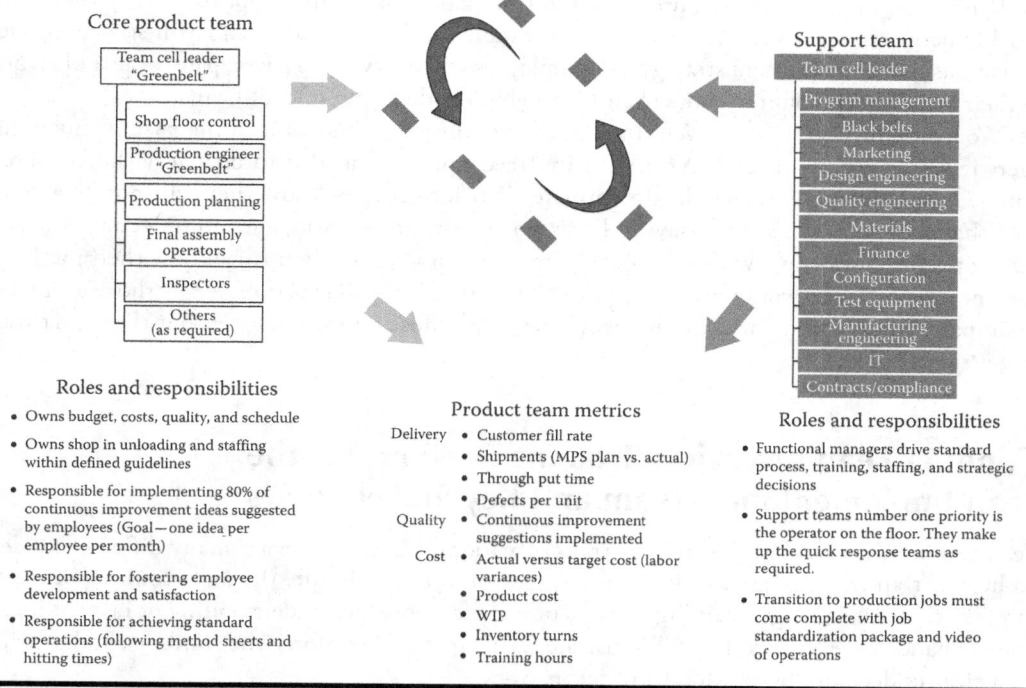

Figure 5.15 Roles and responsibilities and deliverables for core team versus support team.

Meeting with All Team Members in the Pilot Area

When: This is done prior to starting implementation.

    Purpose: This is to present a brief overview, sequence of events, and expectations.

    Attendees: These include the director/manager of operations, HR, Lean team, and pilot area team.

Daily or Weekly Meetings with the Implementation Team

We generally conduct daily or weekly meetings with the implementation teams, or line leaders, to monitor their progress and discuss problem opportunities.

Develop Exit Strategy for the Pilot Team

There should be a set of deliverables that must be met before the pilot team returns to their day-to-day tasks (see Figure 5.15).

Has the Leadership Agree to a No-Layoff Strategy Regarding Any Improvements Implemented (Does Not Refer to Layoffs Necessitated Due to Business Conditions)

This is a very important condition as Lean improves productivity, and the elimination of steps and streamlining processes often frees up labor. If frontline staff and supervisors engage in Lean initiatives and management requires laying off the labor that is freed up, the word layoffs will quickly permeate the organization. The organization will look at Lean as a layoff strategy rather than a business improvement strategy and employees will not want to participate for fear of layoffs in their area. This is counterproductive to achieving the desired results of Lean.

We have ended up in some very intense discussions over this point in the past. Many managers insist on laying off employees who are freed up. We find this to be a very short-sighted policy. Employees will not work to eliminate their jobs if they know they will not be able to feed their families. We are not saying Lean won't work or you won't see improvements if you lay people off, but people will only contribute so much voluntarily if they know their job is on the line. We prefer to work with companies that really value their people versus those that have a company value statement claiming people are their most important asset, but they can't wait to get rid of them.

Conduct Lean Overview Training Sessions for the Lean Implementation Team and Key Stakeholders

Lean training is critical to the cultural transformation of Lean. There are many different models on how to train. In general, as with learning most new things in life, the more training or exposure, the better it is; longer training sessions provide for a broader understanding of Lean as it can provide hands-on exercises that will illustrate Lean concepts, reinforce the concepts, and provide for a clear understanding of why the concepts work.

Your training plan will be influenced by who in the organization is driving the Lean initiative as noted earlier. When possible, providing access to a five-day course (minimum of 40 hours in length), with the purpose of introducing strategic and competitive advantages inherent in Lean thinking concepts, is recommended. The course walks through the implementation approach and provides a foundation for the pilot team to implement Lean product and process improvements with some mentoring by a trained LP. The course should cover Lean culture, history, principles, tools and systems thinking (in the ordered domain) with several practice sessions. It should also include Lean implementations (system kaizens), team building, TQ tools, styles, change management, 5Ss, TPM overviews, empowerment, Lean organizational overview, Lean organizational structure, Lean materials, supply chain management, implementation process map review, video comparisons of batch to one-piece flow environments, Lean industrial and process engineering analysis, standard work, job standardization, setup reduction, layout and cell design, line balancing, performance management, two-bin material systems and Kanban, change management, and Lean implementation strategy. In our courses, we also include Myers-Briggs Styles Indicator and half-day workshop and world-class and other relevant videos. Participants receive a broad-based overview of Lean manufacturing and Lean thinking fundamentals, typical results of Lean implementations, and videos of world-class operations. The differences between kaizens, demand flow, and other implementation approaches are discussed in detail. Team building and TQ exercises are woven into the course. The attendees will create and run a synchronized assembly line on the shop floor:

■ Benefits: Provides training and education through hands-on demonstration of Lean principles at work. Course is 60% lecture and videos and world-class examples and 40% hands-on. This course will teach you how to identify waste and give techniques to eliminate it.

It has tremendous opportunities for process improvements and proven implementation approaches that yield tremendous savings.
■ This course is a prerequisite for LP certification.

Document the Site in Video and Digital Pictures

This is a critical step in the baseline process and should be performed on every project no matter how small. Take video and photos of all areas under consideration for change (and even those that aren't). Take pictures from every angle and note the angles so you can take pictures in the after condition. It is important to note where the pictures are taken because in the after condition, it may be so different, and the landmarks used in the base condition may not exist in the after condition.

Lesson Learned: You can never take enough pictures. We use the pictures for many reasons, such as before pictures, to support visual aids on the floor, to support training and in presentations. Once the implementation is complete and the new process is up and running, the staff often do not remember the original current state of the process. The pictures are very useful to remind the staff of where they started, the progress of the journey, and how far they have evolved.

Summary

Remember it has taken Toyota decades of deploying Lean concepts and tools to progress on the never-ending path of continuous improvement and the journey to delivering excellence in products for its customers. The Lean project implementation plan can follow the model the organization has leveraged for problem-solving as discussed earlier. They should use the BASICS® model, PDCA, and DMAIC if there is not a standard model. Whatever the model selected, planning is critical to any successful implementation. As you roll out Lean, it is key to be able to clearly understand and articulate what you are trying to accomplish, track activities to deliverables, adhere to a timeline and milestones, make calculated revisions as needed, remove barriers, communicate findings, pilot and re-pilot if needed, implement, communicate results, and celebrate and establish the model for ongoing activity. Taking lessons learned and sharing with others to disseminate Lean across the organization will reinforce the cultural transformation needed in developing a Lean organization.

Chapter Questions

1. Explain ETDBW. Name a company that is ETDBW and one that is not.
2. Why does everything start with the customer?
3. How do you get VOC?
4. Who obtains VOC information?
5. List two key attributes to exhibit if you are trying to get an honest assessment of an area.
6. List three plans you should consider for your implementation.
7. List four criteria that an area should meet to be considered for a pilot.

8. What are some key plans that need to be put together prior to starting your Lean project?
9. Put together a high-level implementation plan. What are the two key components of the plan?
10. List three characteristics of a team member.
11. What are the different types of teams?
12. How important is communication and why?
13. What should be communicated and to whom
14. What is a contract for change? Why is it important?
15. What is the Lean Leadership roadmap?
16. Who should make up the Lean steering committee?
17. What did you learn from this chapter?

Notes

1. Michael Hammer, The Agenda, 1st edn. (Crown Business), April 23, 2002. Random House LLC.
2. Jim Womack and Dan Jones, Lean Thinking (New York: Simon and Schuster), 1996.
3. http://nraoiekc.blogspot.com/2021/05/seven-flows-of-manufacturing-toyota.html.
4. Avoiding the Continuous Appearance Trap: 12 Questions to Understand What's Truly Underneath Your Culture, Patrick Adams Consulting Services, LLC ©February 10, 2021.
5. http://abc.go.com/shows/shark-tank/about-the-show. The critically acclaimed business-themed show, Shark Tank, has the Sharks continuing the search to invest in the best businesses and products that America has to offer. The show received a nomination for a Producers Guild Award in 2013. In 2012, "Shark Tank" received an Emmy nomination for Outstanding Reality Program and a nomination for a Critics' Choice Television Award for Best Reality Series. The Sharks—tough, self-made, multi-millionaire and billionaire tycoons—will once again give budding entrepreneurs the chance to make their dreams come true and potentially secure business deals that could make them millionaires. They are billionaire Mark Cuban, owner, and chairman of AXS TV and outspoken owner of the 2011 NBA championship Dallas Mavericks; real estate mogul Barbara Corcoran; "Queen of QVC" Lori Greiner; technology innovator Robert Herjavec; fashion and branding expert Daymond John; and venture capitalist Kevin O'Leary.
6. http://www.surveymonkey.com/.
7. http://www.surveygizmo.com/survey-blog/question-scale-length/ need a 5- to 7-point scale. Information about both the new Kano model and Blitz QFD® can be found at http://www.qfdi.org and free-to-download case studies at http://www.mazur.net/publishe.htm. The authors have not used and have no opinion on this model at this time but found it while doing research on the topic. Michael Hammer, The Agenda (New York: Crown Business), 2001. Harvard Business Review; Michael Hammer, The Agenda (Crown Business Publishing), 2001.
8. https://thecynefin.co/.
9. Strengthening Stamping Capability for Competitiveness in a Global Marketplace, Toyota Presentation, http://www.icospa.com/2008/pdfs/Krinock.pdf, public domain.
10. Scope creep is defined where management continues to add to the project whether it be in additional processes, levels of processes, etc. For example, "Since you are looking at that, why don't you also look at this?"
11. Russ Scaffede, The Leadership Roadmap: People, Lean & Innovation (North River Press, 2008).
12. "Black Belt for Sale," Quality Digest, www.qualitydigest.com/print/4366, October 18, 2009, Mike Micklewright with permission.
13. Jeffrey Liker, Toyota Culture (New York: McGraw-Hill), 2008, pp. 29–30. Jeffrey Liker, The Toyota Way (New York: McGraw Hill), 2004. Matthew May, The Elegant Solution (New York: Free Press), 2007.

14. Contribution from Mike Chan, President Lean Focus LLC.
15. Source: (Excerpts from) Target Magazine, Vol. 22, No. 3, Third Issue, 2006.

Additional Readings

Bradley, T.G. 1994. Managing Customer Value. New York: The Free Press.
Colombo, G. 2003. Killer Customer Care. Irvine, CA: Entrepreneur Press.
McNealy, R. 1996. Making Customer Satisfaction Happen. London, UK: Kluwer Academic Publishers.
Shingo, S. 1987. Key Strategies for Plant Improvement. Cambridge, MA: Productivity Press.
Solomon, J. 2005. Leading Lean. Durham, NC: WCM Associates.

Chapter 6

BASICS® Model

BASELINE the Process

If you continue to evolve and never look back change will still happen... If you accept change as inevitable it won't crush you when it comes...every technology age... the only thing that never gets old is connecting with people.[1]

Baseline the Process/Metrics

As we move through the first or BASELINE phase of the BASICS® model, we need to gain an understanding of the current or as-is process. We accomplish this by going to the place where the process occurs and walking the process with the frontline staff, managers, and team members. The team needs to put their Lean glasses on, noting how the product or information moves from beginning to end, or for a service, what it takes from request to delivery. This allows the opportunity to start asking why five times as we search for root causes and begin to identify waste and opportunities for improvement.

Lesson Learned: This baseline is driven by actual versus perceived customer value. If you do not know what your customer finds valuable or is willing to pay for, you cannot have a true vision of what to improve.

The first hurdle we find at most companies is the lack of process metrics and industrial engineering data. Many times, there are no standards, and if there are, they have not been updated in some time, often years. Some companies have significant data, but the premise of the data is wrong. For instance, if you are measuring customer delivery, are you measuring to customer-promised date or customer-requested date? The other issue we run into is when we are working on a line in an area where the only data for the area exists, not for the individual lines. Batch environments are particularly challenging because many times they flex people in and out of different lines. If we require 20 steps to build a product with people flexing in and out of the line, it becomes very difficult to determine the labor hours. This sometimes means going back to manual logs or overall shipping schedules and timecards or labor records to estimate how many people were working on the line and what the output was; however, in most cases, we never know for sure. Every company is quick to tell us how much they have improved over the years. "You should have seen

DOI: 10.4324/9781003185772-6

what this place used to look like!" We ask these companies, if you do not have process-related metrics in place, how can you possibly know (measure) if you have improved? This does not necessarily mean there was no improvement, but how does one know if they improved and if so by how much?

During this baseline phase, we develop the Lean roadmap by determining the business problem(s) that need solving as defined by the customer and capturing the current state of the process. Capturing the current state includes observing, mapping, and videoing the process; understanding current metrics; potentially developing new or revising existing process metrics; and outlining the initial goals and objectives of the proposed initiative. During the baseline phase, create a project charter that outlines the Lean initiative, including problem statement and proposed scope, baseline data (including current metrics), and target condition including the executive sponsor or champion and the pilot team. The champion and team leader should select and interview the team members.

Collecting data is extremely challenging in companies and, when data is obtained, one must really question if the data collected are reliable. We find many organizations collect data, and accuracy is assumed, which can be a misguided assumption. We often scrutinize or scrub data during Lean projects, surfacing data inaccuracies and challenging the organization that has been utilizing the data for years to make decisions. In general, we find that when we receive historical data, these need to be validated, for example, if we receive a material requirement planning (MRP) file with data in total columns, we will enter the formula in the total column to make sure it is correct. One would be surprised how often we end up with questions regarding the totals columns where we can't come up with a formula that makes sense or works on the whole column. Despite the challenges, this process helps the Lean practitioner (LP) understand the data and the calculations behind it.

Lesson Learned: If you don't document the baseline data ahead of time, prior to implementing the new system, the old numbers will suddenly and magically be remembered as much better than they were once Lean is implemented. It is funny how people in batch environments always remember the most they ever completed in a day. "I remember when this line did 2,200 parts a day." "What they do not tell you about are the days they completed no product because it was all still in some stage of work in process (WIP)."

Typical Baseline Continuous Improvement Metrics

Listed below is a table of the typical CI metrics we utilize (Table 6.1):

It is important with Lean to act on fact and question the data presented for baseline metrics. Many times, we assume what makes up a number, statistic, or ratio and feel we may appear ignorant if we ask the makeup of the number, statistic, or ratio. What is interesting is we often find that even the person giving us the numbers does not necessarily know how the number is calculated or acknowledges that it is too complicated to explain the calculations. Many times, we find that something even as simple as inventory turns can have several definitions depending on the company.

Data and What People Think

In the quest of gathering accurate data, repeatedly, we ask people how long things take, regarding performing activities within a given process. Most managers and staff provide an estimate; however, when we video or use a stopwatch on the process, they are almost never correct. They are very surprised, once we provide the real data, how far-off their calculation or guess was. As soon as

Table 6.1   Before Versus After Metrics

Lean Metrics: Baseline versus After			
Baseline Metrics		Actual Lean JIT Metric	
Operators	23	12	−48%
Hours per unit	1.36	0.54	−60%
WIP (pieces)	4082	1295	−68%
WIP dollars	$326k	$103k	−68%
Floor space (Sq Ft)	1642	962	−41%
Throughput time (minutes)	21	10	−52%
CT (batch secs est)	214	120	−44%

Source: BIG Archives.

someone says, "I think" or "it was" or "it should be," then we know the person is not sure. If our goal is to act in fact then this becomes a problem. Data must be accurate to provide a measurable baseline. Why go into all this with Lean? The baselining phase sets the stage for the Lean initiative. The executive sponsor and operational managers should understand the problem, key process indicators (KPIs), and their targets.

Collection and Analysis: Current State

Lean is about being able to manage by fact and understanding all the data related to the as-is or current state process and what it can deliver. Next, we will go through the types of data needed to develop a true picture of the best way to deliver customer value. The data captured in the baseline phase provide the foundation for the calculations and comparisons for the improvements as we methodically move through the phases. Although we will not be able to go through every item and tool mentioned in the baseline phase (B) of the BASICS® model, we will introduce you to the key pieces of data and calculations in the baseline phase. The metrics can also be collected in conjunction with creating a VSM.

Determine Current State and Future State Customer Demand

Whether leveraging the BASICS® model, plan–do–check–act (PDCA), or DMAIC, they all begin with the ability to understand your current or as-is state, applying tools, and determining what should and should not continue in any process. The data elements described previously are key components to assessing what is currently occurring so we can develop the future state. Without following a roadmap or model, it is difficult to stay on track to achieve the desired outcome.

The first piece of data we need to determine is true customer demand which is critical since it affects what hours we need to operate, and the number of staff required. It is an integral part of many of our other calculations. In a nutshell, the best or most accurate demand numbers are current (actual) and future (or projected) forecasted demand. If we cannot obtain or project these numbers, we must rely on historical data if these exist. Sometimes history is not a good predictor of the future, as product mix, new services, and business development may alter demand. We capture demand yearly, monthly, daily, by day of week, etc., and it is important to understand demand at the lowest possible level, especially if there are wide swings in demand cycles, such as in a seasonal business. One of our rules with Lean is to convert our calculations into a day's worth or sometimes an hour's worth of demand. This is because it is easier for people to understand and manage a days or hours' worth of something versus a week's, months, or years' worth. This will also make it easier to calculate the rest of the formulas as we work through the implementation.

As we begin to relate demand to activities performed, we must be able to analyze demand in terms of how and when it is needed, that is, if a customer wants 1,000 pieces per month and we have 20 working days, then the daily demand is 50 pieces per day. This is called production smoothing or leveling:

$$1,000 \text{ pieces/month} \div 20 \text{ working days/month} = 50 \text{ pieces/day.}$$

Many times, this can prove to be very challenging even though one might assume it would be straightforward. Most companies really do not know and assume that customer demand is what is in the production schedule. However, the production schedule does not necessarily reflect the customer need date and is typically based on our negotiated promised date to the customer. In some cases, sales may have offered a quantity discount, expedited delivery, or padded their lead time by giving the factory a delivery date several weeks earlier than what was needed by the customer. These actions drive more demand than the customer really needs. Likewise, if the customer is using an MRP system or batch-based production system, they may think they know but really do not know their true needs. To determine customer demand, it sometimes requires contacting the customer. During the initial implementations, we generally default to whatever management's best guess is and put the customer demand in terms of what is required daily or sometimes hourly. In one case, we were told our baseline was three employees doing a job. When we reached the end of the project, we reduced the number to two and were told that "we could have done that ...." So don't you want to ask them "why didn't you do that?"

Lesson Learned: If everyone does not agree to the baseline data up front, in writing, you will be surprised to find, later, after you have implemented Lean, how all the previous numbers start to change. Then all these caveats begin to appear like "we could have done that before without Lean!" or "our numbers were better prior to Lean!"

The Lost Customer Premium Story

At large fabrication and manufacturing company in Delaware, we had just implemented a Lean line and could produce six or seven units per day versus the past production rate of two or three units per day. Due to the past production problems, the ordering system at this company regularly included the salespeople padding their dates (requesting units two to four weeks before needed) to ensure they produced the parts on time. The units would sit in credit hold until the salesperson was ready for them to be delivered to the customer's job site. With the implementation of the Lean line, we quickly ran out of room to store all the credit hold units. In addition, a call came in from a customer who really needed a unit right away. We could now build a complete unit in a day versus the weeks it took before, and the customer was willing to pay a 30% premium for the unit. The decision went to the production-scheduling department for analysis. Since they had so many units already on backorder, they turned the customer and the premium down. They lost this customer permanently to their competition! Meanwhile, everything we produced on the schedule went to credit hold and sat for days or weeks waiting for shipping.

Lesson Learned: When you are working on what you do not need, you cannot be working on what you do need! Batch and queue or even one-piece flow systems that do not work to real-time customer demand can result in lost opportunities for customer satisfaction and delivery premiums. Once we install the Lean line, we need to reeducate the marketing and sales force, so they do not pad their dates in the future.

A Project Plan May be Necessary

Depending on the size of the line, a project plan may be required or desired. We suggest creating a short timeline or Gantt chart for an area-focused project and a more formal or detailed plan for a large-scale project we call a project control matrix. See table 6.2 The project control matrix captures the results of the analysis providing milestone dates, a timeline, and status for the ongoing project to ensure the scope and project achieve the desired results.

Progression from Baseline to Benchmark

An important concept in continuous improvement (CI) is realizing the progression from baseline to entitlement to benchmark performance:

- Baseline performance is a measure that indicates where the process is today, defined as the current state, via hard measurement, in terms of performance.
- Entitlement requires iteration after iteration of CI techniques. However, in theory, the best performance the current process can reach is normally three times value-added time with the rest being required work and transportation.[2]
- Benchmark performance is finding and implementing a totally new paradigm to solve the problems associated with the current state process. We define this as the ideal state. The goal of the ideal state is to ask what is not being done or cannot be done today, but if it could be done, it would fundamentally change what we do.[3]

Available Time

The next thing we need to calculate is available time. This is equal to real work time of the team members. It is determined by taking the total time per shift, less breaks, meetings, cleanup, lunch (if included in the 8 hours, but most are not), etc., where the entire work area shuts down. In some continuous manufacturing processes (i.e., casting or government or health-care environments), there is no total shutdown time so available time equals the total shift time as staff and managers cover breaks. If a normal shift is 8 hours with an hour for breaks, meetings, exercise, etc. (again normally, lunch is not included in the 8-hour day), the available time would be equal to

$$8\,\text{hours} - 1\,\text{hour for breaks etc.} = 7 - \text{hour available time.}$$

See the more detailed example in the following where we assume an 8 hour or 480 minutes shift.

Table 6.2 Project Control Matrix Example

Project Control Matrix Example for Large Lean System Implementation Projects

Operation	Units per Product	Build Location	Sub Assy	Video	Full Work	Total Labor Time					Job Standardization Package			Milestones
						Was (minute)	Was Actual (minute)	Is (minute)	Can Be	Goal 80% Reduction	Standard Work Sheet Completed	(CTs)	Tasks	
Operation 1	1	la	Sub assy	9/30/1999	9/30/1999		21.1	10.2	8.0	0.0	10/4/1999		Project control matrix	10/4/1999
Operation 2	1	la	Sub assy	10/5/1999	10/5/1999		9.0	8.1	0.8	0.0	10/5/1999		PPF	10/12/1999
Operation 3	1	la	Module	10/5/1999	10/5/1999	98.0	44.4	25.1		19.6	10/6/1999		Full work completed	10/15/1999
Operation 4	2	lb	Sub assy	10/5/1999	10/5/1999		16.2	4.8		0.0	10/7/1999		Materials review	10/15/1999
Operation 5	1	lb	Module	10/5/1999	10/6/1999	35.0	15.6	11.6		7.0	10/8/1999		JSP	10/19/1999
Operation 6	1	lb	Module	10/5/1999	10/6/1999	36.0	13.6	8.0		7.2	10/9/1999		Draft layout	10/19/1999
Operation 7	1	2	Module	10/5/1999	10/6/1999	19.0	22.7	13.0		3.8	10/10/1999		Workstations design	10/17/1999
Operation 8	1	2	Module	10/5/1999	10/6/1999	50.0	49.6	27.3		10.0	10/11/1999		Update layout	10/22/1999
Operation 9	1	2	Module	10/5/1999	10/7/1999	76.0	66.2	45.7		15.2	10/12/1999		Review layout with line personnel, maintenance, and hse	10/22/1999
Operation 10	1	3a	Sub assy	10/6/1999	10/8/1999		2.7	1.9		0.0	10/13/1999		Review layout with leadership	10/22/1999

Table 6.2 (Continued) Project Control Matrix Example

Project Control Matrix Example for Large Lean System Implementation Projects

Operation	Units per Product	Build Location	Sub Assy	Video	Full Work	Total Labor Time					Job Standardization Package			
						Was (minute)	Was Actual (minute)	Is (minute)	Can Be	Goal 80% Reduction	Standard Work Sheet Completed	(CTs)	Tasks	Milestones
Operation 11	1	3a	Sub assy	10/6/1999	10/8/1999		4.7	2.1		0.0	10/14/1999		Approve layout	10/22/1999
Operation 12	1	3a	Sub assy	10/6/1999	10/8/1999		4.6	2.7		0.0	10/15/1999		Fit up	10/22/1999
Operation 13	1	3a	Sub assy	10/6/1999	10/8/1999		14.6	8.4		0.0	10/16/1999			
Operation 14	1	3a	Sub assy	10/6/1999	10/8/1999		6.3	3.3		0.0	10/17/1999			
Operation 15	1	3a	Module	10/6/1999	10/8/1999	108.0	25.5	15.5		21.6	10/18/1999		Operator training	10/21/1999
Operation 16	1	4a	Sub assy	10/6/1999	10/7/1999		5.9	4.6		0.0	10/19/1999		Planning and scheduling	10/22/1999
Operation 17	1	4a	Sub assy	10/7/1999	10/11/1999		23.6	17.8		0.0	10/20/1999		Visuals	10/29/1999
Operation 18	1	4a	Sub assy	10/6/1999	10/7/1999		9.0	6.8		0.0	10/21/1999		Move line	10/24/1999
Operation 19	1	4a	Sub assy	10/6/1999	10/8/1999		18.7	15.2		0.0	10/22/1999		Run line	10/25/1999
Operation 20	1	4a	Module	10/7/1999	10/11/1999	188.0	18.9	13.7		37.6	10/23/1999		Hand back to supervisor or team leader	10/29/1999
Operation 21	1	4a	Sub assy	10/6/1999	10/8/1999		8.2	6.7		0.0	10/24/1999		Sales review update	
Operation 22	1	4a	Sub assy	10/6/1999	10/8/1999		6.3	4.0		0.0	10/25/1999			

We subtract the following:

- 20 minutes—two 10 minutes breaks
- 10 minutes—morning exercise break
- 5 minutes—cleanup time
- 10 minutes—daily + QDIP or Huddle meeting

This equals 45 minutes of the daily lost time from the workday, so we would subtract it from the 480 minutes:

$$\text{Available time} = 480\,\text{minutes} - 45\,\text{minutes lost time} = 435\,\text{minutes}.$$

Note: Planned downtime should be excluded from the available time calculations. If the cell is planned to be shut down, it does not count as available time; however, setup times and unplanned downtime are all included in available time. Setup time and poor maintenance of machines will count against you, which should help to drive improvement in these areas. Examples of planned cell downtime include monthly safety, all hands, and benefits meetings. There is an impact to available time when setup and non-planned activities are reduced or eliminated, and these need to be addressed immediately as changes occur.

Takt Time Calculation

Many people, while they are familiar with the term takt time (TT), cannot tell you about the formula for it. TT allows us to look at a process or a group of activities and determine, based on customer demand and available time, how a process needs to run related to time. TT is equal to the available time to produce a product or service divided by the customer demand required during the available time:

$$\text{TT} = \text{available time} \div \text{customer demand}.$$

Here is an example (Table 6.3).

If the customer demand is 8,700 units per month, we derive daily demand by dividing by the number of working days in the month (in this case 20), which equals 435 units/day. If there is

Table 6.3 Takt Time Example

Time Available	
One shift	480 minutes
Breaks	−20 minutes
Exercise	−10 minutes
Clean-up	−5 minutes
Daily meeting	−10 minutes
Total available work time	435 minutes

Source: BIG Archives.

one shift then we need 435 units/shift. Takt time = 435 minutes available time/435 units/day = 1 minute/unit

This calculation shows we must produce one unit every minute to meet the customer demand. However, what does this really mean? Let's assume it takes 5 minutes of total labor time to build our product. If the TT is 1 minute, many of you may at first think we cannot meet the TT because it takes longer than 1 minute to build the product. However, this is not the case. If it takes 5 minutes to build the product, you will have to staff the line with five people, each with 1 minute of work. Let's think about what TT is really calculating, as it is not really measuring anything. When we calculated 1 minute per unit, it must be looked at for what it is, which is customer demand: no more...no less. TT can initially be a very confusing concept. It helps to remember:

TT is the customer demand rate.

TT describes the time needed for the system, whether on the floor or in the office, to complete one unit of product or one paperwork task. Whatever system we create, it must result in one unit completed every minute to meet the customer demand from our example. This metric takes nothing else into account. It does not consider the current labor time, machining times, layout, number of people in the area, or current production system. It simply says you must design a business delivery system that will result in meeting the TT or customer demand of 1 minute per unit!

Lesson Learned: It is not unusual to hear there is no way we could double or even increase production the way things are now. It is very difficult for anyone to perceive the Lean environment when their only frame of reference is the current batch environment.

Cycle Time

Cycle time (CT) is calculated in different ways, but each should have the same result. There are two types of CT, desired and actual. Desired CT is like TT but is computed by dividing available time by factory demand (versus customer demand). The actual CT can be determined as follows:

1. The time each team member/operator on the line must be able to meet.
2. The amount of time each person spends completing their part of the operation if the work is evenly distributed.
3. It can be computed by dividing the total labor time by the number of operators, assuming the work can be balanced evenly (i.e., there is no idle time).
4. The amount of time between units coming off the end of the line or out of the process. This is the real, actual CT.
5. It can be dictated by the time of the slowest machine in the line environment.

Determining the CT early in the Lean initiative provides a baseline of the activity or process. It is a very important data point since it can be used as an in-process metric versus a results metric. Once all or part of the waste is eliminated, CT will be monitored in the C or check phase (BASICS®). The current CT data will be compared to the future state target CT of the proposed new process during the S or sustain phase of the BASICS® model.

Cycle Time and Takt Time: What's the Difference?

To begin to put the puzzle together, we differentiate between CT and TT (see Table 6.4). CT is the actual working rhythm of the cell or area and the amount of time each person must meet to complete their part of the operation. Many use TT synonymously with CT, but we differentiate

Table 6.4   Lean Definitions

Lean Definitions For Takt Time and Cycle Time Analysis	
Operators (DL)	The number of direct labor operators building product or assigned to the line on a daily or hourly basis.
Cell leads or indirect labor (IL)	The number of indirect labor employees (hourly or management), who can be wholly assigned or some fraction of their time can be assigned to the line. The ultimate goal would be to account for everyone in the focused factory or product line. In the Lean accounting, we look at total labor time; there is minimal distinction between direct or indirect.
Units per day	The number of units produced per shift or per day.
Throughput time	This is the total time it takes to get one unit through the entire process from raw material (RM) to finished goods and is developed from the process flow analysis. It can also be roughly calculated by taking the total number of WIP and multiplied by the cycle time.
Actual CT	This is equal to how often a unit comes off the line or average time per unit completed. For example: if there are 450 minutes available time in a shift and 150 units completed, the cycle time would have averaged 3 minutes per unit. It is also the amount of time each person must meet to complete their part of the operation. It is calculated by dividing the available time by factory demand. It also equals the total labor time divided by the number of operators (if work is balanced evenly).
Overtime hours	The number of hours worked on paid overtime (i.e., 1.5 paid hours for every hour worked).
Total labor time (TLT)	The total labor time (touch labor) that it takes to build one unit. This number comes from the workflow analysis.
Changeover time	Total time from last good part to completion of first good part (includes first piece verification unless the part is immediately known to be good).
Space	Total space currently utilized by the product line.
Travel distance	The travel distance for the product comes from the PFA.
Operator travel distance	The distance the operators have to travel comes from the workflow analysis (WFA) number of subassembly units (any RM that has had labor added to it).
Wip #	Number of subassembly units (any RM that has had labor added to it).
WIP $:	Number of WIP multiplied by the wip cost per part at that stage
Productivity	The number of total paid worked hours including overtime divided by the number of units produced. Overtime hours should not be factored by time and 1/2 since the 1/2 hour is not worked. Total paid hours is calculated by taking the DL + IL times the number of hours paid per day and divided by the number of units completed per day or per shift.
Rolled throughput yield	Equals Is the multiplication of the percentage yield of good parts produced at each station.
OEE	Reflects actual utilized percentage of capacity. Available time × operating rate × quality.

Source: BIG Archives.

between the two as they are different. TT is a calculation based strictly on customer demand, where CT is based on the cell's demand for a day or hour and/or the time it takes you to complete a particular activity. Very few companies work to true takt time. Therefore, we end up with a factory/process desired CT, which we then must compare to actual CT at which the process is running. They must compute their desired cycle time at which to run.

Our goal is to match the desired and actual CT to TT, but this may not always be possible due to all the variations in most processes. For instance, the desired CT would be based on the factory demand we choose to run for the day. However, in some companies, due to scheduling limitations, equipment limitations, hours one can work, and job skill sets one can perform, it can be difficult to equalize CT and TT. For example, we may have a TT of 1 minute, but someone is out that day, so the CT is running at 2 minutes. In this case, we know we are not meeting the TT and we are going to underproduce to customer demand. The next day, we have two people working on a line to produce more parts than customer demand to catch up. CT and TT can initially be confusing concepts. TT is based on averages and assumes everything is level loaded (or evenly distributed). If our available time was one shift or 450 minutes, and the customer demand was 45 parts per day, we would need to process a part every 10 minutes:

$$\text{Available time} \div \text{customer demand} = TT,$$

$$450 \,\text{minutes/day} \div 45 \,\text{parts/day} = 10 \,\text{minutes/part}.$$

Again, it is important to note this has nothing to do with how long it takes to build the part or how many people work in the department. If the demand changes each day, the TT and CT would need to be adjusted. TT will also vary based on the number of shifts. For two shifts assuming the demand stays constant at 45/day, the TT would be 20 minutes:

$$\text{Available time} \div \text{customer demand} = TT,$$

$$900 \,\text{minutes/day} \div 45 \,\text{parts/day} = 20 \,\text{minutes/part}.$$

This is because the available time increases but the demand remains the same. The same effect of a 20-minute TT can be achieved by running two parallel lines for the same part on one shift.

$$\text{Line 1} - TT = 450 \,\text{minutes/day} \div 22.5 \,\text{parts/day} = 20 \,\text{minutes/part},$$

$$\text{Line 2} - TT = 450 \,\text{minutes/day} \div 22.5 \,\text{parts/day} = 20 \,\text{minutes/part}.$$

Author's Note: In the two-shift example, the CT is 20 minutes/part; however, in the one shift example with 2 lines, the overall CT considering both lines is 10 minutes/part. Again, this has nothing to do with our CT, and, for various reasons, we may choose to run the line at a CT that is not equal to TT.

We need to be able to balance the line or spread the work evenly across the line and flex resources to achieve maximum output. Sometimes, using these techniques helps to better balance work from shift to shift. Balancing the work has a corresponding effect on the number of people required. Some examples that may impact our decision are as follows:

■ We may choose to run at a faster or slower CT. This will cause us to over- or underproduce. For example, we may have had a person out yesterday and need to increase output today.

- We may be short parts, so we must underproduce one day and overproduce the next day when the parts come in.
- Management may decide to move something due next month into this month, so they can get more sales in the month (not a Lean solution, but it will happen nonetheless).
- Someone may be out on vacation, medical leave, in training, etc.

It can become very difficult to work strictly to TT, especially in low-volume high-mix environments or where lines have products that have designs with a lot of variation. To design a process leveraging CT information, we can make changes that will alter the available time to run the process. We can do this by:

- Working overtime
- Working weekends
- Working over lunch and breaks
- Adding or taking away shifts (extending or decreasing the workday)
- Adding lines or equipment or speeding up machines
- Running more or fewer hours per day
- Combining or separating products/services on a line or in a work area

Remember to assess everything that may impact the line or area. If we only focused on TT and determined we had enough capacity based on demand, we would be missing the opportunity to eliminate waste, optimize productivity, and grow our business within the current space.

Lesson Learned: Many times, we throw dollars away but watch the pennies.[4]

Three Types of Inventory

Inventory is divided into three basic types:

1. Raw material (RM)
2. Work in process/progress (WIP)
3. Finished goods (FGs)

Raw Material

Raw material (RM) is material that has no direct labor added to it. Indirect labor will have already been added to receive, move, and stock the material prior to its use.

Work in Process Inventory

Work in process (WIP) inventory is any RM with direct labor added but not completed. A good WIP inventory analogy is our laundry example. If we do our laundry every two weeks, how many days of clothes do we need? We need at least 2 * 7 days/week or 14 days' worth of clothes plus the time it takes to launder them. If it takes 3 days to launder them, we need a total of 17 days of clothes inventory. If we do our laundry once a week and it now takes a day to launder them, we can cut the inventory required from 17 days to 8 days.

Finished Goods Inventory

FGs are any materials that have had all the direct labor added. Indirect labor will still be required to pull it out of stock and ship it to the customer.

Measuring Inventory and Cash Flow

Most companies track inventory dollars; however, it is typically not very accurate even though they think it is! Many times, inventory is not truly based on the earliest due date (EDD) or FIFO[5]; much is obsolete; some is damaged, mislabeled, or stocked in the wrong location; and many times, the amount you have is not what the system says you have. Many times, the part master is not up-to-date, or the part is planned incorrectly. We have seen parts planned as MRP but with min/max information entered, which results in the system overriding one or the other. We find that the minimum lot sizes, average price, min/max levels, or other information in the record are incorrect. We particularly see this when data are transferred from one enterprise resource planning (ERP)/MRP system to another where the data loaded were incorrect or a flag was not set. Had we not questioned the data when developing the plan for every part (PFEP), the site would have gone on thinking the system was accurate. We will discuss the PFEP later in the book. Many times, scrap is not entered, and orders are closed out partially or in error. Some systems cannot tie the lower levels to the upper levels in the work orders correctly.

As a result, most companies have little or no idea of their true inventory costs. To figure out a day's worth of inventory, we need to calculate the inventory used over a specified period and divide it by the number of days in the period. For example, if a department has $6 million in RM inventory and they use an average of $1.2 million per month, we will take $1.2 million per month and divide by 30 calendar days per month:

$$\$1,200,000 \div 30 \text{ calendar days} = \$40,000 \text{ per calendar day.}$$

If we take the $6,000,000 supply inventory on hand,

$$\$6,000,000 \div \$40,000 / \text{day} = 150 \text{ calendar days of supply (DOS).}$$

Once we have DOS, we can calculate inventory turns:

$$\text{Inventory turns} = \text{calendar or annual working days} \div \text{DOS.}$$

For example,[6]

$$365 \text{ days in the year} \div 150 \text{ DOS} = 2.43 \text{ turns per year.}$$

When figuring out what individual part levels should be, we call this part of the PFEP.[7] In the PFEP, we will use the most recent pricing and multiply by average daily part usage to determine a days' worth of supply. Using the formulas previously, we can determine a true days' worth of usage for any product line or program.

Throughput Time: A Key Metric

Throughput time is calculated by adding the total processing, inspection, transport, and storage time or the sum of all the process flow analysis (PFA) CTs. Once we have throughput time, we can divide it by the TT or desired CT to determine the standard amount of work in process inventory required (SWIP) to meet the CT. We will discuss this more later in the chapter when we discuss Little's law. We recommend throughput time as a key Lean productivity metric. This metric is important because in Six Sigma terms where $Y = f(x)$, almost every other metric (x's) is somehow related to or ends up impacting throughput time, which would be our big Y or output metric. The longer the product stays in any type of inventory storage situation:

- The greater the danger of damaging the parts
- The more opportunity for defects
- The more we tend to batch produce
- The more it costs to house the parts
- The more supplies are required over the length of production
- The more labor required to handle the inventory
- The fewer products we can produce
- The need for more space and warehouses
- The more it raises our costs, which can reduce our market share
- The potential for parts not being counted or double counted—incorrect inventory

Every leader should understand that each extra second of throughput time adds costs, which can be defined in a variety of ways. This is seldom tracked and mostly hidden in traditional cost accounting methods.

Understanding and managing throughput time is critical to most companies as it impacts whether they can ship the next product, satisfies an urgent customer need, or performs the next service on time. Managing throughput time means the difference between whether we need to build new plants, buy more equipment, work overtime, retain existing business, or gain new business. Managing throughput time can positively impact the financial viability of any organization and should be a key metric for every line manager's performance review or bonus criteria. The example (see Figure 6.1) shows an example of materials management CTs that can be used to manage overall throughput time. Performance reviews can be tied to the ability to meet the targets for reducing CTs throughout the year.

Throughput Time and +QDIP

+QDIP is an acronym for safety, quality, delivery, inventory, and productivity, which all tie to the throughput time metric. We find, in every company, if we shorten throughput time, safety improves as we get the operators involved in making their job easier. The first things we look for during video analysis are safety and ergonomic issues. Quality generally improves because we are eliminating steps from the process so there are fewer opportunities for defects. Fill rate or on time delivery improves because we get the product out quicker and more predictably. Inventory along with inventory costs go down and productivity goes up. So, the by-products are that your costs decrease and customer satisfaction increases. To top it all off, we now gain capacity to potentially generate more revenue. The longer the throughput time, the more complex our processes seem to become and the more frustrating it is for our team members who are trying to move products

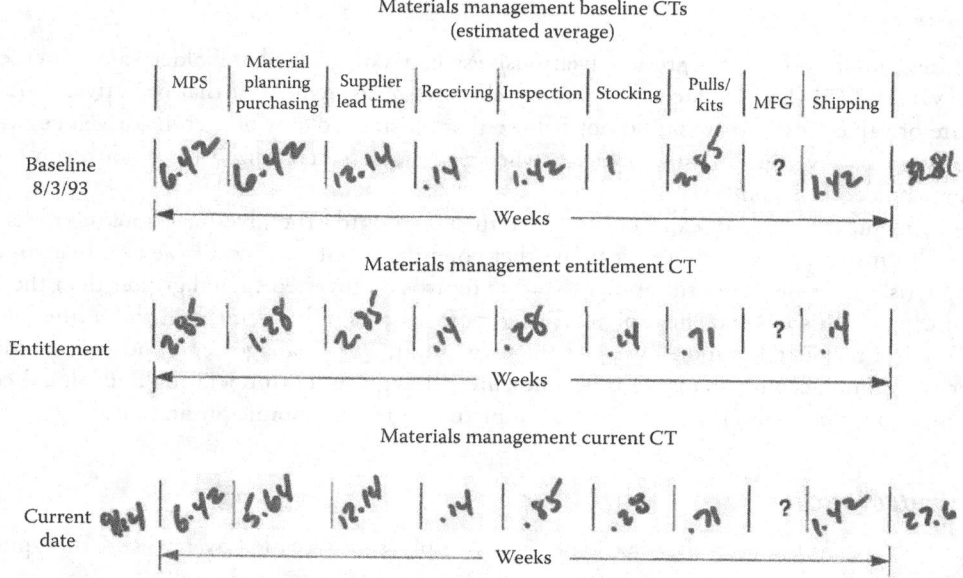

Figure 6.1 Throughput time example—Every manager had to identify their process and capture their process times.

through the system and keep them flowing. In the batch world, we just keep throwing people and parts at it trying to get something out the door.

How do we reduce throughput time? First, we must understand what comprises our throughput time. Remember, it is made up of all the individual process CTs. So, we must look at total throughput time for a product to get through our business processes from order entry to revenue collection and work to understand the drivers. Next, we reduce the individual CTs with point kaizen events or attack the overall process in one fell swoop through a system kaizen implementation.

Homework: One action you can immediately take is to have all your managers and supervisors define throughput time in their areas and calculate and understand what their CTs and resulting throughput times are for the processes for which they are responsible. The more we reduce the CT for each process, the less inventory we need, the less rooms we need, etc. We place a cautionary note, however, on metrics such as customer satisfaction and throughput time as there are a substantial number of contributing factors (x's) to both metrics. One isolated Lean initiative may not—and we have found through experience will not be able to—impact all the contributing factors to significantly move the needle on these metrics for the overall plant. A carefully planned sequential series of point kaizens or an overall system kaizen is required.

Financial Metrics

Being able to articulate and quantify financial metrics can be important, especially early in Lean implementations when organizations are still trying to prove the value of adopting Lean. One challenge outlined in the following highlights some of the data points one might consider gathering during the initial phases of the initiative to begin to construct the financial component of the return on investment (ROI) calculation.

EVA[8]

Assuming the objective for a profit-driven business is maximizing shareholder value, then economic value added (EVA) is a clear and comprehensive measurement of that objective. EVA is a measure of value creation. If you do not believe that all stakeholders of a profit-driven company in the long run have their claims furthered when shareholders maximize their claims, you forget that shareholders are paid last.

Investments are made in expectation of a return or reward. The investor is looking to have a yield on his investment that is greater than other potential investments available to him assuming the same risk. EVA measures the ability to create returns on invested capital greater than the cost of that capital. This has the effect of attracting more sources of investment in the future and so on. EVA as a metric takes more variables (namely, profit, asset management, and risk) of shareholder value into account than any other measures. It captures both operating and capital costs consumed to generate revenue. This provides a picture of true economic profitability.

EVA Calculation

$EVA = $ net operating profit after tax $-$ (net assets employed $\times$ weighted average cost of capital).

The operating profits are adjusted for an after-tax cash basis. Net operating profit after tax (NOPAT) represents cash flow from operations available for reinvestment or distribution: Operating income $\times$ (1 − tax rate) can be used as a proxy for NOPAT,

$$NOPAT = Operating\ income \times (1 - tax\ rate).$$

Net assets employed: The amount of capital invested in the business. This includes operating capital in the form of working capital plus net property, plant, and equipment plus goodwill.

Weighted average cost of capital (WACC): The opportunity cost to all capital investors weighted by the relative (market value) contribution to the company's total capital. The opportunity cost is the rate of return the investor could expect to earn on other investments of equal risk. An example of WACC is as follows:

Type of Capital	% of Total Capital Structure	Required Return %	WACC
Equity	40	10	0.04
Short term	25	3.5	0.00875
Long term	35	7	0.0245
Return requirement			0.073 or 7.3%

Some conclusions to be drawn on the WACC include the following:

1. It is influenced by the capital structure and hence can be managed through financial engineering (managing structure and debt rates).
2. As the ratio of debt-to-equity increases for a company, its WACC decreases.
3. As the ratio of debt-to-equity increases for a company, the risk of default increases.
4. The lower the WACC, the better.

The original formula of EVA = NOPAT – (net assets employed × WACC) goes beyond most of the traditional measures that focus on the income statement. It gives a broader indicator of economic value by including investments represented in the balance sheet. As written, the results would be in units of dollars $$ or EVA in an absolute dollar. If one divides the formula by net assets employed, the result is an EVA spread or ROI over the cost of capital.

$$\text{EVA} = \left(\text{NOPAT} - \left(\text{net assets employed} \times \text{WACC}\right)\right) \div \left(\text{net assets employed}\right),$$
$$= \text{return on invested capital} - \text{WACC}.$$

Author's Note: The purpose here is to merely introduce the reader to this concept. There are books written on EVA and it is too complex to describe here in its totality.

EVA is an excellent way to determine the economic value of an opportunity relative to alternatives. It is applicable for strategic level decisions of acquiring and divesting of business units to the more tactical decisions of which product lines to grow and which to manage for cash or discontinue. It can be used with some data gathering effort to prioritize customers. It also brings into perspective relative risk and effort associated with a particular opportunity. If a strategic option only provides an EVA spread of 1.5% versus an investment in US bonds, and it demands resources in the form of time and talent, it may be more advantageous to buy bonds and wait for a better opportunity or return the capital to shareholders. EVA is used by some of the world's leading companies including Coca-Cola, ITT, Whole Foods Markets, Hewlett Packard, London-based Diageo PLC, Herman Miller, GE, and AT&T.

Return on Net Assets[9]

Another perspective on EVA can be gained by looking at a firm's return on net assets (RONA). RONA is a ratio calculated by dividing a firm's NOPAT by the amount of capital it employs (RONA = NOPAT/capital).

$$\text{EVA} = \left(\text{net investments}\right) \times \left(\text{RONA} - \text{required minimum return}\right).$$

If RONA is above the threshold rate, EVA is positive.

What Is MVA?

Market value added (MVA) is a measure of wealth a company has created for its investors. It is a cumulative measure of corporate performance that looks at how much a company's stock has added to (or taken out of) investors' pocketbooks over its life and compares it with the capital those same investors put into the firm. Maximizing EVA and MVA should be the primary objective for any company concerned about its shareholders' welfare.

MVA Calculation

First, all the capital a company has acquired from inception is added up. This includes equity and debt offerings, bank loans, and retained earnings. Some adjustments are made that capitalize certain past expenditures, like R&D spending, as an investment in future earnings. This adjusted capital amount is compared to a firm's total market value that is the current value of a company's stock and debt to get MVA or the difference between what the investors can take out and the amount investors put in.

$$
\begin{aligned}
MVA = \big[&(\text{shares outstanding} \times \text{stock price}) \\
&+ \text{market value of preferred stock} \\
&+ \text{market value of debt} \big] - \text{total capital}.
\end{aligned}
$$

When calculating EVA and MVA, the amount of equity equivalent reserves for certain accounts must be determined first. Equity equivalents are adjustments that turn a firm's accounting book value into economic book value. This economic book value is a truer measure of the cash that investors have put at risk in the firm and upon which they expect to accrue some returns.

Using EVA and MVA within a Company

All managers have the same goal of obtaining capital and earning a rate of return on it that exceeds the return offered by other seekers of capital funds. EVA can be used as a financial management system, which allows managers and employees to focus on how capital is used, and the cash flow generated from it. There are two benefits from focusing on growth in EVA: management's attention is focused more on its primary responsibility that is increasing investors' wealth and, secondly, distortion caused by using historical cost accounting data is reduced or eliminated so managers can spend their time finding ways to increase EVA. This increased awareness of the efficient use of capital will eventually produce additional shareholder value. Managers can do a better job of asset management, and EVA can be used to hold management accountable for all economic outlays whether they appear in the income statement, on the balance sheet, or in the footnotes to the financial statements. This is possible because EVA creates one financial statement that includes all the costs of being in business, while making managers aware of every dollar they spend. Another benefit of using EVA is it creates a common language for making decisions, especially long-term decisions. Examples are resolving budgeting issues and evaluating the performance of organizational units and managers. EVA quantification of results in financial terms also helps to energize other management programs such as total quality management (TQM), quick response, and customer development by demanding and getting continuous financial improvement. Managers and employees adopt a long-term focus and begin to think more like owners as they start to feel responsible for and take part in the economic value of the firm.

Benefits of EVA Incentive Plan

One effective way to align employees' interest with investors is to tie their compensation to output from the EVA metric. People are paid for sustainable improvements in EVA. The behavior within a company is changed through the understanding of what drives EVA and economic returns. Necessary properties for the incentive system to work are as follows:

■ Have an objective measure of performance that cannot be manipulated.
■ Plan must be simple so everyone in the organization can understand it.
■ Significant bonus amount to alter employees' behavior.
■ Keep the target fixed and do not move the goalpost after the plan gets under way.

Strongly recommended properties are as follows:

- No limits should be placed on the plan.
- Include cancellation clause whereby a banked bonus is lost if a person resigns.
- Incorporate long-term perspective into the plan.
- Structure of the plan should be team based.
- Both management and labor must agree to the plan details.

At company in upstate New York, we used EVA as the measurement target in our Scanlon-based gain-sharing program for a small, $75 m in revenue business unit in a several billion-dollar public company. Two-thirds of the roughly 240 people were represented by the United Steel Workers (USW) union. It started slow due to the erosion of trust between employees and management over the prior decade, high targets due to the turnaround environment of the business, and a lack of financial backing. However, after a couple of years, the bonus was 5% of each employee's pay and topped out at over 10% per year.[10]

Implementing value-added measures into a company is a costly and timely process. Supporters justify the substantial costs and time by pointing out the benefit of optimizing the company's strategy for value creation. A transition to value-added measurements requires serious commitment of the board of directors and senior management to use these measures to manage the business. Every individual in the company must buy into the plan to make it successful. It will also require extensive training and communication effort directed to everyone in the company. Everyone must be educated on the basic theory underlying the notion of creating economic value. Nonetheless, EVA should not be viewed as the answer to all things. It doesn't solve business problems, which is the manager's responsibility. In conjunction with MVA, it provides a meaningful target to pursue for both internally and externally oriented decisions.

Sales per Employees

Sales or revenue by itself can be a misleading metric for companies, as the prices charged or product mix can change from year to year or during a year; however, sales per employee is a pretty good overarching metric for companies implementing Lean. This is determined simply by dividing the sales dollars for a given period by the number of employees working.

Contribution Margin by Employee

Contribution margin or gross profit per employee is also a good overarching metric for Lean. This is a high-level look at the contribution per employee, and we should set a percentage goal to increase this each year.

Peak Demand

Peak demand is a phenomenon all around us. There is a peak demand for amusement parks on certain holidays. Restaurants or kitchens refer to peak demand as being slammed. In many manufacturing companies, it is referred to as end of the month. Companies can experience peak demand at various times throughout a shift, day, month, or year. Sometimes we call it seasonal variation. Spikes in demand can make it difficult to level load the schedule. For instance, Kawasaki used to build snowmobiles in the summer and motorcycles in the winter.

Ski demand varies based on the weather. To level out demand, ski resorts manufacture their own snow if the temperature allows.

If not carefully planned, peak demand can drive a tremendous amount of waste. Supporting peak demand requires extra staffing, overtime, and sometimes extra equipment or lines. Once peak demand ends, what do we do with the extra staff and equipment? Sometimes we utilize temporary labor to flex up and down as peak demand varies. Our Lean principle's goal is to level load demand, but until that can be done, we need to account for normal variation or peak demand in our TT and CT to provide services to meet the demand. We may need a couple of TTs due to variation and the ability to accommodate fluctuations in customer demand and product.

Note: Customer demand must be analyzed in the same increment of time as available time to be compared with TT.

Little's Law and Queuing Theory[11]

A key to each Lean journey is to minimize (preferably eliminate) waste, which increases speed in the system. Increasing speed (velocity) will equate to reducing customer lead time, which improves customer satisfaction and provides for secondary financial benefits, such as the potential to charge a premium for faster deliveries and likely improvements in inventory turns (cash conversion). Minimizing waste must include a detailed review of inventory and steps to reduce the inventory. Little's law provides the relationship between the following:

1. The average number of items in a system
2. The average waiting time (or flow time) for a given item
3. The average arrival time to the system to help understand queuing (i.e., waiting within a system)

Of importance is if you know two of the three, the relationship allows for calculating the third.[12] Leveraging Little's law can allow one to understand wait times or expected wait times (WIP) or being in the queue or flow time, with only a couple of pieces of data. Additionally, one can leverage this relationship to predict a quality of service related to calculated times in a system based upon the number of arrivals and arrival time into the system. Little's law provides a simple but powerful method to understand the relationship of steady-state production systems. The law has deep-rooted mathematical underpinnings; however, we can use the law as a tool for Lean. The textbook by Hopp and Spearman refers to Little's law as "… an interesting and fundamental relationship between WIP, CT and throughput." They go on to state the law as

$$TH = WIP \div CT$$

where they define throughput (TH) as "the average output of a production process (machine, workstation, line, plant) per unit time," WIP as "the inventory between the start and end points of a product routing," and CT as "the average time from release of a job at the beginning of the routing until it reaches an inventory point at the end of the routing (is the time the part spends as WIP)." They note that "CT is also referred to as flow time, throughput time, and sojourn time, depending on the context."[13] Another way to look at it is as follows:

$$Inventory(WIP) = Throughput(TH) \times Cycle\ Time(CT).$$

A simple examination of the law shows that reducing WIP (which is a Lean goal) while holding throughput steady will result in reduced CT. We could conclude that reducing WIP will always reduce CT; however, we need to be careful in the application as reducing WIP without changing other factors will usually reduce throughput (i.e., output). We need to focus on the total system, including reduction in variability (i.e., improved quality) to ensure the line (process) can achieve higher levels of throughput with much lower levels of WIP. A simple illustration is a line that produces one unit per hour (CT) with a throughput time of 16 hours; in this case, the WIP should equal 16 units. Another way to look at the formula is as follows: the longer the throughput time, the more inventory (WIP) must exist in the system. For a queuing system in steady state, the average length (L) of the queue equals the average arrival rate (Y) times the average waiting time (W). More succinctly,

$$L = Y \times W.$$

Example: If it takes 60 days to get a product through your factory and you ship (steady state) 100 units per day, then 100 units per day × 60 days = an average of 6000 units in WIP inventory at any given time. This would equate to 6 WIP inventory turns per year.

The law appears very intuitive, and, in general, there are very few constraints when using the relationship. We can use the relationship for any system, including manufacturing, administration, or transaction, including both systems within a system. The system must not be a start-up or shutdown system or a system that is unstable (in transition or not in control). This theory is the underpinnings of standard work in process (SWIP). If an emergency room waiting area has an average length of 1 hour and our arrival rate/CT is 10 minutes, we need a waiting room that can hold six people. In manufacturing, if an oven has a 60-minute throughput time and we are producing at a CT of one every 2 minutes then we need 30 in the oven.

Lesson Learned: As we cut our throughput time and increase our first pass yield (FPY, the total throughput yield of the system), our costs will be reduced.

Tom Peters[14] said, "in their book, Stalk and Hout say the consumption of time should become the primary business measurement performance variable,"[15] i.e., ahead of the 'P' word profit. Sounds silly at first blush, sounds brilliant at second blush because if you get the 'T' word right then the 'P' word takes care of itself. In addition, if we can reduce our throughput time, we can now increase our capacity (assuming we have the demand).

Weighted Average Demand Calculations

Let's say we have baseline data for three different products being manufactured on one line:

- Demand for product A is 50 units/day, and it takes 4 people 8 hours to make 100 units.
- Demand for product B is 25 units per day, and it takes 2 people 8 hours to make 100 units.
- Demand for product C is 25 units, and it takes 3 people 8 hours to make 100 units.
- Total demand = 50 (product A) + 25 (product B) + 25 (product C) = 100 units

To calculate average hours per unit day, we would first add up the hours per day:

- Product A takes 32 hours (4 people × 8 hours)/100 units or 0.32 hours per unit
- Product B takes 16 hours (2 people × 8 hours)/100 units or 0.16 hours per unit
- Product C takes 24 hours (3 people × 8 hours)/100 units or 0.24 hours per unit

If we were to average this, it would come out to 0.24 hours per unit. However, our demand is not split up evenly. So, we must figure out the demand for each product. Total demand is 100 units so product A equals 50/100 or 50% of the demand, product B = 25%, and product C = 25% demand. So, the weighted average hours per unit are as follows:

- Product A = 0.5 × 0.32 hours per unit = 0.16 hours per unit
- Product B = 0.25 × 0.16 hours per unit = 0.04 hours per unit
- Product C = 0.25 × 0.24 hours per unit = 0.06 hours per unit.

We add these together to get 0.26 hours/unit, which is the weighted average per unit based on the product mix of products A, B, and C (Table 6.5). Mixed model lines typically require this weighted average applied globally to determine the baseline metrics since the data are normally not kept by the product line.

Homework: Let's say you could produce 32 of product A in 8 hours, 16 of product B in 8 hours, or 24 of product C in 8 hours. What would the weighted average hours per unit be?

Answer: See Table 6.6.

Each organization must decide what confidence level can be placed on the accuracy of the data. The bottom line is that having data is great, but it is the human interpretation of this data that is critical. Sometimes, it helps to have a couple of people looking at the data as you progress through the implementation to make sure the formulas are correct. The team that includes the executive sponsor and Lean initiative owner must understand the information and determine what is reasonable to accomplish in relation to the organizational goals. In addition, as situations change like product mix or total labor content improves, the calculations must be revised/updated to make sure everyone continues to manage by fact, or the system will break down.

Table 6.5   Weighted Average Example

			Weighted Average				
1	A	B	C	D	E	F	G
2				Col B ÷ Col C		Col E ÷ E7	Col D * Col F
3		Hours per	Hundred Units	Average Hours per Unit	Demand per Day	Percent of Daily Demand	Weighted Average Hours per Unit
4	Product A	32	100	0.32	50	50	0.16
5	Product B	16	100	0.16	25	25	0.04
6	Product C	24	100	0.24	25	25	0.06
7	Totals			0.24	100	100	0.26

Source: BIG Archives.

Table 6.6 Answers to Weigthed Average Quiz

	A	B	C	D	E	F	G
				Answers to Weighted Average Quiz			
1				Col C ÷ Col B		Col E ÷ E6	Col D * Col F
2		Demonstrated Units per Day	Paid Hours per Day	Average Hours per Unit	Demand per Day	Percent of Daily Demand	Weighted Average Hours per Unit
3	Product A	32	8	0.25	5	21	0.05
4	Product B	16	8	0.50	12	50	0.25
5	Product C	24	8	0.33	7	29	0.10
6	Totals	24		0.36	24	100	0.40

Source: BIG Archives.

What Is a Second Worth?

What is a second worth? We could have picked almost any race from swimming to running to illustrate the point (Table 6.7). In the Olympics, in a 400-m dash, six of eight runners were within a second and the seventh was 4 1/100ths over a second. In any process, seconds over the course of a year add up to hours, and sometimes days or more of savings. Improve your seconds, inches, cm, and pennies; a little bit every day and watch the savings add up.

Homework: Find out what every extra second of throughput time costs you in your business, hospital, and government office or service industry. What is every second worth in dollars? This will help people on the front lines to relate to the benefits of providing suggestions and ideas on how to reduce throughput time.

Table 6.7 What is a second worth?

2012 Summer Olympics London: 400 m Dash Results		
Rank	Athlete	Mark
1	James Kirani	43.94
2	Santos Luguelin	44.46
3	Gordon Lalonde	44.52
4	Brown Chris	44.79
5	Borlee Kevin	44.81
6	Borlee Jonathan	44.83
7	Pinder Demetrius	44.98
8	Solomon Steven	45.15

Source: BIG Archives.

Value Stream Mapping

VSM has become an important tool in Lean implementations particularly in understanding the current state of a process and identifying the opportunities in which a process can be improved. VSM techniques are explained in two books, Learning to See[16] and Seeing the Whole.[17] Since the introduction of these books, many subsequent books utilize VSMs as part of their instruction. This book is no exception. VSM is included initially as part of the baseline toolset (the B in the BASICS® model), but it can also be used as an assessment tool (an A in our BASICS® model).

We have included VSM in the baselining tools as the first step to documenting the system or process steps for an administrative process. But VSMs can also be used as an analysis tool to determine if steps can be eliminated or simplified to create the future state. Often there are quick wins identified, which can jump-start a project and allow teams to see immediate results. Additionally, we find that people work in silos and many times they do not understand the entire process; creating a VSM can be eye-opening as the entire process is unveiled, and it is easier to see waste in the process. They are also a good tool to keep track of your progress during your Lean journey. Why start with VSM? The reason is if one can eliminate a step at the value stream level, no further analysis (i.e., product, operator, or setup) is needed for that step and it hastens the improvement process. This reasoning cascades to the next step that is the product flow analysis (PFA). If we can eliminate a step at the PFA level, we don't have to do the next step of the analysis that is the operator analysis. As we make improvements throughout the process, we should go back and update the VSM.

Lesson Learned: At many companies during the TQM phase in the late 1990s, anywhere from one to several total quality (TQ) teams were launched each week or month to go make improvements to processes. When we went back and reviewed these projects, we found that had we looked at the entire process up front at the VSM level, we could have just eliminated many of the projects because we eliminated those project steps. This could have saved a team of 4–8 people working on improving them and essentially wasting many months of the company's resources.

The On-Time Delivery Metric Story

At a company in Phoenix, AZ, we were working on an aircraft engine line. Prior to our implementation, the previous manager of the area changed the production process to separate the subassembly operations from the final assembly operations. Prior to this, each operator built their own engine, including the subassemblies, from start to finish. This manager was a Six Sigma black belt and wanted to make their mark as a manager. They had no experience in assembly operations and had never seen an engine manufactured prior to being assigned as manager to the line. They baseline their metrics from the start of an engine to its completion, then, under the auspices of Lean, created a separate subassembly area and assigned operators to just build subassemblies. The operators' objections to the changes were not solicited, and unsolicited objections went unheeded.

After a month, the on-time delivery (OTD) of the area was reduced to zero, but the project and the new manager's time spent managing her new area was regarded as a huge success. How could this be? Well, they manipulated (gamed) the metrics. They took the old final assembly time, which included the subassemblies, and compared it to the new final assembly time, which excluded the subassemblies and took credit for a 50% CT reduction. Amazing, isn't it? But it is not as uncommon as one might think. When we arrived to work with the company, there were subassemblies everywhere and virtually no room to build the final assembly; but the area "looked good to the untrained Lean eye." They had visual metrics boards, but they couldn't ship anything on time!

They promoted the manager and put a new manager in charge, again with no experience, and that is the environment in which we had to kick off our pilot true Lean project. Within 12 weeks, with much resistance due to the black belt's implementation, we were able to involve everyone in the area and set up a true Lean subassembly line and increased the real OTD to over 40%.

Lesson Learned: Figures don't lie but liars do figures.[18]

As the value stream evolves from current state to ideal state and then back to future state, it can be used as a method to keep track of progress throughout your Lean journey. The VSM is one of the tools that crosses the steps of the BASICS® model and is included as a tool in Check or the C in the BASICS® model. As improvements occur, the value stream should be updated to reflect the new current state. The VSM (see Figures 6.2 and 6.3) is much more powerful than a flow chart and has been successfully applied across many types of business, such as manufacturing on the shop floor, to office settings, in health care, and government processes. The VSM is a good tool for virtually any type of manufacturing process; however, it is also one of the best tools for mapping transactional administrative processes including order entry, scheduling, human resources, purchasing, sales, marketing, engineering, finance, and new business development. The VSM allows one to see the overall systems and clearly understand the components of a process, subsystems, and interrelated dependencies at work as it follows the value stream across departmental silos. VSM also helps one visualize more than a single-process level. It links both information and material flows across many departments (see Figure 6.4).

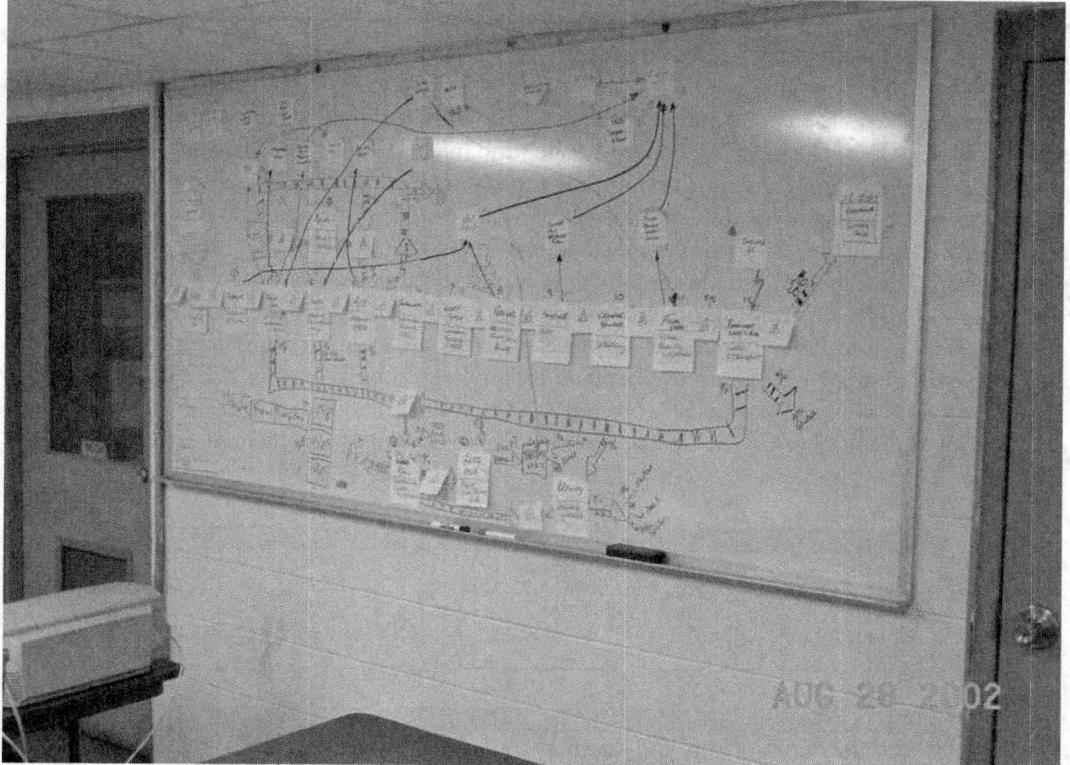

Figure 6.2   VSM example.

Figure 6.3 VSM example.

Lesson Learned: There is an inherent danger in initially mapping a sublevel process or subassembly process. This danger presents itself in the fundamental concept of the value stream itself. If we only look at a small part of the value stream, we are not necessarily seeing the big picture. Therefore, it is important to do a high-level VSM for the overall organization, which depicts how all the individual value streams work together. There should be an executive position in the organization that is assigned to always look at how all the value streams (processes) function and work together and assess improvement opportunities to streamline the overall organization. The master layout should be considered at this level. If areas are creating VSMs of their individual area, they will be working on improvements in isolation; essentially, we are still supporting silos. This often yields some improvements, but not the improvements needed to yield the results that occur when the entire value stream is assessed. We see layouts implemented by well-meaning

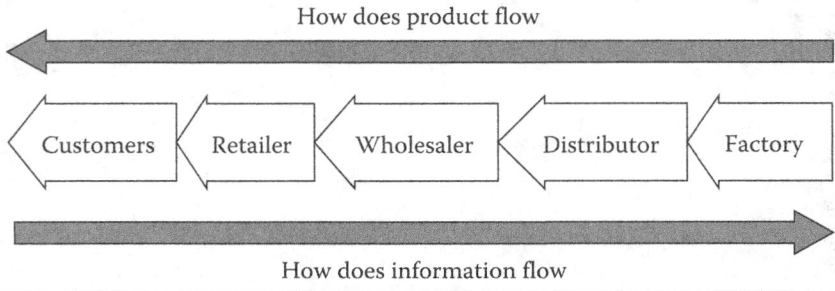

Figure 6.4 VSM tracks both product flow and information flow.

managers or teams, but because there is no knowledgeable Lean review, they are not Lean but still implemented.

Value Stream Discussion

A VSM is like a process map on steroids. The VSM has all the elements of the Six Sigma SIPOC (an acronym for suppliers–inputs–process–outputs–customer) tool where SIPOC is a high-level picture of the process depicting how the given process is servicing the customer. However, it provides an enhanced view of the process by looking at how the product or information flows through the process, as well as the flow and interrelatedness of the information necessary to process the part, paperwork, or electronic/paperless transaction. The VSM combines traditional process flow mapping focusing on the flow of the process, with data to create a roadmap to help identify improvement opportunities. When creating a VSM, it is often the first time that cross-functional managers and teams begin to understand the impact of the process in handing off from one area to another. It can be very eye-opening. The VSM:

- Visualizes the flow
- Focuses on the big picture/system(s)
- Helps identify areas to improve across silos
- Identifies the current state of the process
- Helps highlight the waste in the process
- Helps determine the sources (causes) of waste
- Provides a common language for discussing problems and improvements
- Makes necessary decisions about flow very apparent
- Enables innovation—brainstorm ideal and future states that leave out wasted steps while introducing smooth flow and leveled pull
- Provides a visual roadmap of prioritized opportunities to the strategic plan (i.e., projects and tasks) necessary for improvement as a management tool to track progress

There are hundreds of processes in any company or government entity. There are high-level steps/activities, process level, and sub-process levels. A process box in a high-level VSM, if further decomposed, could result in being its own process or sub-process VSM (see Figure 6.5). The level and details depicted in VSM will depend on the business problem you are trying to solve. The VSM outlines the process and categorizes what amount of the overall time is process time and storage (waiting) time for the product or information going through the process. It also shows the information flow, materials flow, and a timeline with a results box that shows the overall process versus storage time. The value stream lends clarity to the process, helping to reveal process steps that impede throughput and highlight where waste and non-value activity are prevalent.

Lesson Learned: Many times, we hear someone say the VSM shows how much value added exists in the process. This is not the case. A step that is classified as a process step does not mean it is value added. Most process steps consist of many non-value-added steps. So, at this level, VSMs mix up value-added and non-value-added activities in the process steps. VSMs do show process times versus inventory/storage times. The VSM can help a team assess a process and directionally determine how much of the process is of value and what needs to be improved.

The current state VSM is the first layer of the onion. It shows the as-is processes, which make up the overall system, and provides focus on opportunities for improvement. VSM an information

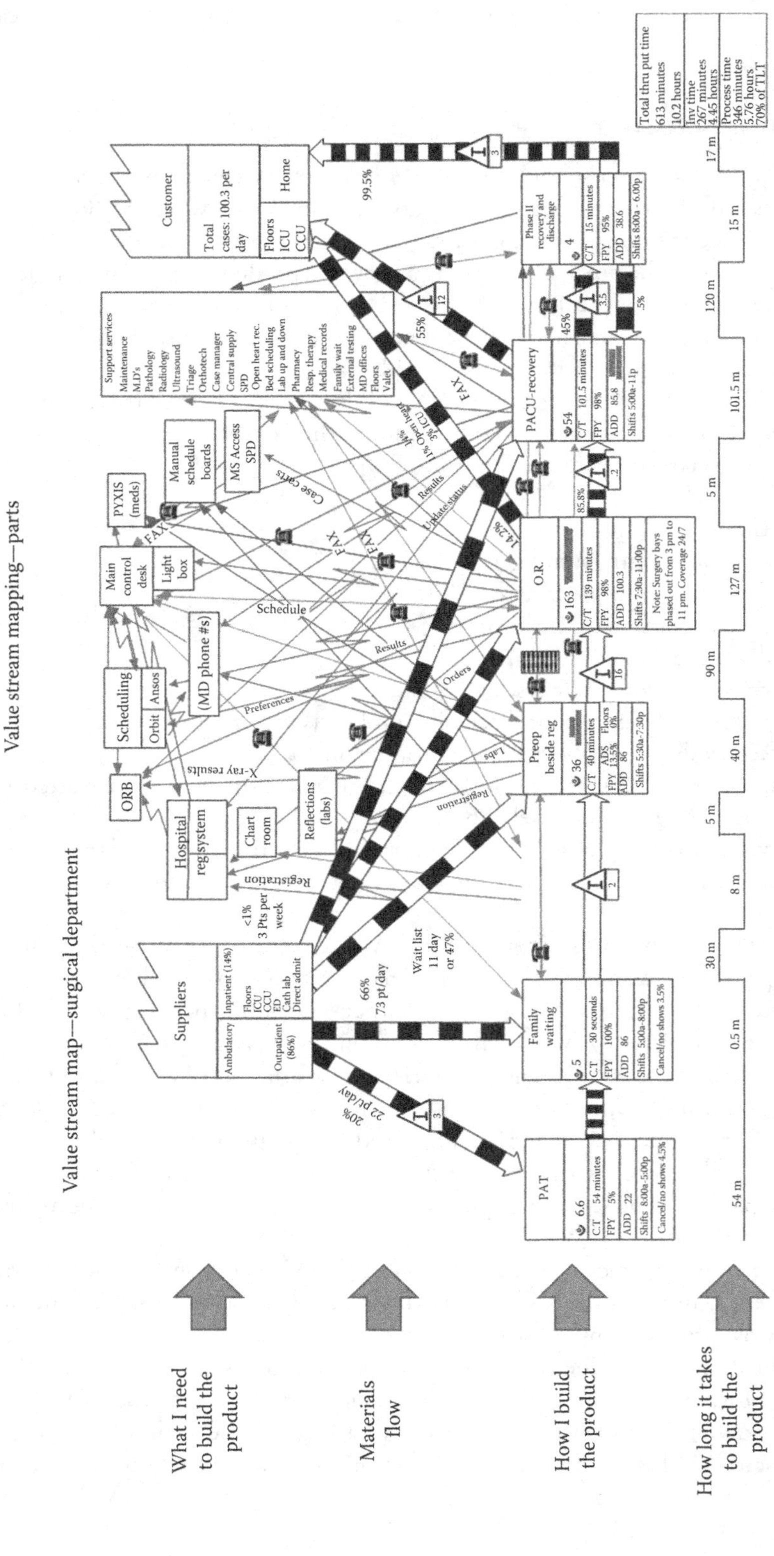

Figure 6.5 VSM Parts.

flow process is very tricky because we are mapping information process flow boxes that interact with information flow system boxes at the top of the map. VSMs:

- Visually identify process versus storage steps
- Help to identify which steps can be eliminated, rearranged, combined, or simplified (ERSC)
- Facilitate opportunities to improve flow
- Enable opportunities to see where information systems should be able to talk to each other
- Identify where we can create pull systems
- Provide a vehicle to manage the area and feed materials or information
- Create employee objectives for their evaluations
- Enable one to strive for perfection
- Create a management roadmap to track the elimination of waste and improvements

Updating your value stream maps is a great way to keep track of your progress over time.

Lesson Learned: We all want to think everything we do adds value, so some of us will play with the definitions of value added to make us feel better. This can do more harm than good. The goal of any process improvement tool is to highlight the waste in the process and expose variation. If we end up deceiving ourselves or work to make audit tool standards lower so we feel better, we are degrading the improvement process and lowering our standards. To be value added, it must meet the three criteria discussed earlier in the book:

1. Customer cares
2. Physically changes the product or transaction (or patient) for the better
3. Done right the first time

Value Stream Mapping

At a large foundry, each step of the process was captured on a VSM in addition to the changeover times. We did the map a little differently in that we overlaid the VSM over their layout. Each process in the plant had a process data box on top of it. As they decreased their CTs through ongoing every-day improvements and occasional events, they would update their VSM and pass their learning's on to the other plants.[19] This created a continuous learning environment across the company. The maps were reviewed by the senior leadership during each visit where the question was not how have you done but what are you planning to do next? Where is your bottleneck? How can we help you?

There is a saying that goes "minutes count but seconds rule."[20] This could be no truer than at their manufacturing plant where saving a second in the process could literally result in a million dollar across the company. Since we started with them, they are now averaging over a 50% increase in productivity. This increase in production allowed them to shutter one plant and stop work on a new plant.

The Hoshin Plan and VSM Story

Back in the late 1990s Donnelly Mirrors utilized VSM as a working tool for supervisors and teams to constantly monitor their progress and identify new opportunities for improvement. They integrated this approach with their Hoshin Planning System. It was very easy for anyone, even a stranger, to see the linkage between the Hoshin goals the team had and the goals of the senior leadership team.

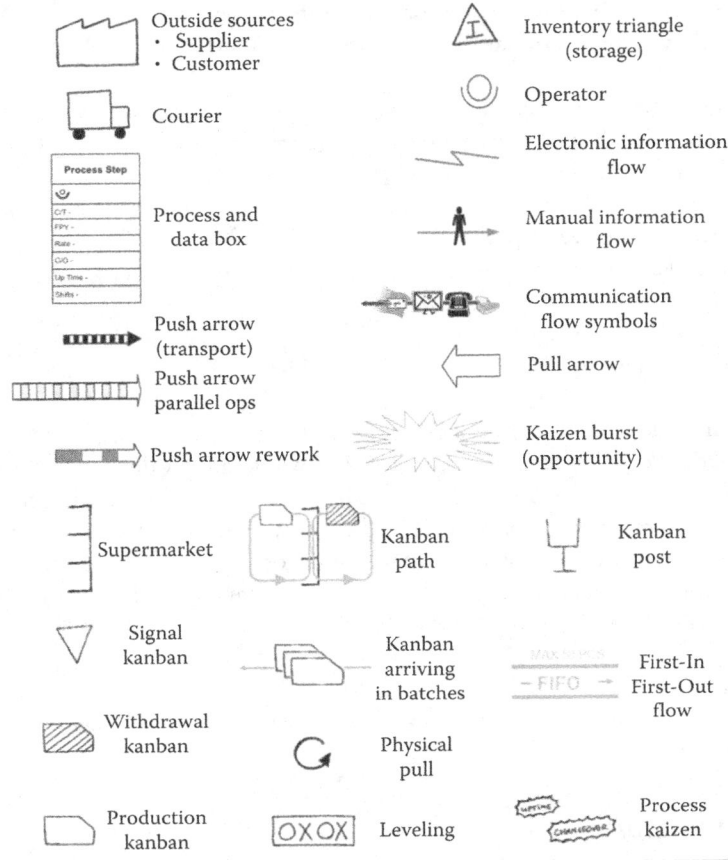

Figure 6.6 VSM surgery example with parts of a VSM noted.

Parts of a Value Stream Map

VSMs have four major parts (Figure 6.6). In the middle of the map are the process boxes, which is how the part, product, or information flows. At the top of the map are information system boxes that outline what information, whether it be electronic or paper, is required to make each process work and the connection to the process box. The third part is the timeline information at the bottom of the map. The timeline is a sawtooth, which includes the storage times on top and process CTs on the bottom. The results box shows the overall storage time (non-value-added time) versus the process time. The fourth part is the materials flow from supplier to customer.

Value Stream Map Icons

There are many references to VSM icons.[21] Figure 6.7 depicts some standard icons we utilize, as well as lines to show manual information flows (i.e., someone hand-carrying information verbally or written and communication, such as fax, e-mail, snail mail, and telephone). We use colored lines for information flow. We use red for automated, green for manual, and blue for snail mail, e-mail, fax, text, etc.

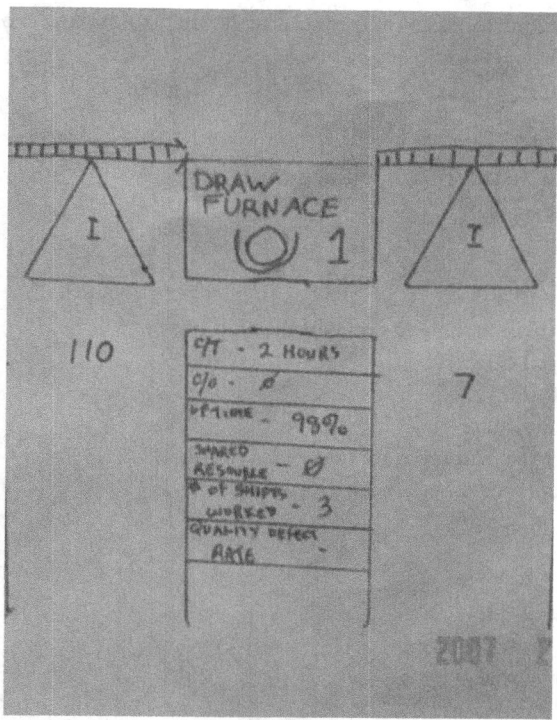

Figure 6.7 VSM icons.

Value Stream Map Definitions

Our approach is to make the VSM as realistic as possible. The process box also includes a data box. We try to get statistically accurate data to populate the boxes where we can; however, the entire process map is a snapshot in time. While some simple maps can and have been done in a day, we find that when combined with teaching a VSM team and collecting real data, doing the ideal and future states, and developing a list of projects tied to the strategic plan, it normally takes a week. On the outside, it sometimes could take up to two to three weeks for a very large process.

We normally create the map with paper and pencil and Post-it® notes. We send the team out to walk the process and interview the staff to begin the outline of process and storage boxes. The basic current state map can almost always be drawn in less than a couple of hours and sometimes less than an hour. Then we send the team out to collect data for each process and storage box. Throughout the data collection process, we find that the map undergoes constant changes. Collecting accurate data for the process boxes can take from several hours to several days depending on the VSM scope. The maps are next reviewed by the major stakeholders. The team then creates a project prioritization schedule which is reviewed at the senior leadership debriefing. A normal schedule for a weeklong VSM event would be as follows:

Day 1

- VSM training class.
- Walk the process and interview staff.

- Use yellow stickies and flip chart paper to outline the process and storage boxes.
- Fill in information boxes and lines to boxes.

Day 2

- Collect data and fill in information flow system boxes.
- Revise map as necessary.

Day 3

- Collect data and finish arrows to communication boxes.
- Draw in the material flow.
- Brainstorm ideal state.
- Create the ideal state map.
- Brainstorm project list and separate task versus project.
- Note which projects could be done within the year.

Day 4

- Create a future state map.
- Complete project prioritization.
- Complete data collection.
- Develop the final report out.

Day 5

- Leadership presentation and team celebration.

The VSM event deliverables include three maps: current state, ideal state, and future state, in that order, which result in a prioritized project list of tasks and projects. A task is anything that can immediately be assigned to an individual to complete. Projects generally involve some type of study and require a team. We review the map with the leadership team and key stakeholders at the end of the week or when the map is completed. This provides the opportunity to fully walk through the current state or reality and focus on what it will take to improve the product or administrative process. Many times, we use value stream maps in place of or as part of a Lean assessment. It is a great way to figure out where to start a Lean project. We are often asked what the rules are for developing VSMs. Since the books on VSMs are based on very simple examples, we tell companies that the rules are to accurately depict your processes in whatever way makes the most sense. There are no hard, rigid guidelines.

Drawing the Current State Value Stream Map

As discussed previously, the first step is to create the VSM based on the current state (see Figure 6.8); this requires walking the process pretending to be the "thing" (or information) going through the process with a team of subject matter experts consisting of frontline staff and those familiar with the process. The VSM must describe what occurs in the process, not what is written in policies or how supervisors or managers may believe the process is occurring. It is critical to

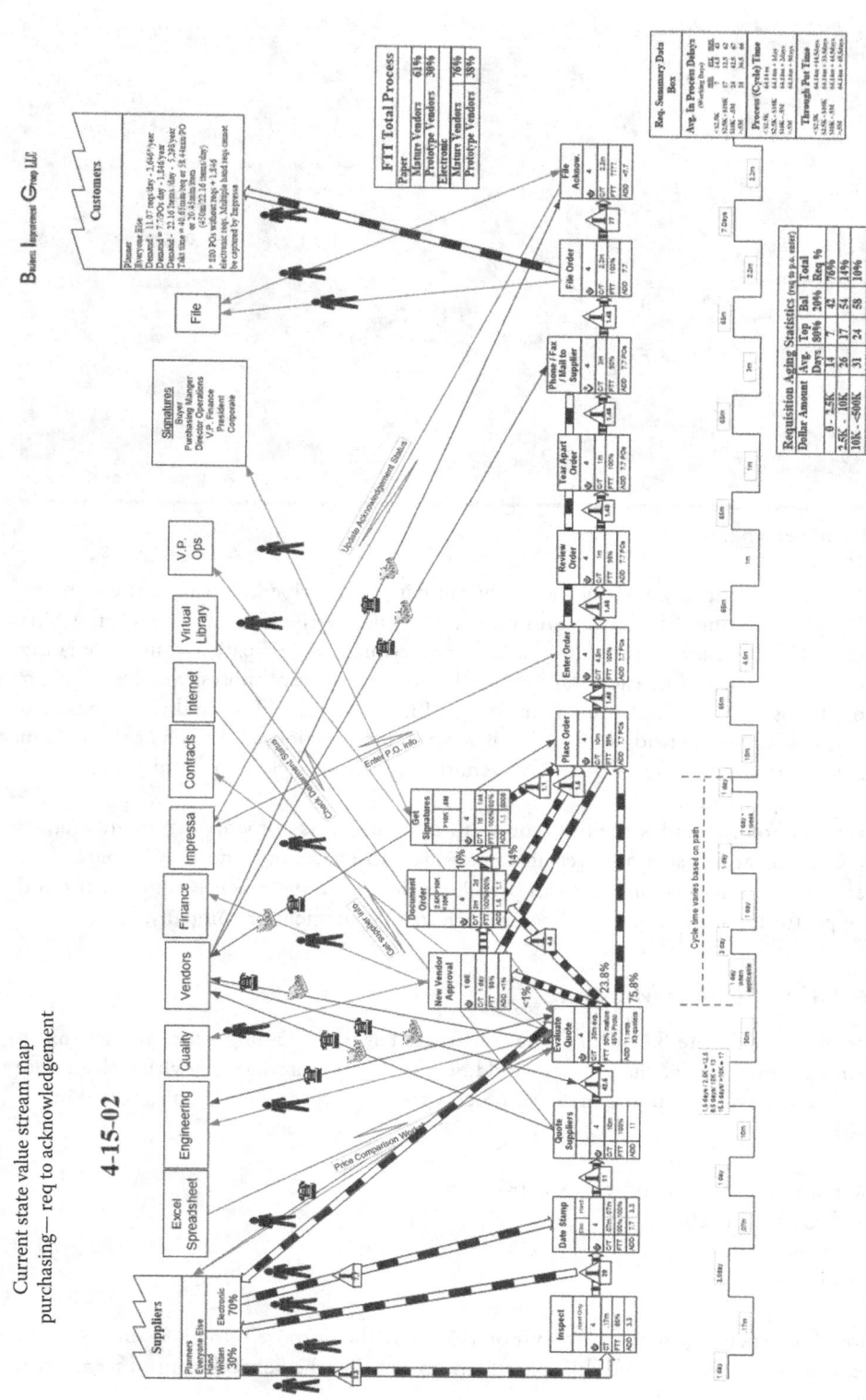

Figure 6.8   Current state purchasing department VSM.

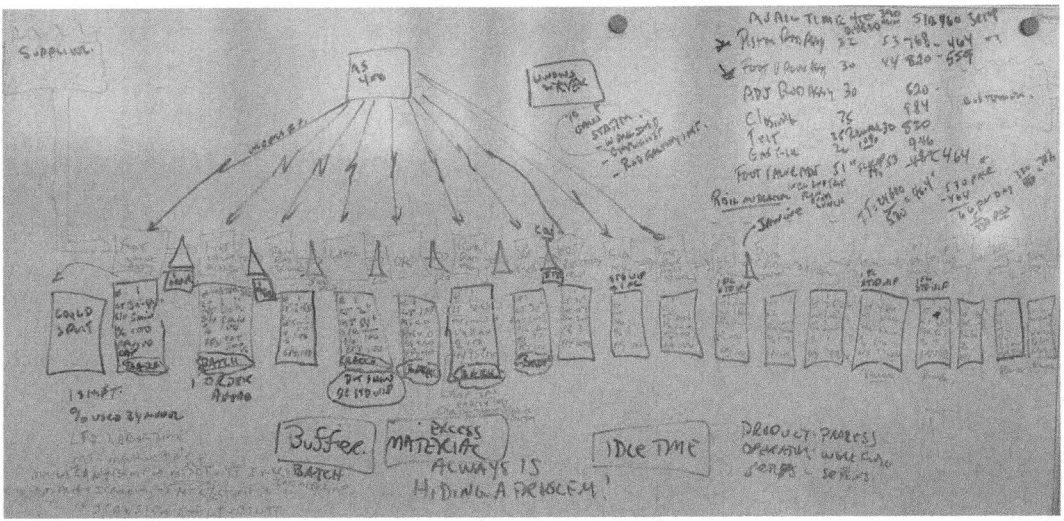

Figure 6.9 Hand drawn VSM.

capture reality to truly identify waste and non-value activity as described, as well as the supporting data. Once this is accomplished, the team moves on to define the ideal state. All our VSMs are initially hand-drawn. This is because it is easier for everyone to participate and make ongoing changes as the map is reviewed by each stakeholder. For presentation purposes, we often convert these maps to Microsoft Visio® and print them out to flip chart size. Most traditional business executive cultures are not quite ready for hand drawn VSM presentations and often criticize them for being messy or unreadable (see Figure 6.9). Another good example of a hand-drawn value stream is shown in Figure 6.10.

Lesson Learned: You must pick the hills you want to die on. It is not worth trying to change executives' perceptions at a first-time meeting to consider A3 charts or hand-drawn maps. It is sometimes better to compromise on the Lean principles than have the executives lose focus and not have the opportunity to expose or implement Lean in a department or company.

Ideal State Value Stream Mapping

The ideal state map (see Figure 6.11) should be constructed as part of a brainstorming session in which the team determines what the process would be like if they were starting with a clean slate and all barriers are removed. Mapping the ideal process sets the target condition and is looking at the process with:

■ What it could look like five or ten years from now
■ All sacred cows removed
■ All the money in the world
■ All the technology available

Teams should not spend more than an hour on this step. The purpose is to get teams to brainstorm, get the team out of the box, and shift paradigms to envision the possibilities and set an ideal state target condition.

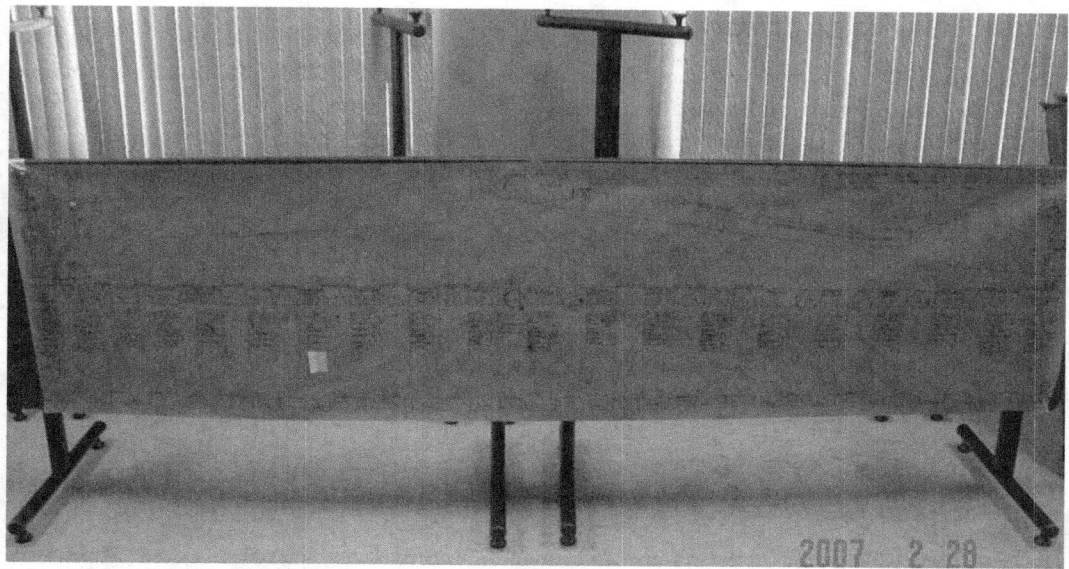

Figure 6.10 Hand drawn VSM used to track company progress each year.

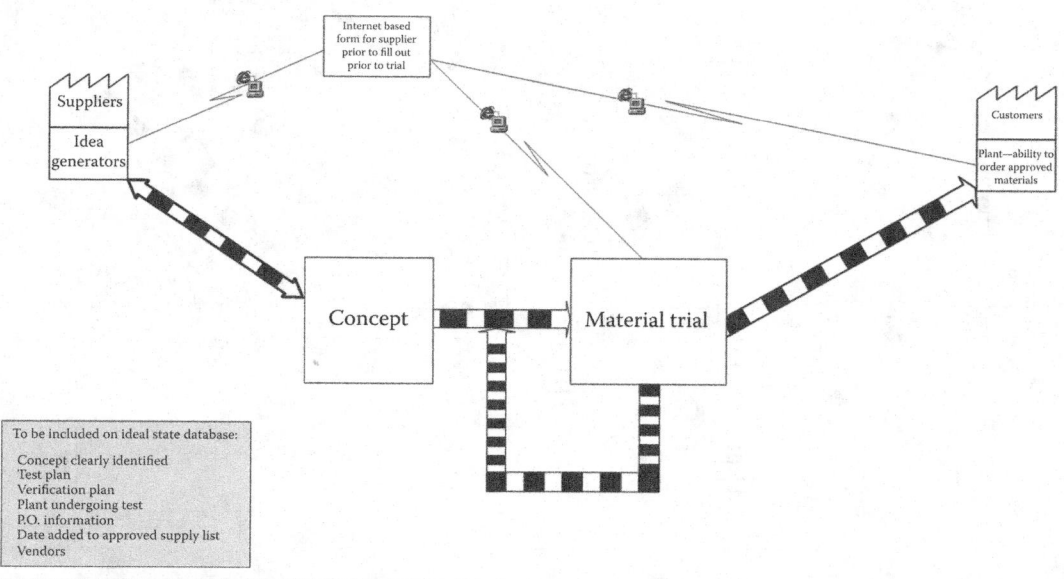

Figure 6.11 Ideal state VSM.

Future State Value Stream Mapping

The final step is to construct a future state map (see Figures 6.12–6.14). The future state map is created by the same team and normally determines what could realistically be accomplished from the ideal state map over the next year but can look out even two years. This is accomplished by reviewing the current state map to determine the following:

- Which activities can be eliminated, rearranged, simplified, or combined? *
- Which events can be done in parallel?
- What is the critical path?
- How many people must really touch the product or information?
- Where are there handoffs between participants? (mistakes, waits)
- Are there activities duplicated by the same or another person or department?

Value Stream Map Project Lists, Prioritization Matrix, and Tracking

The team creates kaizen bursts (sometimes known as improvement bursts) or potential projects and identifies quick wins (immediate changes to improve the process, usually unnecessary waste activities), which can be implemented, to get the process from its current state to future state. As the team reviews and designs the future state process, the opportunities are placed in a project list.

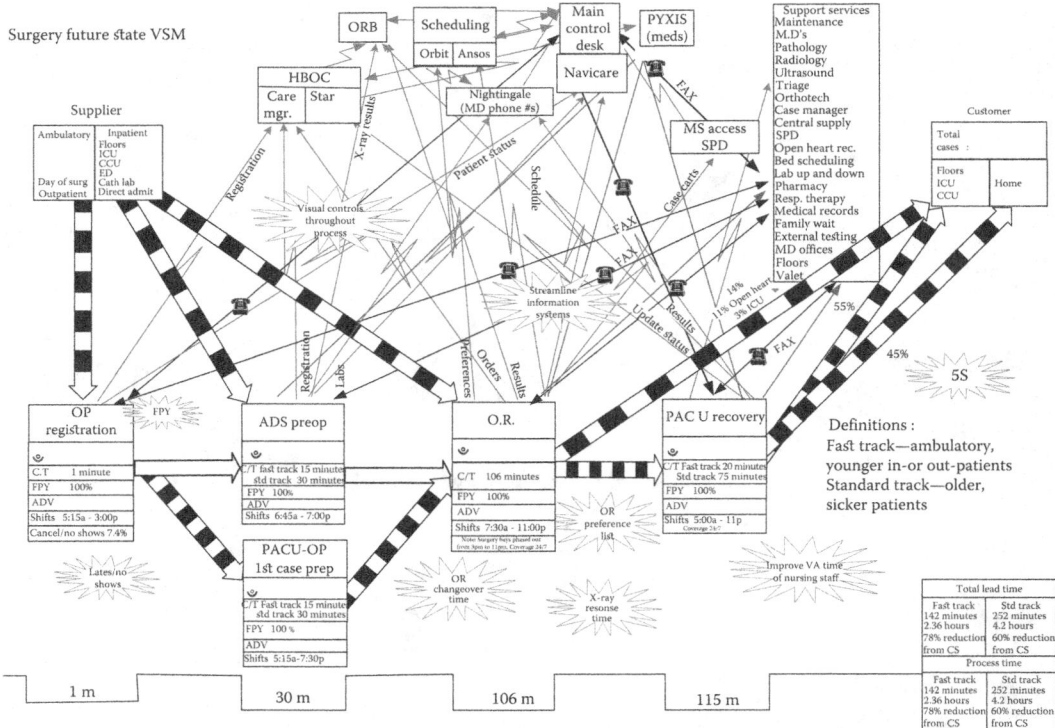

Figure 6.12   Future state example surgery process.

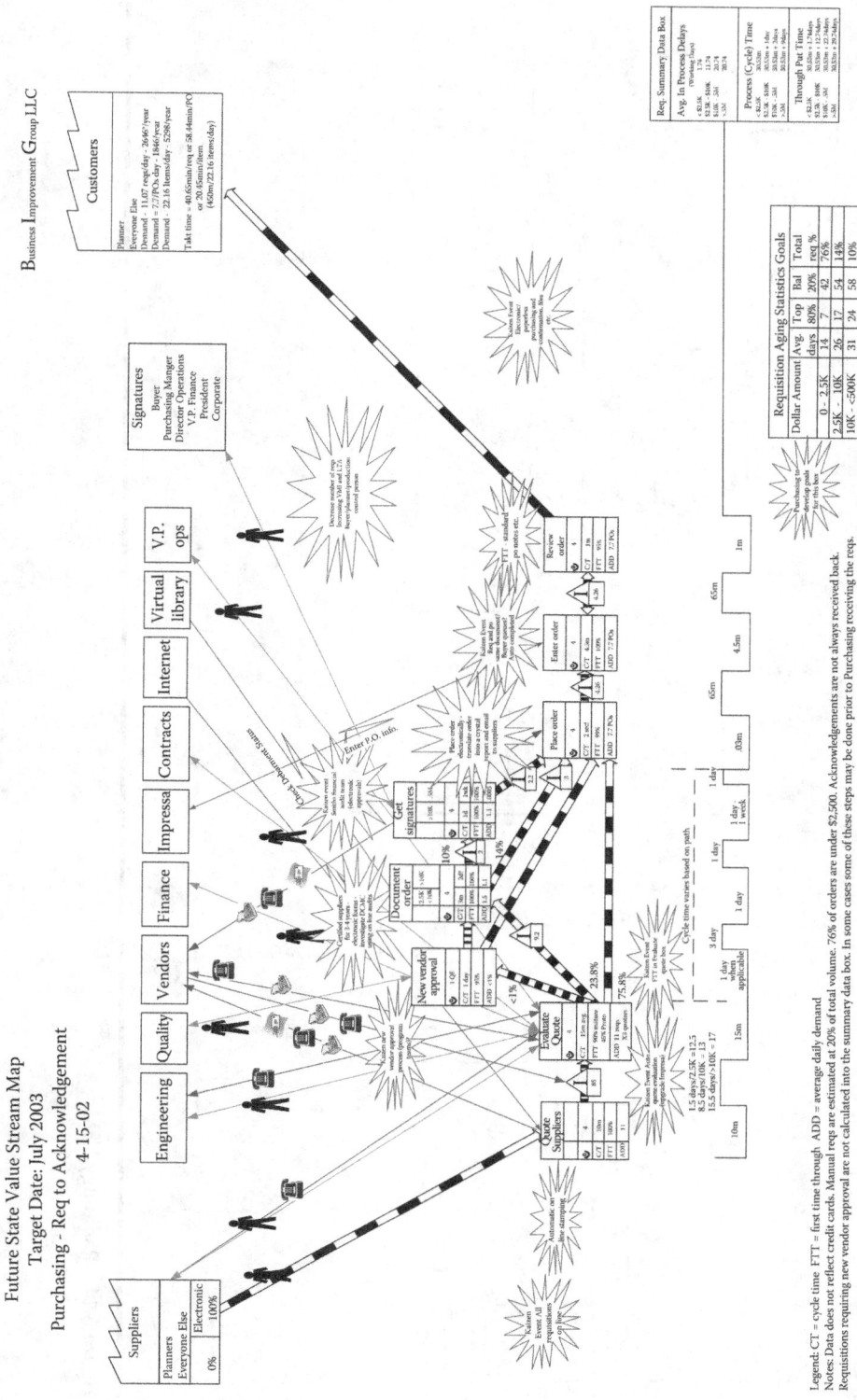

Figure 6.13   Future state purchasing department example.

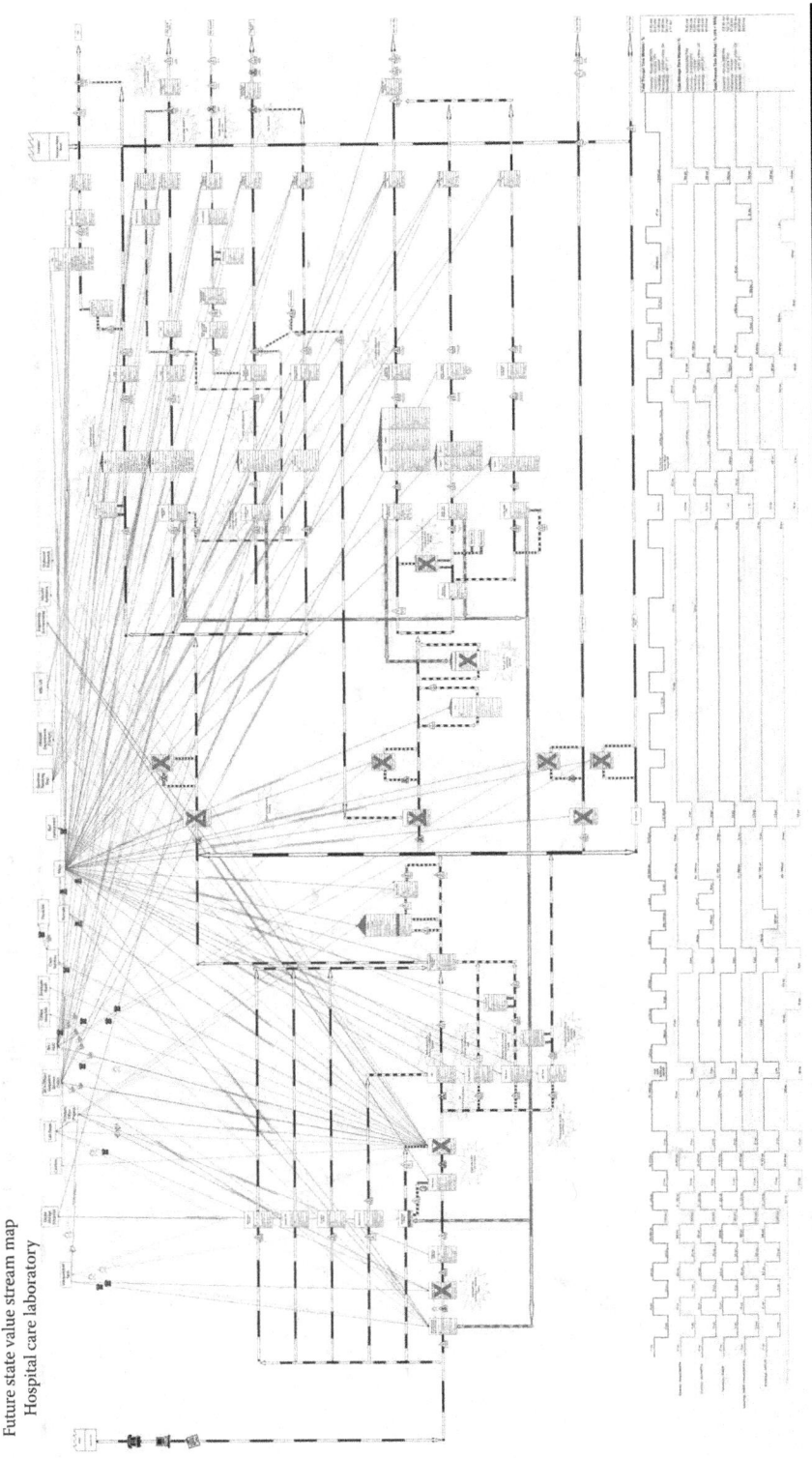

Future state value stream map
Hospital care laboratory

Figure 6.14 Radiology VSM.

Proposed Projects	Ranking 1-low impact 3-medium impact 5-high impact Project or Task	Owner	Resources Required	Financial Perspective	Internal Business Process Perspective	Improve External Customer/Stakeholder Perspective	Organization Enabler Perspective	Future Perspective	Totals	Costs	Potential Savings/ROI	Benefits
1 Kaizen event—Auto quote evaluation, (upgrade Impressa, requires $30K Oracle update, Impressa is included in maintenance contract) and electronic/paperless purchasing & confirmation, files, etc.	Project	Purchasing	IT	5	3	3	1	5	17	$30K		Improved data collection
2 Buyer/planner/production control person	Project	Purchasing	Operations, L&P	5	3	1	5	1	15			
3 Kaizen event—FTT in evaluate quote process	Project	Purchasing	Cross functional	1	3	1	3	1	9			
4 Kaizen Event—All requisitions on line	Project	Purchasing	IT	1	3	1	1	1	7			
5 Kaizen new vendor approval process, investigate program teams, standard form or	Project	Purchasing	Quality	1	3	1	1	1	7			
6 Kaizen event Smiths financial audit team—signature authority	Project	Purchasing	Smiths financial	1	1	1	1	1	5			
7 Place order electronically—translate order into a crystal report and email to suppliers	Task	Purchasing	IT						0			
8 Req and po same document? Buyer queues? Auto completed	Task	Purchasing	IT						0			
9 FTT—standard po notes, etc.	Task	Purchasing	IT						0			
10 Decrease number of reqs—Increasing VMI and LTA	Task	Purchasing	Purchasing						0			
11 Certified suppliers 3-4 years to cut down paperwork, on-line DCAA audits	Task	Purchasing							0			
12 Purchasing to develop goals for this CT/baging req box	Task	Purchasing							0			

Figure 6.15   Example of project priorities matrix using company strategic plan goals to prioritize.

Each opportunity is ranked based on impact to the strategic planning goals (Figure 6.15) (which may include service, people, finance, clinical, operations, ease of deployment, and cost). In addition, priority ranking is used to understand the risk and impact to other departments for each solution that is proposed. The list of potential opportunities provides a roadmap of CI activities the team can work on and track progress over the next year.

Value Stream Layout Maps (Sometimes Referred to as Skitumi Maps)

During our VSM teachings, we always use the phrase; the process boxes are a process, not a place. However, the information in VSMs can help guide layout revisions to help optimize flow. Skitumi maps leverage the VSM data by overlaying the process boxes (data) on top of the existing master layout (see Figures 6.16a and 6.16b). This is an excellent way for leaders to help visualize how their overall layouts create bottlenecks and waste. This is also a good way to look at your overall master layouts or block diagrams of the company overall and develop high-level systemic approaches to improvement.

Some Key Points about Value Stream Maps

■ You must walk the process! This is also true in the office. The VSM cannot be done in isolation in a conference room, on a computer, or in a cafeteria.
■ Become the product as you outline the process. Make sure everyone is clear on what you are following (i.e., the product) otherwise everyone will get confused and discouraged.

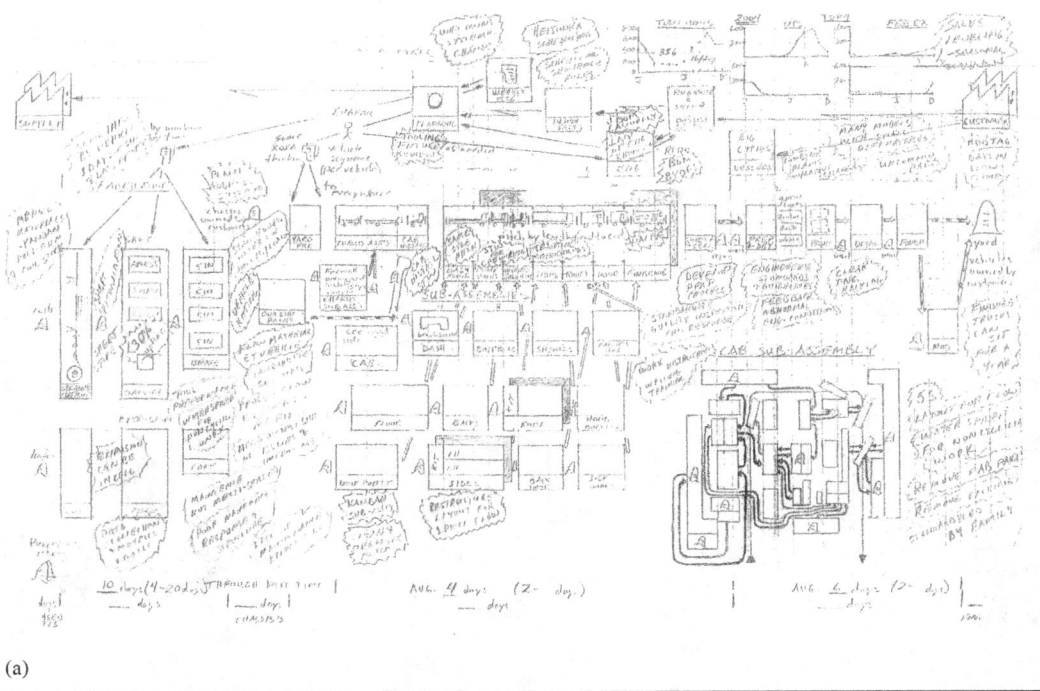

(a)

Figure 6.16a   Skitumi map current state.

Source: BIG Archives.

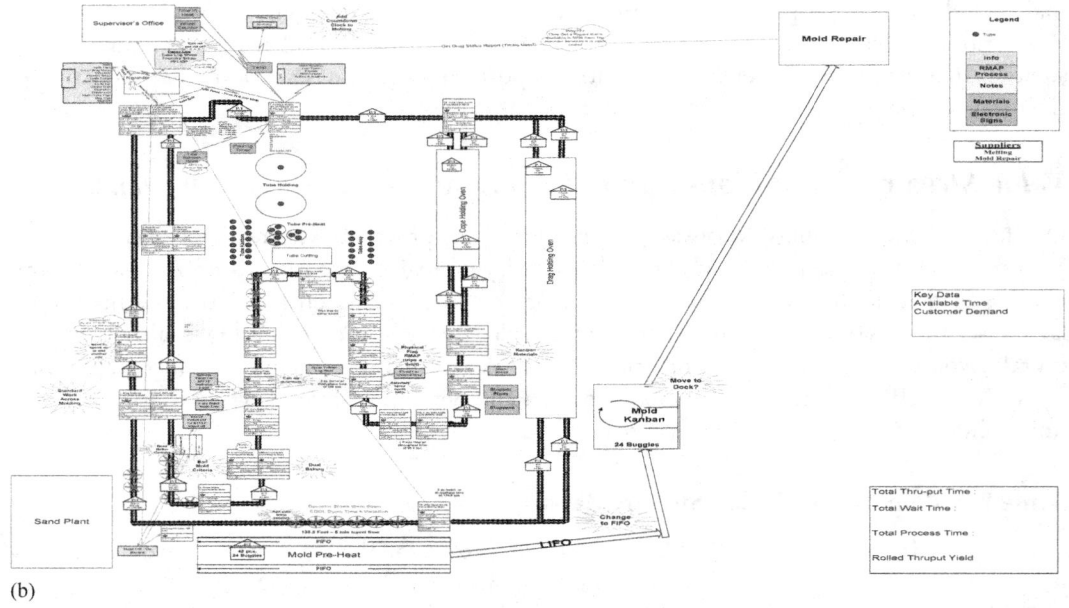

(b)

Figure 6.16b   Example of a VSM superimposed over a layout.

- We find it is best to do it by hand first and obtain agreement from everyone involved in the process.
- While some insist on only doing hand-drawn maps, we do many times put VSMs into the computer using Visio™ or PowerPoint™. People are more computer literate today and it is easier to communicate the process via e-mail versus taking a picture of the hand-drawn map. We also find the hand-drawn version occasionally is lost or torn, stickies fall off, etc. They are also easier to update as the process changes in the future.
- It is best to map the current or baseline state by reviewing the entire process versus a piece of the process.
- Don't confuse value added and process times. They are different. At the VSM level, process CTs include both value added, and non-value added.
- Don't be afraid to change or update the map during the year. It is good practice to have every stakeholder review the map, make changes, and track their progress throughout the year.
- Ensure the map is as close to reality as possible. If you can acquire accurate historical data, it is better than timing the process and calling it a snapshot in time; however, sometimes there is no other choice.
- Hold the process owner accountable to run the VSM event and to meet the actions agreed upon during the mapping event. Accountability means to truly own the process and its performance because they either have everything they need to achieve realistic goals or have access and authority to ensure goals are met in an efficient and effective manner. If the process owners cannot achieve agreed upon metrics, it could mean it is a bad fit for the person or an indication some other process is not providing inputs in an efficient manner or effective manner.

Chapter Questions

1. List three benefits of creating a VSM.
2. What are the four parts to a VSM?
3. How does the VSM differ from traditional SIPOC?
4. What are the three types of value stream maps?
5. What is the value in creating an ideal state map?
6. What is the definition of TT?
7. What is the definition of CT?
8. CT must always be greater than the TT to keep up with customer demand. Is this statement true or false?
9. How do you determine the available time when calculating TT?
10. Why is it important to determine the baseline metrics for an area before starting a Lean implementation? What industries does Lean business delivery system (LBDS) work in?
11. What is a future state map and how does it relate to value stream maps?
12. Who is responsible for developing value stream maps?
13. What did you learn from this chapter?

Notes

1. Influenced by Person of Interest, season 2 Ep 14 "One Percent" 2/72013 CBS.
2. Allied Signal Training Manual.

3. Video by Joel Barker, The New Business of Paradigms ©2001. Joel Barker—Original Business of Paradigms, 1989, Charthouse International Learning, Distributed by Star Thrower, and Joel Barker Video Paradigm Pioneers, produced by Chart House Learning, Distributed by Star Thrower ©1993.

4. David Beels.

5. FIFO stands for first in first out. In the past, this was how we recommended inventory be used so we were always using the oldest material in stock first. This obviously helps when working with materials with shelf lives or expiration dates. However, in today's literature, using FIFO does not always mean we are using the oldest material first. So, we need to account for the "born on" or expiration dates on our material and always use the oldest product first based on its expired date or mfg. date (if no expiration date exists). We use FIFO in the text assuming the reader realizes we want to make sure we rotate our stock based on its date not necessarily when it was received. A good example of this is to check supermarket shelves. Many times, the "best if used by dates" are completely out of order on the shelves. So, if you were to use FIFO (on this small scale) it would not necessarily reflect "the best if used by date."

6. Erich Helfert, Techniques of Financial Analysis (Chicago, IL: Irwin Publishing), 1997, p. 110; also http://www.inventoryturns.com.

7. Rick Harris, Making Materials Flow (Cambridge, MA: Lean Enterprise Institute [LEI] 2006).

8. Contributed by Joe McNamara via personal correspondence 2-23-13, during the 1990s residual income (RI) has been refined and renamed as EVA by the Stern Stewart consulting organization. Although the EVA model was thoroughly applied by Stern Stewart & Co., for the first time, in the 1919s, a similar concept had been contemplated by economists for many years before. It was the famous economist Alfred Marshall in 1890 who first spoke about the notion of economic profit, in terms of the real profit that a company makes when it covers, besides the various operating costs, the cost of its invested capital. Based upon the previous meaning of economic profit, Stern Stewart & Co. developed the concept of the EVA model. The basic difference between the notions of economic value and RI concerns the method for calculating profits and invested capital. The EVA concept extends the traditional RI measure by incorporating adjustments to the company financial performance measure for distortions introduced by GAAP. There are three basic inputs needed for EVA computation: the capital invested, return on capital, and the cost of capital.

9. RONA and MVA were based on an article on http://maaw.info/ArticleSummaries/ArtSumDierksPatel97.htm, Dierks, P. A. and A. Patel. 1997. What is EVA, and how can it help your company? Management Accounting (November): 52–58. Summary by Zuwena De Freitas, Master of Accountancy Program, University of South Florida, Summer 2002.

10. Story submitted by Joe McNamara—personal correspondence February 27, 2013.

11. Little's Law, Queuing Theory—Factory Physics, Hopp & Spearman, McGraw Hill, © 1995, 2000, 2001, Public Domain (no © on site).

12. Chapter 5—Little's Law John D.C. Little and Stephen C. Graves Massachusetts Institute of Technology http://web.mit.edu/sgraves/www/papers/Little's%20Law-Published.pdf.

13. Chapter 5, p. 92—Little's Law John D.C. Little and Stephen C. Graves Massachusetts Institute of Technology http://web.mit.edu/sgraves/www/papers/Little's%20Law-Published.pdf.

14. Speed Is Life, Tom Peters, a co-production of Video Publishing House and KERA© 1991.

15. George Stalk and Thomas Hout, Competing Against Time (New York: MacMillan), 1990.

16. Mike Rother and John Shook, Learning to See, Lean Enterprise Institute (LEI), 2003 www.Lean.org.

17. Jim Womack and Dan Jones, Seeing the Whole (LEI) 2002.

18. (Congress 1852, sometimes credited to Mark Twain).

19. Companies can take credit for this as preventive action in their QMS per editorial comment from Ken Place

20. Shawn Noseworthy.

21. Mike Rother and John Shook, Learning to See, Lean Enterprise Institute (LEI), 2003 www.Lean.org; Lean Lexicon, by and published by the Lean Enterprise Institute (LEI), 2003 www.Lean.org, Jim Womack and Dan Jones, Seeing the Whole (LEI), 2002.

Additional Readings

Hopp, W.J. and Spearman, M.L. 2011. Factory Physics, 3rd edn. Long Grove, IL: Waveland Press Inc.
Rother, M. and Shook, J. 1999. Learning to See. Brookline, MA: LEI.
Shook, J. 2004. Lean Lexicon. Brookline, MA: Lean Enterprise Institute.
Tapping, D. and Shuker, T. 2003. Value Stream Management for the Office (Aug 31, 2011). New York: Productivity Press.
Womack, J.P. 2002. Seeing the Whole*. Brookline, MA: LEI.
Womack, J.P. and Jones, D.T. 1990. The Machine That Changed the World: The Story of Lean Production. New York: HarperCollins.
Womack, J.P. and Jones, D.T. 1996. Lean Thinking. New York: Simon & Schuster.
Womack, J.P. and Jones, D.T. 2005. Lean Solutions. London: Simon & Schuster.

Appendix A - Study Guide

Chapter 1 Questions and Answers

1. What is the five-step thought process for Lean?
   - Specify value from the standpoint of the end customer by product family.
   - Identify all the steps in the value stream for each product family, eliminating waste whenever possible as those steps do not create value.
   - Make the value-creating steps occur in tight sequence to ensure the product flows smoothly toward the customer. Ensure the process steps flow without going backward.
   - As flow is introduced, let customers pull value from the next upstream activity.
   - As value is specified, value streams are identified, wasted steps are removed, and flow and pull are introduced. Begin the process again and continue it until a state of perfection is reached in which a perfect value is created with no waste.

2. Where did Lean thinking begin? Where are its roots?
   Lean has its roots in the United States, not Japan. Japan learned from the United States. Frank and Lillian Gilbreth, Frederick Taylor, and Henry Ford all practiced principles that comprise Lean today.

3. What results can you expect from implementing Lean?
   Companies that implement Lean experience the following common results:
   - Reduce direct labor by 50% or more.
   - Reductions in indirect labor of over 30% or more.
   - Increase output to 50%–70% or more resulting in similar productivity gains (hours per unit).
   - Reduce time from order entry to cash and concept to market that is throughput time, by up to 80%, sometimes days or weeks to hours.
   - Reduce hospital emergency department wait times by 90% and increase physician productivity. Surgeons increase their cases per day in less time.
   - Reduce changeover times by 50% or more, many times to less than 3 minutes or even eliminating them altogether.
   - Free up cash by increasing inventory turns.
   - Reduce monthly accounting closings from weeks or days to hours.

4. What role does the CEO play in Lean transformations?
   The CEO must embrace the concept that Lean is a journey and not a one-time quick fix. The CEO must not allow dabbling in Lean and must be prepared to make a multiyear commitment. The CEO must have the support of the board of directors (BOD). The best results occur when the CEO and BOD understand Lean and preferably have been trained in Lean.

The CEO must buy in and lead by example to be successful and be prepared to dedicate the best employees in the organization to the Lean journey. If you have a CEO and board of directors that support Lean and put some of their best people into the effort, they will initially see good results but struggle to sustain them. If you have a CEO and board of directors that do not understand Lean or support it properly and put people on it that are the easiest to free up, they will see spotty results, not sustain them and then blame the Lean practitioner(s) and Lean in general for their poor results.

5. Explain the impact or ROI on Lean transformations.

Organizations must realize there will and should be successes on each Lean initiative; however, the correct infrastructure and budget must be in place to train, implement, and sustain the gains. The most successful ROIs are recognized when there is a cultural shift and the entire organization, both vertically and horizontally, embraces and buys into Lean.

Focus on continuous improvement every day should outweigh the insistence on implementing only those perceived large ROI projects first. The solution to this sole ROI focus is simple yet takes great patience to achieve. Ultimately, it is the efficiency of the process and layout that dictate how many FTEsare required. Once waste is removed, the process and the layout, designed for flexing, define what one needs to effectively run that particular operation.

If one focuses on improving the process, the ROI will take care of itself. Once reductions are identified, management must have the fortitude to act on facts and make the changes without laying off permanent team members.

For CEOs, patience and perseverance is the key. What is really required is upper level executive leadership to drive culture change, adoption, and deployment. Toyota did not get there in a month! It took many years to implement the TPS, and they are still working on perfecting it today many decades later. As organizations embark on their multiyear Lean journey, they will need to determine if they need or what they will accept as their ROI and how to articulate the benefits of Lean across the enterprise and to the board members to sustain ongoing cycles of continuous improvement.

Companies that are Lean no longer use ROI as the main decision-making tool or keep track of ROIs. They implement Lean because focusing on continuous process improvement is the right thing to do for their organizations survival.

6. What is big company disease? Does your company have it?

The big company disease has characteristics such as ignorant about their processes, poorly documented processes, batch-based organizations designed in functional silos, executive leadership located far from the manufacturing floor, leaders not engaged in the business with no time to walk the floor (Gemba), and leadership teams generally do not have a clear understanding of their business delivery systems (value streams) or the interconnectivity of their processes and have difficulty giving tours by themselves.

7. What are some differences between batch and one-piece flow?

Batch produces items or services by repeating the same operation for each piece until the lot is complete and then moving on to the next operation. One-piece flow is producing a completed item or delivering a completed service one at a time.

Characteristics and lessons learned are as follows:

- Batching environments are fraught with waste, lack of space, and delays.
- Batch systems have little control over their processes.
- Once you "Lean out" an area, the supervision of the area is much easier, thus creating time to work on small improvements.

- Space, which seems initially to be at a premium, is available and empty resulting in "excess" space.
- Results can be obtained quickly within a specific area or process.
- Root cause analysis and management by fact may initially solve the problem, but you cannot switch back to the old ways of doing things if one wants to avoid reoccurrence of the problem.
- Installing carousels and automated material storage equipment makes it much harder to implement Lean.
- Introduction of automation and new software does not always solve the problem.

8. Where can one apply Lean principles and tools?

Lean processes can be applied anywhere and across all sectors of the economy from manufacturing to hospitals. Any process can be improved by applying Lean tools. If the CEO buys in and drives Lean as part of the strategic plan and incorporates Hoshin policy deployment or bottom-up planning, they will see excellent results in bottom-line improvement. Results will be direct cost savings and significant cost avoidance. We define cost savings as those that directly hit the bottom line, whereas cost avoidance refers to items that would have increased costs had we not alleviated the need for them. In addition, the elimination of waste in a process will decrease the process steps and reduce the opportunities for errors, thereby improving customer satisfaction and, ultimately, quality.

9. What are four principles of the Toyota philosophy?

The Toyota philosophy is embodied in the following four steps:

1. Customer first.
2. People are our most valuable resource.
3. Kaizen (activities that cause improvement).
   a. Create a learning organization.
   b. Create a problem-solving environment.
   c. Surface problems quickly with swift solutions and countermeasures.
   d. Standard work—(there cannot be improvement without a standard in place).
4. Go and see.
   • Shop floor focus.
   • Everyone in the organization is a resource that supports the floor (Gemba).
   • Build and encourage a supportive culture.

10. What is important to remember as a Lean practitioner?

We are all introduced to Lean in a different way, sometimes from a friend, reading an article or a book, or simply by visiting a company where Lean was implemented. Many of us have to be exposed to Lean principles and some of us just naturally think Lean, yet we don't even realize it.

Implementing Lean requires a counterintuitive paradigm shift in thinking to offset the ever-prevalent resistance to change from the current system. This requires an ongoing shifting of attitudes during the transition from the old batch business model. This includes the need to adopt new accounting techniques and instituting significant structural organizational changes. In short, developing a new way of thinking.

A consistent theme throughout is the balance required between philosophy and tools. As such, about 50% is based on Lean tools, system thinking, and practical application, while the other 50% is associated with value systems, strategic thinking, creative thinking, respect for people, change management, value of the person (VOP), the Harada method, leadership, and sustaining the Lean culture. This overall theme while not always stated is underlying every chapter and is referred to interchangeably in a different way (i.e., tasks vs. people, tools vs. people, etc.).

Focusing on return on investment (ROI) can be frustrating and distracts from the goal of helping to support the Lean journey. Companies that truly comprehend Lean don't go after ROIs; they go after improving the process, which they know will result in improvements in quality and financial savings to the bottom line (ROI).

11. What did you learn from this chapter?

Lean can be applied across all sectors of the economy. CEO involvement is critical to the success of the journey. One-piece flow is a foundational principle and system thinking will help to visually understand the process. Both Lean tools and involvement of the employees is critical for success. Successful journeys occur when the relentless pursuit of waste elimination is the priority and not ROI calculations.

Chapter 2 Questions and Answers

1. What are the main benefits of an assessment?

There are many facets to assessing or evaluating the adoption or deployment of Lean and most organizations find that they want to make an assessment of where they are on the Lean maturity curve and the benefits they still have left to achieve. The assessment provides focus for management, is absolutely critical for any successful change program, and provides insight to the desired outcome, which is a business, built on lean principles.

2. What is an LMP?

A Lean maturity path provides the steps toward a Lean mature organization from realization (having a compelling need to change) to lean adoption (which is very rare).

3. Name and describe five of the ten assessment categories.

 – Management effectiveness—current business environment, commitment from management, management involvement, implementation strategy, and employee rewarding
 – People and organizational culture—on-the-job training, PDCA, policy deployment, leadership and training
 – Sustainability components—visual management systems and process and leader standard work
 – Equipment—TPM and equipment efficiency
 – Value stream flow—customer feedback, supplier programs, and Kanban

4. Can assessment be performed in the office areas? What should be considered when conducting such assessments?

Yes, office assessment can (and should) be conducted. Typical areas to assess are:

 – Standard work
 – Accountability
 – Visual controls
 – Number of reports
 – Cycle time/throughput time
 – Office waste
 – Overtime
 – Reasons for outsourcing
 – Cutting overhead without understanding the impact on the processes and value stream

- Vendor payments exceeding purchase order commitments (usually indicates cash flow management issues)
- Constant need or desire to have meetings
- Excessive e-mails
- Failed audits
- Customer complaints
- Low morale and office turnover

5. Who should conduct the assessments?

Lean assessments can be conducted internally (known as a self-assessment) and an outside consultant can be used. The advantage of the outside consultant is the internal bias that is removed from the assessment process.

6. What is a self-assessment? What is the value?

A self-assessment can be defined broadly as a self-appraisal or evaluation with respect to worth. There are many facets to assessing or evaluating the adoption or deployment of Lean and most organizations find that they want to assess where they are on the Lean maturity curve and the benefits they still have left to achieve.

7. What should management do with the results from an assessment?

Management should use the assessment result as a tool to help drive the Lean journey. Lean has a greater chance of being successfully deployed if it is viewed as strategic and that is driven from the top by the CEO and board level that have established a compelling reason to engage in Lean. Management must become fully engaged in the Lean process to be successful and the CEO should be the executive sponsor.

8. What is a pre-Lean assessment? What is the information used for?

The Pre-Lean Assessment is performed prior to engaging in a Lean implementation. These are geared to help the organization understand what opportunities exist and the act as a guide for preparation to starting their Lean journey.

9. What did you learn from this chapter?

Chapter 3 Questions and Answers

1. Is OPF really better than batching? What are typical benefits?

One-piece flow (OPF) is better than batching and typical benefits are less space, reduced size of the equipment required, improved quality, and lower costs.

2. What are the problems that come with a batch system?
- Quality—Problems aren't found until the batch is completed forcing the whole lot to be scrapped or reworked.
- Waste of longer lead times delaying product or service to customers.
- Space—Batching creates the perception of the need for more space that is driven by all of the stored inventory collected during and between processes.
- Tracking information—Batching forces us to create cost accounting standards, labor collection processes, and tools to track the standard cost of the batches as they move through the factory.
- Resources—Batching results in more production and inventory control people to schedule, expedite, and track the product as it moves through the factory.
- Respect for people—Batching leads to repetitive motion problems and often requires sit-down operations that result in increased health issues.

– Delivery—Batching slows down product velocity and throughput time resulting in longer lead times and repair times for our customers.
– Customer satisfaction—Batching results in poor customer satisfaction due to missed schedules.
– Cash—Batching companies have low inventory turns tying up precious company cash.

3. What are the eight reasons that force us to batch?

The following eight major forces force batching:

i. Our minds (brains)
ii. Setups/changeovers
iii. Travel distance
iv. Equipment
v. Processes
vi. Idle time
vii. Space
viii. Variation

4. What is a segmented batch?

Segmented batching is processing a batch of products one piece at a time, for example, running only one type of model down the line at a time and then converting the line over to run another model type. For example, this would entail building all Camry's on the same line in the morning using OPF, and then building all Corollas on the same line in the afternoon using OPF.

5. What is the difference between batching and working in parallel?

Batching processes are created by adding the same input to several parts in sequential order and then adding a second input to each of the parts sequentially until the parts are completed. Batching often uses more space and is inherently less efficient than parallel processing.

Continuous flow processes are one-piece or multiple-piece flow processes in parallel where each input is added sequentially on an assembly or manufacturing line.

6. Why is Lean so hard to implement?

Our minds seem to be programed to believe working on more than one piece or activity at a time is better. People defend their batching behavior as being the most efficient and hence the most productive way to do the job. They reason that if they are working on one piece, they should continue to do the same operation to all the other pieces before moving onto the next operation.

Inherent in batching is the illusion we are working faster and more efficiently. This illusion is so prevalent that it drives most of the eight wastes in our factories, hospitals, government, retail industries, and service sectors.

7. Think of examples where you batch at home or at work. Why do you batch? What would it take to flow?

At home, we often bake cookies. We mix the ingredients in batch and bake the cookies in batch. To obtain OPF, we would need an oven that processes (bakes) on a conveyor in an ONP method, which would not be practical in a home but such a process is used to bake pizzas in many of the pizza chain stores.

8. What is a mixed model? When would you use a mixed model? Discuss why a mixed model might be selected.

True mixed model sequencing is working OPF regardless of the type of product. An example in the automotive industry is when any model type can be produced, one behind the other, on the same line. We would use a mixed model to allow for continuous flow of finished goods without setting up different lines or factories. An example is Harley-Davidson in York, Pennsylvania. The assembly line is run in a mixed-model mode such that each motorcycle off the line is different, thus satisfying customer demand using an OPF strategy.

9. What is parallel processing and what are the advantages, if any? Describe an example in a manufacturing environment and an example in an office environment.

The key is to understand in the long run anything high volume runs OPF or multiple pieces in parallel (i.e., traffic lanes). Many times, companies mistakenly feel they are performing work or steps in parallel when in fact they are still batching.

If two of us are each working on the same unit at the same time, then we are working in parallel. Traffic lanes run in parallel. Manufacturing or processing in parallel is different from processing in a batch. Running in parallel means we can run multiple products at the exact same time through the process or operation. Many high-volume food and beverage production lines run this way.

10. If batching is bad, why is it so hard to stop? What are the barriers of resistance that support batching?

OPF is very counterintuitive to most individuals. The single biggest incentive to batch comes from our minds. Humans are made to batch and batching must be an innate quality we all possess, and for some reason, we are all hardwired to think batching is better. Many times, it may be part of your organizations' vision that drives batching (i.e., We've always done it that way—WADITW) resulting in a natural cultural resistance to change.

11. What did you learn from this chapter?

Chapter 4 Questions and Answers

1. List and describe two fundamental principles when developing a single-piece flow line.

Single-piece or OPF refers to the processing or servicing of each component part, product, or piece of paper, one at a time, through each step until it is completed. Another principle is to work toward cellular lines, with all the dedicated tools, instructions, and staff on the line, to avoid wasted time looking for parts (materials), tools, or instructions.

2. Describe the BASICS® Model.

The BASICS Model was constructed to provide a practical guide (or framework) to approaching a Lean implementation and to present an easy-to-use roadmap in which the terminology helps guide the users on what should be occurring as you move through the roadmap.

The BASICS Lean system implementation approach is based 50% on the principles of scientific management, developed primarily by Frank Gilbreth and taught by Dr. Shigeo Shingo, and 50% on change management discussed throughout the book. BASICS is:

Baseline (B):

- Charter the team and scope the project.
- Baseline metrics.
- Map the process using value stream map (VSM).
- Determine the customer demand and takt time (TT).

Assess/analyze (A):

- Process (product) flow analysis—become the customer or product.
- Group tech analysis.
- Full work analysis of the operator.
- Changeover analysis.

Suggest solutions (S):
- Develop block diagrams—make and approve recommendations.
- Create the optimal layout for the process.
- Design the workstations.
- Create standard work.
- Determine the capacity and labor requirements.
- Train staff in the new process.

Implement(I):
- Implement the new process—use pilots.
- Implement Lean metrics.

Check (C)
- Incorporate 5S and visual controls.
- Mistake proof and implement total productive maintenance (TPM) the process.

Sustain (S):
- Build standard work into your existing quality system, i.e., ISO 9000 so it becomes part of your company's infrastructure and gets audited.
- Kaizen, kaizen, kaizen.
- Suggestions implemented from the floor are part of the culture.
- PDCA—over and over and over again.
- Update standard work.
- Implement leader standard work and a Lean Management System.

3. What is the BASICS Lean® Business Delivery System?
The BASICS Lean® Business Delivery System (BLBDS) is a learning organization without waste and is fueled by continuous daily improvement.

4. Explain the high-level BASICS Lean® Business Delivery System Model (see Appendix A.1).

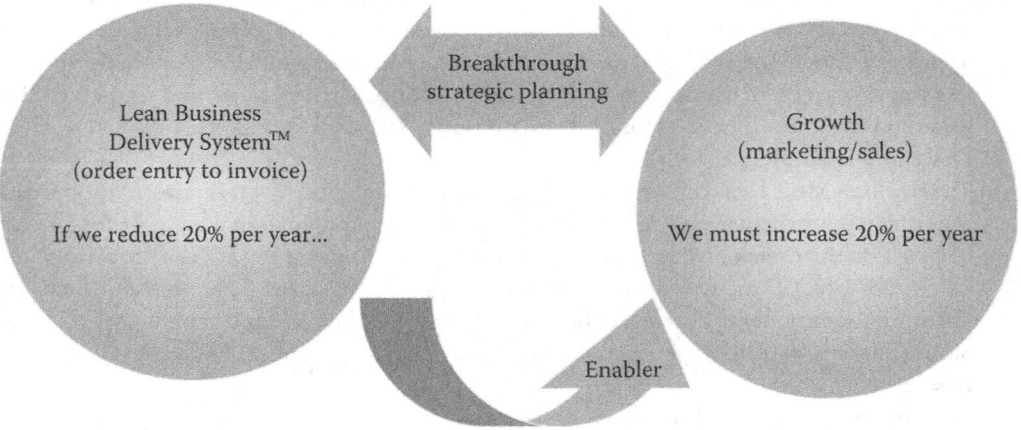

Appendix A.1 Lean business delivery system overview—Lean is an enabler but doesn't guarantee growth.

On the left side is the BLBDS, which comprises all the processes required from order entry to shipping, invoicing the customer, handling returns, and ultimately recycling. Lean tools can be applied to anything, which is a process. This side can be further divided into the task (scientific management) and people (respect for humanity) pieces of implementation.

On the right side is the marketing and growth piece. The goal is to grow the business at the same rate we are improving the business. The model works as follows:

Lean is an enabler for growth but does not guarantee growth. Lean is applied in organizations to take advantage of being able to do more, with the same or less resources.

Organizations must proactively have a plan for sales in order for their business to grow. Growth must be part of the overall Lean initiative in order to succeed. When a company can produce its products with less waste than its competition, it has a distinct advantage. The increased profits can be invested in research and development, capital equipment, higher wages, or passed on to customers to undercut the competitor's price.

5. Why do we say Lean is a journey?

Lean is a journey that has no real end as there are always continuous improvement projects that can be accomplished noting very mature Lean companies, such as Toyota, still have significant levels of CI to pursue during the lean journey.

6. How does the BASICS® Model compare to PDCA or DMAIC?

The BASICS® Model provides a practical guide, an overall framework, to approaching a Lean implementation in which the terminology helps guide the users on what should be occurring as you move through the roadmap. During the implementation process, various tools are used, and there are a variety of problem-solving models utilized, such as plan–do–check–act (PDCA), and define, measure, analyze, improve, control (DMAIC).

7. Is Lean about working smarter and not harder?

Yes, working smarter is favored over working harder. A main thrust of Lean is efficiency through a relentless pursuit of waste removal in the value stream. This approach works in manufacturing products as well as the services industry.

8. Why do people always think they are working harder when implementing Lean?

People are producing the goods or services and are often asked to support and be involved in the Lean implementation, which often involves training on the front end. From an employee's perspective, they can feel overwhelmed, and it is critical that leadership understand this will occur and provide support to those involved in lean implementation projects, especially those tasked to continue to provide customer support during the journey.

9. What is the difference between one-piece flow and batching?

One of the key concepts in Lean is one-piece flow (OPF), or small-lot processing. OPF refers to the processing or servicing of each component part, product, or piece of paper, one at a time, through each step until it is completed. Batch is the opposite of OPF and processing occurs on more than one piece at the same time in a batch mode. A simple example is a batch of cookies cooking in an oven.

10. What did you learn from this chapter?

Chapter 5 Questions and Answers

1. Explain ETDBW. Name a company that is ETDBW and one that is not.

The term ETDBW means an organization is easy to do business with. The book The Agenda inspires this discussion. ETDBW means the business accepts orders or requests for service when and by whatever means is most convenient for the customer. It means the orders or services are provided in the customer's terminology. It means the organization makes it painless for a customer to check the status of an order or result. A company that is ETDBW is L.L.Bean. The firm is open 24 hours per day, offers one of the best return policies in retail, provides status very easily and delivers high-quality products that customers enjoy. Most people consider the Internal Revenue Service (IRS) to be an organization that is not ETDBW. Many citizens have complained about delays, difficulty reaching knowledgeable staff, and not having a customer-friendly experience.

2. Why does everything start with the customer?

   A firm must clearly understand customer needs to ensure the customer and business are aligned. A firm that is not aligned with the customer will not win new customers and could be faced with customer loss, leading to loss and revenue that stifles investment in people, processes, and new products.

3. How do you get VOC?

   VOC must come directly from the customer and we must solicit feedback directly from our customer to determine their real needs. There are many ways to obtain VOC, such as holding focus groups, leveraging subject matter experts, and conducting customer surveys.

4. Who obtains VOC information?

   There are many ways to obtain VOC, such as holding focus groups, leveraging subject matter experts, and conducting customer surveys. Various individuals in an organization can obtain the information to include business development, program management, executive management, customer relations, staff or any person or team that has direct contact with the customers. The customer survey can be done face to face, via e-mail, via Internet (i.e., Survey Monkey), by phone, etc.

5. List two key attributes to exhibit if you are trying to get an honest assessment of an area.

   Observe and take in as much information (which we call data) as possible. The first thing is to observe who is conducting the tour. If it is a lower level person, it can potentially reveal the following:

   - The plant manager does not think the tour is important.
   - The plant manager does not feel confident enough to take us around the plant.
   - Lean is not important to the plant manager.
   - The plant manager is just too busy (which is data).

   A plant manager far down the Lean maturity path would welcome the chance for outsiders to highlight problems and opportunities to improve and insisted they provide a list of problems/opportunities either immediately after or upon return to their companies. The questions we ask vary based upon who is taking us around. If the plant manager is leading the tour, we ask more detailed questions to determine the extent to which he or she is familiar with the plant floor and office areas. We may also ask some strategic questions and about plant metrics. If a lower level person is taking us around, we ask questions geared toward the level of the person, their role, and perceived level of knowledge. The first part of the assessment is to observe whether there is any flow, if work cells are in place, if visual controls exist, and how much inventory is lying around. If they told us they have some Lean experience, we ask to see what they have done in Lean to date and how long they have been working on it. Some companies start Lean by working on the culture piece in which case they may have some visual controls, or employee teams, which might have done some point kaizen events. During the tour, you can start looking for what might be a good pilot line on which to begin your Lean implementation. We also inquire about on-time deliveries (OTD), quality, material requirement planning (MRP) system, parts shortages, kitting, Kanbans, vendor-managed inventory (VMI), various cycle times, etc. If there is a Lean line in place or they conducted a point kaizen event, we walk through their accomplishments, how it was done, over what time frame, and who participated. We observe if people are sitting or standing and if they are batching and how the line is balanced. We look for production planning information and see if any standard work exists. Try to ask the same questions at all levels of the organization and then compare the responses.

The key is to listen, listen, and listen. This is an information-gathering exercise.

6. List three plans you should consider for your implementation.

    Communication Plan, Training Plan, Resource Plan, and Change Management Plan should be considered for the lean implementation.

7. List four criteria that an area should meet to be considered for a pilot.

    The pilot area must meet the following criteria:
    - Be representative of most areas in the company.
    - Be strategically key to the business.
    - An environment where the implementation has the best chance of success and sustaining.
    - The supervisor and staff are willing to make the necessary changes and lead the area with the new changes in place.
    - People in the pilot area have a positive attitude toward change.
    - Have a way to measure before and after results and set targets for implementation.
    - It should test the new tools being utilized.
    - Solutions should be transferred to other lines.

8. What are some key plans that need to be put together prior to starting your Lean project?
    a. Lean Implementation Plan
    b. Communication plan
    c. Training plan
    d. Resource plan

9. Put together a high-level implementation plan. What are the two key components of the plan?
    - The factors critical to quality (CTQ)
    - The baseline or current state of what is going to be addressed and targets if known
    - The potential impact on key corporate strategies
    - What's included in the scope (input and output boundaries)
    - An outline of what is out of scope
    - The target customers
    - The risks

10. List three characteristics of a team member.

    Team Members should have the following characteristics:
    - Good communication skills
    - Good interpersonal skills
    - High energy, provide 110% effort, and ability to work long hours
    - Ability to receive constructive critical evaluation of their own work
    - Positive attitude
    - Willingness to accept change
    - Strong computer skills: a good working knowledge of Microsoft Excel and Project preferred but not required. (Note: We do everything on pencil and paper or whiteboards first, nothing has to be done on a computer. Many times we just take pictures of the papers or whiteboards to preserve them)
    - Team player attitude

11. What are the different types of teams?

   We have found dedicated teams to be a best practice for companies starting with Lean. The teams can change from project to project. However, if you are bringing in a consultant, it is extremely important to have people designated for the consultant to transfer knowledge. One of the goals should be to have the knowledge and resources to phase out the consultant over time. These designees should be selected carefully so as not to invest a lot of time and money in training and experience only to have the person take it to another company or worst case—competitor. We have found part-time (non-dedicated) teams generally don't work well. The day-to-day business always wins out and Lean gets put on the back burner.

12. How important is communication and why?

   The communication plan is a critical part of Lean implementation. It should be created initially and actively worked throughout the entire Lean initiative in order to ensure a successful transition post pilot. It is culturally important to have the appropriate level of communication related to the activities to help disseminate Lean across the organization.

13. What should be communicated and to whom?

   A Lean model site implementation plan should be developed using a project management tool such as Microsoft Project that is a project management software, developed and sold by Microsoft, designed to assist a project manager in developing a plan, assigning resources to tasks, tracking progress, managing the budget, and analyzing workloads. This plan can be developed and used at any level for any project. The plan should be communicated in accordance with the table to include kick-off and ongoing communications.

14. What is a contract for change? Why is it important?

   The contract for change has been extremely useful from a culture standpoint to ensure all stakeholders are on the same page and having them literally sign and date the contract for change document. The contract for change should contain the vision, goals and objectives, an escalation plan, methodology, and commitment.

   The contract for change allows for an escalation process to help the improvement teams or supervisors remove barriers to improvement. Failure to have this process in place will force these issues to be hidden and not come to the surface. The escalation process should proceed all the way to the CEO.

15. What is the Lean Leadership roadmap?

   This is the plan outlining the high-level steps. We suggest that once a pilot implementation is conducted, the senior leadership meet and form a steering committee to develop their roadmap with deliverable milestones. This Lean Leadership roadmap typically should be a three- to five-year plan and should contain a communication plan and a training plan for the site.

16. Who should make up the Lean steering committee?

   The Lean steering committee's makeup will depend on the size of the firm. We recommend making the senior leadership team the Lean steering team. We also recommend one of the board members be designated as an executive sponsor for the overall Lean program as we do not recommend this to be a new or separate committee. If Lean is going to be our culture, then Lean becomes the way we do business. Therefore, implementing Lean should become the job/mission of the CEO, the board, and the senior leadership team. For ongoing Lean projects, it helps to assign a different executive to sponsor each team (where it makes sense). At a smaller plant level, the plant manager would be the executive sponsor of each team.

17. What did you learn from this chapter?

Chapter 6 Questions and Answers

1. List three benefits of creating a VSM.

   There are many benefits of VSM, to include:
   - Visualizes the flow
   - Focuses on the big picture/system(s)
   - Helps identify areas to improve across silos
   - Identifies the current state of the process
   - Helps highlight the waste in the process
   - Helps determine the sources (causes) of waste
   - Provides a common language for discussing problems and improvements
   - Makes necessary decisions about flow very apparent
   - Enables innovation—brainstorm ideal and future states that leave out wasted steps while introducing smooth flow and leveled pull
   - Provides a visual roadmap of prioritized opportunities to the strategic plan (i.e., projects and tasks) necessary for improvement as a management tool to track progress

2. What are the four parts to a VSM?

   VSMs have four major parts. In the middle of the map are the process boxes, which is how the part, product, or information flow. At the top of the map are information system boxes, which outline what information, whether it be electronic or paper, is required to make each process work and the connection to the process box. The third part is the timeline information at the bottom of the map. The timeline is a sawtooth, which includes the storage times on top and process CTs on the bottom. The results box shows the overall storage time (non-value-added time) versus the process time. The fourth part is the materials flow from supplier to customer.

3. How does the VSM differ from traditional SIPOC?

   VSM has all the elements of the Six Sigma SIPOC (an acronym for suppliers–inputs–process–outputs–customer) tool where SIPOC is a high-level picture of the process depicting how the given process is servicing the customer. However, it provides an enhanced view of the process by viewing how the product or information flows through the process, as well as the flow and interrelatedness of the information necessary to process the part, paperwork, or electronic/paperless transaction. The VSM combines traditional process flow mapping focusing on the flow of the process, with data to create a roadmap to help identify improvement opportunities.

4. What are the three types of value stream maps?

   Value stream maps can be used for many processes including transactional administrative processes including order entry, scheduling, human resources, purchasing, sales, marketing, engineering, finance, and new business development as well as production/manufacturing processes.

5. What is the value in creating an ideal state map?

   The purpose is to get teams to brainstorm, get the team out of the box, and shift paradigms to envision the possibilities and set an ideal state target condition. The ideal state map should be constructed as part of a brainstorming session in which the team determines what the process would be like if they were starting with a clean slate and all barriers are removed. Mapping the ideal process sets the target condition and is looking at the process with:
   - What it could look like five or ten years from now
   - All sacred cows removed

- All the money in the world
- All the technology available

Teams should not spend more than an hour on this step.

6. What is the definition of TT?

   Takt time (TT) is the customer demand rate and describes the time needed for the system, whether on the floor or in the office, to complete one unit of product or one paperwork task.

7. What is the definition of CT?

   Cycle time is calculated in different ways, but each should have the same result. Desired cycle time is similar to takt time and is computed by dividing available time by factory demand (vs. customer demand).

8. CT must always be greater than the TT to keep up with customer demand. Is this statement true or false?

   This is false as our goal is to match the desired and actual CT to TT. We differentiate between CT and TT noting CT is the actual working rhythm of the cell or area and the amount of time each person must meet to complete their part of the operation. Many use TT synonymously with CT, but we differentiate between the two as they are different. TT is a calculation based strictly on customer demand, where CT is based on the cell's demand for a day or hour and/or the time it actually takes you to complete a particular activity. Very few companies work to true takt time. Therefore we end up with a factory/process desired cycle time which we then have to compare to actual cycle time at which the process is running.

9. How do you determine the available time when calculating TT?

   The calculation for available time is intuitive and straightforward. Available time is equal to the real work time of the team members and is determined by taking the total time per shift less breaks, meetings, cleanup, lunch (if included in the 8 hours, but most are not), etc., where the entire work area shuts down. In some continuous manufacturing processes (i.e., casting or government or healthcare environments), there is no total shut down time so available time equals the total shift time as staff and managers cover breaks. If a normal shift is 8 hours with an hour for breaks, meetings, exercise, etc. (again normally, lunch is not included in the 8-hour day), then the available time would be equal to

   $$8\,\text{hours} - 1\,\text{hour for breaks etc.} = 7\,\text{hours available time.}$$

10. Why is it important to determine the baseline metrics for an area before starting a Lean implementation? What industries does Lean business delivery system (LBDS) work in?

    In the first or B phase of the BASICS® Model, we must gain an understanding of the current or as-is process. If you don't document the baseline data ahead of time, prior to implementing the new system, the old numbers will suddenly and magically be remembered as much better than they were once Lean is implemented. If everyone does not agree to the baseline data up front, in writing, you will be surprised to find, later on, after you have implemented Lean, how all the previous numbers start to change. Then all these caveats begin to appear such as "we could have done that before without Lean!" or "our numbers were better prior to Lean!" The LBDS can be used in all industries. The principles can be applied across all industries and the process used should be consistent with the teachings in this book and the book entitled The Lean Practitioner's Field Book.

11. What is a future state map and how does it relate to value stream maps?

    The future state map is the final step and is created by the same team and normally determines what could realistically be accomplished from the ideal state map over the next year but can look out even two years. This is accomplished by reviewing the current state map to determine the following:

- Which activities can be eliminated, rearranged, simplified, or combined?
- Which events can be done in parallel?
- What is the critical path?
- How many people must really touch the product or information?
- Where are there handoffs between participants? (mistakes, waits)
- Are there activities duplicated by the same or another person or department?

12. Who is responsible for developing value stream maps?

There should be an executive position in the organization that is assigned to continuously review how all the value streams (processes) function and work together and assess improvement opportunities to streamline the overall organization. There is an inherent danger in initially mapping a sublevel process or subassembly process. This danger presents itself in the fundamental concept of the value stream itself. If we only look at a small part of value stream, we are not necessarily seeing the big picture. This is why it is important to do a high-level VSM for the overall organization, which depicts how all the individual value streams work together. The master layout should be considered at this level. If areas are creating VSMs of their individual area, they will be working on improvements in isolation; essentially, we are still supporting silos even though they may have been Leaned. This often yields some improvements, but not the improvements needed to yield the results that occur when the entire value stream is assessed. We see layouts implemented by well-meaning managers or teams, but because there is no knowledgeable Lean review, they are not really Lean but still implemented.

13. What did you learn from this chapter?

Appendix B - Acronyms

5Ws	when, where, what, who, why
5W2Hs	when, where, what, who, why, how, how much
5 whys	asking why five times in a row in order to get to the root cause
AGV	automatic guided vehicle
AI	artificial intelligence
AP	accounts payable
ASL	approved supplier list
AT	actual time
AT&T	American Telephone and Telegraph
BASICS®	lean implementation model for converting batch to flow: baseline, analyze (assess), suggest solutions, implement, check, and sustain
BFT	business fundamental table
BIG	Business Improvement Group LLC based in Towson, MD
BOM	bill of material
BPD	business process development
BRIEF	Baseline Risk Identification of Ergonomic Factors
BVA	business value added
C	Cold
CAD	computer-aided design
CAP	change acceleration process
CEO	chief executive officer
CM	centimeters
COGS	cost of goods sold
CQI	continuous quality improvement
CTP	cost to produce
CTQ	critical to quality
CV	coefficient of variation
CWQC	company-wide quality control
CYA	cover your ass
DBH	day by hour
DFA	design for assembly
DFM	design for manufacturing
DFMA®	Design for Manufacturing and Assembly
DIRFT	do it right the first time
DL	direct labor
DMAIC	design, measure, analyze, improve, control

DMEDI	design, measure, explore, develop, implement
DOE	design of experiments
DPMO	defects per million opportunities
EBIT	earnings before interest and taxes
EBITDA	earnings before interest taxes depreciation, and amortization
ECR	engineering change request
ED	emergency department (emergency room)
EDD	earliest due date
EDI	electronic data interchange
EHS	environmental, health, and safety
ERP	enterprise resource (requirements) planning
ERSC	eliminate, rearrange, simplify, or combine
EHS	Environmental Health and Safety
ETDBW	easy to do business with
EV	earned value
EVA	economic value added
FC	full change
FG	finished goods
FIFO	first in, first out, replaced by EDD, earliest due date
FISH	first in still here
FMEA	failure modes and effects analysis
FPY	first pass yield
FT	feet
FTT	first time through (thru)
FWA	full work analysis
GE	General Electric
GM	general manager
GMS	global manufacturing system
GPI	global process improvement
H	hot
H	hour or hours
HBS	Harvard Business School
HEPA	high-efficiency particle absorption
HPWT	high-performance work teams
HR	human resources
HS&E	health safety and environmental
ICE	SMED formula, identify, convert, eliminate
i.e.	that is
IL	indirect labor
IN	inches
INFO	information
INSP	inspection
ISO	International Organization for Standardization
IS	information systems
IT	information technology (computing/networking)
IT	idle time
ITCS	intelligent tracking control system

JB	job breakdown
JEI	job easiness index
JI	job instruction
JIC	just in case
JIT	just in time
JM	job methodology
JUSE	Japanese Union of Scientists and Engineers
KPI	key process indicators
KPO	Kaizen Promotion Office
KSA	knowledge, skill, or ability
LB	pound or pounds
LBDS	lean business delivery system
LCL	lower control limit
LEI	Lean Enterprise Institute
LIFO	last in, first out
LMAO	laughed my butt off
LMP	lean maturity path
LP	lean practitioner
LP1	lean practitioner level 1
LP 2–5	lean practitioner level 2 through level 5
LRB	lean review board
Max	maximum
MBD	month by day
MBTI	Myers-Briggs Type Inventory—personality styles
MH	man hours
Min	minute or minutes
Min	minimum
MM	materials manager
MPS	master production schedule
MRB	material review board
MSA	measurement systems analysis
MSD	musculoskeletal disorder
MSE	manufacturing support equipment
MSE	measurement system evaluation
MT	meter
MTD	month to date
MVA	market value added
NIH	not invented here
NOPAT	net operating profit after taxes
NOW	not our way
NRE	Nonrecurring engineering
NTED	no touch exchange of dies
NVA	non-value added
NVN	non-value added but necessary
OCED	one cycle exchange of die
OE	order entry
OEE	overall equipment effectiveness

OEE	overall engineering effectiveness scale
OPBSF	one-piece balanced synchronized flow
OPER	operator
OPF	one-piece flow
OPI	office of process improvement
OPS	operations
OR	operating room
ORG	organization
OSED	one-shot exchange of dies
OTD	on-time delivery
OTED	one-touch exchange of dies
OTP	on-time performance
PC	production control
PCDCA	plan–control–do–check–act
PDCA	plan–do–check–act
PDSA	plan–do–study–act
PEST	political, economic, social, and technological
PFA	process flow analysis (following the product)
PFEP	plan for every part
PI	process improvement
PI	performance improvement
PIT	process improvement team
P/N	part number
PM	preventative maintenance
PO	purchase order
POU	point of use
POUB	point of use billing
PPCS	part production capacity sheet
PPF	product process flow, synonymous with PFA
PPM	parts per million
PPV	purchase price variance
Prep	preparation
PSI	pounds per square inch
PWI	perceived weirdness indicator scale (1–10) developed by Charlie Protzman
QC	quality control
QCD	quality, cost, and deliver
+QDIP	safety, quality, delivery, inventory, productivity
QTY	quantity
RC	running change
RCCA	root cause corrective action
RCCM	root cause counter measure
Rchange	resistance to change
REQ	requisition depending on the context
Reqmt	requirements
RF	radio frequency
RFQ	request for quote
RFID	radio-frequency identification

RM	raw materials
ROA	return on assets
ROI	return on investment
RONA	return on net assets
RR	railroad
RTC	resistance to change
RW	required work
S	second or seconds
SASL	signal acquisition source locator
SIPOC	suppliers–inputs–process–outputs–customer
SJS	standard job sheet
SMART	specific, measurable, attainable (achievable), realistic (relevant), timely
SMED	single-minute exchange of dies
SMG	strategic materials group
SOP	standard operating procedure
SORS	standard operation routine sheet, same as SWCS
SPACER	safety, purpose, agenda, code of conduct, expectations, roles
SPC	statistical process control
SPEC	specification
SQC	statistical quality control
ST	storage time
STRAP	strategic plan
SWCS	standard work combination sheet, same as SORS
SWIP	standard work in process
SWOT	strengths, weaknesses, opportunities, threats
TBP	Toyota Business Practice
TCWQC	total company-wide quality control
TH	throughput time
TIPS	transport, inspect, process, store
TL	team leader
TLA	three letter acronym
TLT	total labor time
TM	team member
TOC	theory of constraints
TPM	total productive maintenance
TPS	Toyota production system
TQ	total quality
TQM	total quality management
TT	takt time
UAI	use as is
UCL	upper control limit
UHF	ultrahigh frequency
USW	United Steelworkers
VA	value added
VMI	vendor-managed inventory
VOC	voice of the customer
VOP	Value of the Person

VS	value stream
VSL	value stream leader
VSM	value stream map
W	warm
WACC	weighted average cost of capital
WADITW	we've always done it that way
WE	Western Electric
WFA	Workflow analysis, following the operator
WIIFM	what's in it for me
WIP	work in process
WMSD	work-related musculoskeletal disorder
WOW	ways of working
YTD	year to date

Appendix C - Glossary

5 whys: Method of evaluating a problem or question by asking *why* five times. The purpose is to get to the root cause of the problem and not to address the symptoms. By asking why and answering each time, the root cause becomes more evident.

5 Ws: Asking why something happened—when, where, what, why, or who did the task.

5W2H: Same as the five Ws but adding how and how much.

5Ss: Method of creating a self-sustaining culture that perpetuates a neat, clean, and efficient workplace:

- **Shine:** Keep things clean. Floors swept, machines and furniture clean, all areas neat and tidy.
- **Sort:** Clearly distinguish between what is needed and kept and what is unneeded and thrown out.
- **Standardize:** Maintain and improve the first three *Ss* in addition to personal orderliness and neatness. Minimums and maximums can be added here.
- **Store:** Organize the way that necessary things are kept, making it easier for anyone to find, use, and return them to their proper location.
- **Sustain:** Achieve the discipline or habit of properly maintaining the correct procedures.

Absorption costing: Inventory valuation technique where variable costs and a portion of fixed costs are assigned to a unit of production (or sometimes labor or square footage). The fixed costs are usually allocated based on labor hours, machine hours, or material costs.

Activity-based costing: Developed in the late 1980s by Robert Kaplan and Robin Cooper of Harvard Business School. Activity-based costing is primarily concerned with the cost of indirect activities within a company and their relationships to the manufacture of specific products. The basic technique of activity-based costing is to analyze the indirect costs within an organization and to discover the activities that cause those costs.

Affinity diagram: One of the seven management tools to assist general planning. It organizes disparate language information by placing it on cards and grouping the cards which go together in a creative way. Header cards are used to summarize each group of cards. It organizes information and data.

Allocation: A material requirement planning (MRP) term where a work order has been released to the stockroom; however, the parts have not been picked for production. The system allocates (assigns) those parts to the work order; thus, they are no longer available for new work orders.

Andon: Andon means management by sight—visual management. Japanese translation means light. A flashing light or display in an area to communicate a given condition. An andon can be an electronic board or signal light. A visual indicator can be accompanied by a unique sound as well.

Assembly: A group of parts, raw material, subassemblies, or a combination of both, put together by labor to construct a finished product. An assembly could be an end item (finished good) or a higher level assembly determined by the levels in the bill of material.

Backflush: MRP term used to deduct all component parts from an assembly or subassembly by exploding the bill of material by the number of items produced. Backflushing can occur when the work order is generated or when the unit is shipped.

Backlog: All customer orders received but not yet shipped.

Balance on hand (BOH): The inventory levels between component parts.

Balancing operations: This is the equal distribution of labor time among the number of workers on the line. If there are four workers and 4 minutes of labor time in one unit then each worker should have 1 minute of work.

Batch manufacturing: A production strategy commonly employed in job shops and other instances where there is discrete manufacturing of a nonrepetitive nature. In batch manufacturing, order lots are maintained throughout the production process to minimize changeovers and achieve economies of scale. In batch manufacturing environments, resources are usually departmentalized by specialty and very seldom dedicated to any particular product family.

Benchmarking: Method of establishing internal expectations for excellence based upon direct comparison to the very best at what they do. Benchmarking is not necessarily a comparison with a direct competitor.

Bill of material: A list of all components and manufactured parts that comprise a finished product. The list may have different levels denoting various subassemblies required to build the final product.

Bin: A storage container used to hold parts. Bins range in various sizes from small to very large containers and can be made of plastic, wood, metal, cardboard, etc.

Bin location file: An electronic listing of storage locations for each bin. Generally, locations are designated to the work area, rack, and shelf, and location on the shelf, that is, 1—A—2 defines assembly area 1, rack A, and shelf 2 position on the shelf.

Blanket order: An order generally issued for a year or longer for a particular part number or group of specific part numbers. The blanket order defines the price, terms, and conditions for the supplier, thus allowing an authorized representative of the purchasing team to issue a release against the blanket order to the supplier.

Blanket order release: An authorization to ship from the customer to the supplier a specified quantity from the blanket order.

Block diagram: A diagram where the processes are represented in order of assembly by blocks denoting the process name, cycle time, utilities required, standard work in process (SWIP), etc.

Bottleneck: Generally referred to as the slowest person or machine. However, only machines can be true bottlenecks as we can always add labor. A true bottleneck runs 24 hours a day and still cannot keep up with customer demand.

Breadman: Centralized floor stock systems where the suppliers normally own and manage the material until it is used.

Budget: A plan that represents an estimate of future costs against the expected revenue or allocated funds to spend.

Buffer: Any material in storage waiting further processing.

Buffer stock: Inventory kept to cover yield losses due to poor quality.

Capacity: The total available possible output of a system within current constraints. The capability of a worker or machine within a specified time period.

Carrying costs: The cost to carry inventory, which is usually determined by the cost of capital and cost of maintaining the space (warehouse) and utilities, taxes, insurance, etc.

Catch ball: Communications back, forth, up, down, and horizontally across the organization, which must travel from person to person several times to be clearly understood and reach agreement (consensus). This process is referred to as *catch ball.*

Cause and effect diagram: A problem-solving statistical tool that indicates causes and effects and how they interrelate.

CEDAC: Anachronism for cause and effect diagram with the addition of cards. Problem-solving technique developed by Ryuji Fukuda. A method for defining the effect of a problem and a target effect statement. Through the development of a CEDAC diagram, facts and improvements will be identified that allow action.

Cellular layout: Generally denotes a family of product produced in a layout, which has the machines and workstations in order of assembly. Does not necessarily imply the parts that are produced in one-piece flow.

Chaku-Chaku: Japanese term for *load-load.* Refers to a production line that has been raised to a level of efficiency that requires simply the loading of parts by the operator without any effort required for unloading or transporting material.

Checkpoint: Control item with a means that requires immediate judgment and handling. It must be checked on a daily basis.

CNC: Acronym for computerized machining—stands for computer numerical control.

Consigned inventory: Normally finished goods stored at a customer site but still owned by the supplier.

Constraint: Anything that prevents a process from achieving a higher level of output or performance. Constraints can be physical like material or machines or transactional like policies or procedures.

Continuous flow production: Production in which products flow continuously without interruption.

Continuous improvement (kaizen): A philosophy by which individuals within an organization seek ways to always do things better, usually based on an understanding and control of variation. A pledge to, every day, do or make something better than it was before.

Contribution margin: Equal to sales revenue less variable costs leaving how much remains to be put toward fixed costs.

Control chart: A problem-solving statistical tool that indicates whether the system is in, or out, of control and whether the problem is a result of special causes or common system problems.

Control item: A control item is an item selected as a subject of control for maintenance of a desired condition. It is a yardstick that measures or judges the setting of a target level, the content of the work, the process, and the result of each stage of breakthrough and improvement in control during management activity.

Control point: Control item with a target. A control point is used to analyze data and take action accordingly.

Cost cutting: Eliminating costs in the traditional way, that is, reducing expenses, laying people off, requiring people to supply their own pens, making salary workers work much more overtime, etc.

Cost of capital: The cost of maintaining a dollar of capital invested for a certain period. Normally over a year.

Cost reduction: Reducing costs by eliminating the waste in processes.

Correlation: A statistical relationship between two sets of data such that when one brings about some change in the other it is explained and is statistically significant.

Cp process capability: Process capability is the measured, inherent reproducibility of the product turned out by a process. The most widely adopted formula for process capability (Cp) is

$$\text{Process capability} \left(\text{Cp}\right) = 6\sigma = \text{total tolerance} \div 6$$

where σ is the standard deviation of the process under a state of statistical control. The most commonly used measure for process capability within ASA is a process capability index (Cpk), which is

$$\text{Cpk} = \text{lesser of Cpu or Cpl}$$

where

$$\text{Cpu} = \left(\text{upper specification} - \text{process mean}\right) \div 3$$

and

$$\text{Cpl} = \left(\text{process mean} - \text{lower specification}\right) \div 3$$

Interpretation of the index is generally as follows:

Cpk > 1.33	More than adequate
Cpk ≤ 1.33 but > 1.00	Adequate, but must be monitored as it approaches 1.00
Cpk ≤ 1.00 but > 0.67	Not adequate for the job
Cpk ≤ 0.67	Totally inadequate

CPIM: APICS—acronym for certified purchasing and inventory manager. Rigorous course material required with five modules of testing to be certified.

CPM: Acronym stands for certified purchasing manager—this is a NAPM (national association of purchasing managers) certification for purchasing professionals. Requires passing rigorous testing and experience criteria.

Cross-functional management: Cross-functional management is the overseeing of horizontal interdivisional activities. It is used so that all aspects of the organization are well managed and have consistent, integrated quality efforts pertaining to scheduling, delivery, plans, etc.

Cross-training: Training an employee in many different jobs within or across cells.

Customer relations: A realization of the role the customer plays in the continuation of your business. A conscious decision to listen to and provide products and services for those who make your business an ongoing concern.

Customer service: Any specifications required to meet the customer demands, needs, or requests for information and service. Everyone in the company should be a customer service representative.

Cycle: Completion of one whole series of processes by a part or person.

Cycle time: Available time divided by the factory capacity demand, the time each unit is coming off the end of the assembly line or the time each operator must hit, or the total labor time divided by the number of operators.

Cumulative: The progressive total of all the pieces.

Cumulative time: Is equivalent to adding up the total times as you progress. For instance, if step 1 is 5 seconds and step 2 is 10 seconds, the cumulative time is 15 seconds.

Daily control: The systems by which workers identify simply and clearly understand what they must do to fulfill their job function in a way that will enable the organization to run smoothly. These items are usually concerned with the normal operation of a business. Also a system in which these required actions are monitored by the employees themselves.

Data: Any portrayal of alphabetic or numerical information to which some meaning can be ascribed. Data can be found in a series of numbers or in an answer to a question asked of a person.

Data box: Term apportioned to a box in a value stream map that underlies a process box and contains elements such as process cycle time, number of persons, change over time, lot size, etc.

Demand flow: Material only moves to a work center when that work center is out of work. Subject of the book *Quantum Leap* by the World Wide Flow College of Denver. Layouts are typically a conveyor down the middle of the line with subassembly lines feeding in both sides.

Deming cycle: A continuously rotating wheel of plan, do, check, act.

Demonstrated capacity: Term to depict capacity arrived at by nonscientific means. Generally, it is arrived at by feel or observing actual output without determining what the process could generate if all the waste was removed.

Deviation: The absolute difference between a number and the mean of a data set.

Direct labor: Labor attributable specifically to the product.

Direct material: Raw material or supplied materials that when combined become part of the final product.

Distribution: Term generally refers to a supply chain of intermediaries.

Distributor: A company that generally does not manufacture material but is a middle man. They normally hold some finished goods but not always. Sometimes they may make some modifications to the finished goods.

Dock to stock: Process where suppliers are certified by the company's supplier quality engineers or purchasing and quality professionals that result in the supplier's products bypassing inspection or sometimes receiving to go directly to the stock room or shop floor where it is used.

Download: Transfer of information from a central computer (cloud) to a tablet, PC, phone, or other type of device.

Downstream operation: Task that is subsequent to the operation currently being executed or planned.

Downtime: Time when a scheduled resource is not operating.

Earned hours: Standard hours credited for actual production during the period determined by some agreed upon rate.

Economic order quantity: Model used to determine the optimum batch size for product running through an operation or a line. It is equal to the square root of two times the annual demand times average cost of order preparation divided by the annual inventory carrying cost percentage times unit cost.

Economy of scale: Larger volumes of products realize lower cost of production due to allocating fixed costs against a larger output size.

EDI: Acronym stands for electronic data interchange which is the ability for computer systems between supplier and customer to talk to each other without human involvement. In some cases, this requires programing of an interface between computers so they can talk to each other.

Effectiveness: Is the ability to achieve stated goals or objectives, judged in terms of metrics that are based on both output and impact. It is (a) the degree to which an activity or initiative is successful in achieving a specified goal and (b) the degree to which activities of a unit achieve the unit's mission or goal.

Efficiency: Production without waste. Efficiency is based on the *energy* one spends to complete the product or service as well as timing. For example, we all know of the *learning curve*. The more one performs a new task, the better they become each time the task is practiced. As one becomes more efficient, they definitely reduce stress and gain accuracy, capability, and consistency of action. A person has achieved efficiency when they are getting more done with the same or better accuracy in a shorter period of time, with less energy and better results.

Eight dimensions on quality: Critical dimensions or categories of quality identified by David Garvin of the Harvard Business School that can serve as a framework for strategic analysis. They are performance, features, reliability, conformance, durability, serviceability, esthetics, and perceived quality.

Elimination of waste: A philosophy that states that all activities undertaken need to be evaluated to determine if they are necessary, enhancing the value of the goods and services being provided and what the customer wants. Determining if the systems that have been established are serving their users or are the users serving the system.

Ending inventory: Inventory present at the end of a period. Sometimes validated by taking a physical inventory.

EPE: Acronym stands for every part every—this denotes batch size of lots running through the process.

Ergonomics: The study of humans interacting with the environment or workplace.

ERP: Acronym for enterprise resource planning system. It is a business management software to integrate all business phases to include marketing/sales, planning, engineering, operations and customer support the third generation of MRP systems usually used to link company plants locally, nationally, or globally. SAP, ORACLE, and BPCS are examples of these types of systems.

Excess inventory: More inventory than required to do any task.

Expedite: To push, rush, or walk a product (or information, signatures, etc.) through the process or system.

Expeditor: One who expedites.

External setup time: Time utilized and steps that can be done preparing for changeovers while the machine is still running. Example—prepping for a racing car pit stop like getting tires in place, having fuel ready, etc. Focus of changeovers or setups moving internal elements to external elements.

Fabrication: The process of transforming metals into a final product or subassembly usually by machine. Generally, a term to distinguish activities done in a machine shop versus manually assembling components into a final product.

Facility: The physical plant or office (transactional areas).

Failure analysis: The process of determining the root cause of a failure usually generating a report of some type.

Family: A group of products (or information) that shares similar processes.

FIFO: First in, first out inventory management system.

Flex fence: Purchasing term used in contracts to mitigate demand risk by having the supply chain capable of flexing production plus or minus 10%, 20%, or 30%. This is accomplished by identifying long lead items and developing plans to stock some of those parts at the buyer's expense.

Flexible workforce: A workforce totally cross-trained, capable, and allowed to work in all positions.

Floater: Cross-trained workers moved around throughout the day to different positions depending on the takt time or cycle time and the staffing requirements for the day.

Floor stock: Generally less expensive C-type parts stored centrally on the floor and owned by the company.

Flow: Smooth, uninterrupted movement of material or information.

Flow chart: A problem-solving tool that illustrates a process. It shows the way things actually go through a process, the way they should go, and the difference.

Flow production: Describes how goods, services, or information are processed. It is, at its best, one piece at a time. This can be a part, a document, invoice, or customer order. It rejects the concept of batch, lot, or mass producing. It vertically integrates all operations or functions as operationally or sequentially performed. It also encompasses pull or demand processing. Goods are not pushed through the process but pulled or demanded by succeeding operations from preceding operations. Often referred to as *one-piece-flow.*

FMEA: Failure mode and effects analysis. A structured approach to assess the magnitude of potential failures and identify the sources of each potential failure. Each potential failure is studied to identify the most effective corrective action. FMEA is the process of mitigating risk by looking at a process to determine what is likely to go wrong, the probability of it going wrong, the severity if it does go wrong, and the countermeasures to be taken in the event it does go wrong.

FOB: Free on board—logistics term used to designate where title passes to the buyer.

Focused factory: A plant or department focused on a single or family of products. Where everything can be done within the four walls. Does not necessarily mean cellular or one-piece flow.

Forecast: An attempt to look into the future in order to predict demand. Companies use techniques that range from historical statistical techniques to systematic wild ass guesses (SWAGs). The longer the forecast horizon, the less accurate the forecast.

FTE: Acronym standing for full-time equivalent. The formula is to take the total number of hours being worked by one or multiple people and divide by 2,080 hours (per year) and come up with the equivalent of one person's worth of labor per year.

Functional: Organized by department.

Functional layout: Layouts where the same or similar equipment is grouped together. These layouts support batch production.

GAAP: Acronym for generally accepted accounting principles.

Gain sharing: Method of compensating employees based on the overall productivity of the company. The goal is to give the employee a stake in the company and share based on productivity. Measures and participatory schemes vary by company and philosophy. There are many different methods of gain sharing. Normally differentiated from profit sharing, which is based on formulas relating only to company profits.

Grievance: Term refers to complaint (contract violation) filed by an employee (normally union based) against someone who is union or nonunion in the company.

Hanedashi: Device or means for automatic removal of a workpiece from one operation or process, which provides proper state and orientation for the next operation or process. In manufacturing, a means for automatic unloading and orientation for the next operation or process. In manufacturing, a means for automatic unloading and orientation for the next operation, generally a very simple device. Crucial for a *Chaku-Chaku* line.

Heijunka: Japanese term for level loading production. Necessary to support Kanban-based systems.

Histogram: A chart that takes measurement data and displays its distribution, generally in a bar graph format. For example, a histogram can be used to reveal the amount of variation that any process has within it based upon the data available.

Hoshin: Type of corporate planning, strategy, and execution in a setting where everyone participates in coming up with goals through a process called catchball and everyone down to the shop floor knows what they are doing is directly supporting the top three to five company goals.

Housekeeping: Keeping an orderly and clean environment.

Idle time: When a person is standing around with nothing to do, visible by arms crossed. Also known as pure waste.

Indirect costs: Traditional accounting costs that are not directly related or accounted to the product. Also known as overhead costs.

Indirect labor: Traditional accounting of labor required to support production without directly working on the product.

Indirect materials: Traditional accounting of materials used to support production but not directly used on the product.

Information: Data presented to an individual or machine.

Information systems: Term used to designate manual or computer-based systems, which convey information throughout the department or organization as a whole. Term used in value stream mapping for boxes located at the top of the map with lines to the process (information) boxes with which they interact.

Input: Work or information fed to the beginning of a system or process.

Inspection: The act of multiple (two or more) checks on material or information to see if it is correct. Can also refer to a department of humans that checks incoming materials (receiving inspection), WIP (in-process inspection), or final inspection before the product leaves the plant.

Internal setup time: Term used to designate time when machine or process is down (not running). Example is time when the racing car is in the pit stop having tires replaced and fuel added, etc.

Interrelationship diagram: A tool that assists in general planning. This tool takes a central idea, issue, or problem and maps out the logical or sequential links among related items.

It is a creative process that shows every idea can be logically linked with more than one idea at a time. It allows for *multidirectional* rather than *linear* thinking to be used.

Inventory: Purchased materials used to assemble any level of the product or to support production. Inventory can be in various stages from raw materials to finished goods.

Inventory turnover or turns: The number of times inventory cycles or turns over during the year. Generally calculated by dividing average cost of sales divided by the average inventory (normally three months). This can be a historical or forward-looking methodology. Can also be calculated by dividing days of supply into the number of working or calendar days.

Ishikawa diagram: Referred to as a fishbone used to graphically display cause and effect and to get to the root cause.

Item number: Normally a part number or stock number for a part.

Jidoka: Automation with a human touch or mind, autonomation. Automatic machinery that will operate itself but always incorporates the following devices: a mechanism to detect abnormalities or defects and a mechanism to stop the machine or line when defects or abnormalities occur.

Job costing: Where costs are collected and allocated to a certain job or charge number. Can be based on actual or standard costs.

Job description: List of roles and responsibilities for a particular job.

Job rotation: Schedule of movement from machine to machine or process to process. Used to support and encourage cross-training.

Job shop: Term used for factories that have high mix and low volume typically nonrepeatable or customized products.

Just-in-time manufacturing: A strategy that exposes the waste in an operation, makes continuous improvement a reality, and provides the opportunity to promote total employee involvement. Concentrates on making what is needed, when it is needed, no sooner, no later.

Kaizen (Kai = change; zen = good): The process improvement that involves a series of continual improvements over time. These improvements may take the form of a process innovation (event) or small incremental improvements.

Kanban: Japanese for a sign board. Designates a pull production means of communicating need for product or service. Originally developed as a means to communicate between operations in different locations. It was intended to communicate a change in demand or supply. In application, it is generally used to trigger the movement of material to or through a process.

Kit: Collection of components used to support a sub- or final assembly of a product.

Kitting: Process of collecting the components used to support a sub- or final assembly of a product.

Knowledge worker: A worker, who acquires information from every task, analyzes and validates the information, and stores it for future use.

Labor cost: Cost of labor, can be direct or indirect. In Lean, we look at total labor cost versus indirect or direct associated with traditional cost accounting systems.

Layout: Physical arrangement of machines and materials or offices.

LCL: Lower control limit, used on control charts.

Lead time: The time to manufacture and deliver a product or service. This term is used in many (often contradictory) contexts. To avoid confusion, lead time is defined as the average total lapse time for execution of the product delivery process from order receipt to delivery to the customer under normal operating conditions. In industries that operate in a build-to-order environment, lead times flex based on the influences of seasonal demand loads. In environments where production is scheduled in repeating, fixed-time segments or cycles, the lead time is usually determined by the length of the production cycle (i.e., days, weeks, months, etc.).

Lead time or throughput time: Time it takes to get through the entire process or time quoted to customers to receive their orders (from order to cash).

Lean production: The activity of creating processes that are highly responsive and flexible to customer demand requirements. Successful Lean production is evident when processes are capable of consistently delivering the highest quality (defect-free) products and services, at the right location and at the right time, in response to customer demand and doing this in the most cost-effective manner possible.

Learning curve: A planning technique used to predict improvement based on experience. Uses log charts to trend the data.

Level load: Process of leveling or equally distributing demand or products across a cell or plant. Also known as heijunka.

LIFO: Last in, first out inventory management.

Limit switch: Various electronic devices used to trigger an action when a particular limit is reached. Used to control machines or count parts, used to turn on or off machines, used often for poka yoke, etc.

Little's Law: Throughput time divided by cycle time = amount of inventory in the system.

Logistics: The art and science of shipping materials, distribution, warehousing, and supply chain management.

Lot: Refers to a group of parts or information generally batched together through the process.

Lot size: Number of parts in a batch to be produced.

LTA: Acronym for long-term agreement. An agreement negotiated with a supplier for a longer term and more complex than a simple blanket (pricing) agreement, normally three to five years with other conditions centering on the supplier's improvement, quality and delivery certification, and price reduction goals.

Machine hours: Total hours a machine is running. Can be value-added or non-value-added time normally used for capacity planning. May or may not include setup time or unplanned downtime.

Machine utilization: The amount of time a machine is available versus the amount of time the machine is being used. Includes setup and run time compared to available time. It used to be the *be all and end all* for traditional cost accounting measures. With Lean, it is not as important unless it is a true bottleneck machine.

Make or buy: Study of costs of purchasing a part versus purchasing the raw materials and making it in house.

Make to order: A product that is not started until after the customer orders it. In some cases, a Kanban or inventory of parts produced to a certain level may then be modified to fit the customer requirements.

Manufacturing resources planning (MRP II): A second-generation MRP system that provides additional control linkages such as automatic purchase order generation, capacity planning, and accounts payable transactions.

Master schedule: Schedule with customer orders loaded by due date or promised date.

Master scheduler: Person who enters sales orders into the master schedule.

Material requirements planning (MRP): A computerized information system that calculates material requirements based on a master production schedule. This system may be used only for material procurement or to also execute the material plan through shop floor control.

MBO: Management by objectives—a system where goals are handed down from manager to employee where the employee participates in the process.

Means (measure): A way to accomplish a target.

Min max: Refers to a type of inventory system where once the minimum level is reached or a reorder point is reached, a quantity is reordered, which brings the quantity back up to the maximum level. Some computer MRP systems (Oracle) have this as an option to manage inventory.

Milk run: Term used to identify the path water spider uses to replenish materials for a line.

Mistake proofing: Also known as poka yoke or foolproofing. A system starting with successive checks by humans to inspection devices built into or added to machines to detect and or prevent defects.

Mixed model production: The ability to produce various models with different levels of customization one by one down the production line.

Monthly audit: The self-evaluation of performance against targets. An examination of things that helped or hindered performance in meeting the targets and the corrective actions that will be taken.

MPS: Master production schedule.

MRO: Term used to designate maintenance repair and operating supplies.

MRP: Material requirements planning; a computerized system developed by Olie Wright using lead time offsets, bill of material, and various planning parameters used to predict when to release requisitions or work orders in order to schedule the production floor.

MRPII: Material resource planning; a more advanced MRP system, which ties various systems together within a single company, that is, manufacturing and finance.

MTM: Methods time measurement; system that has studied and determined times for various operations or movements by operators. Generally used with motion study.

Muda: Japanese term for waste.

Multiskilled or process workers: Description for individuals at any level of the organization who are diverse in skill and training. Capable of performing a number of different tasks providing the organization with additional flexibility.

Mura: Japanese term for uneven.

Muri: Japanese term for overburden.

Nemawashi: Refers to the process of gaining consensus and support prior to implementing a strategy.

Net sales: Total sales less returns and allowances.

Noise: Randomness within a process.

Nominal group technique: Process of soliciting information from everyone in the group.

Non-value added: Designation for a step that does not meet one of the three value-added criteria.

Non-value added but necessary (sometimes called business value added): Any step that is necessary but the customer is not willing to pay for it but it is done right the first time.

Normal distribution: Statistical term where most data falls close to the mean (±1 sigma), less fall away from the mean (±2 sigma), and even less fall even further away (±3 sigma), where the distribution when graphed looks like a bell-shaped curve.

NTED: No-touch exchange of dies.

Objective: What you are trying to achieve with a given plan. The desired end result. The reason for employing a strategy and developing targets.

Obsolete: Loss of product value due to engineering, product life decisions, or technological changes.

Offset: Time entered into MRP systems to designate how long it takes to get through a part of the system, that is, purchasing time entered as two days. MRP uses this information to develop a timeline to predict when to release the order or purchase requirement. When added up, it equals the total lead time of the product in the system.

OJT: Acronym for on-the-job training.

One-year plan: A statement of objective of an organizational event for a year.

Operating system: Refers to the type of system computer is using, that is, DOS, windows, etc.

Operation: A series of tasks grouped together such that the sum of the individual task times is equal to the takt time (cycle time to meet product demand requirements). It is important to distinguish between operations and activities. Operations are used to balance work content in a flow manufacturing process to achieve a particular daily output rate equal to customer demand. An operation defines the amount of work content performed by each operator to achieve a balanced flow and linear output rate.

Opportunity cost: Return on capital, which could have been achieved had it been used for something else more productive.

Order policy: Term used in MRP to decide lot sizing requirements.

Organization structure: The fashion in which resources are assigned to tasks. Includes cross-functional management and vertical work teams. Also includes the development of multiskilled workers through the assignment of technical and administrative personnel to nontraditional roles.

Organizational development: Process that looks at improving the interactions within and between departments across the overall organization. Generally led by a consultant or company change agent.

Organizational tools: These provide a team approach in which people get together to work on problems and also get better at what they are doing. Organizational tools include work groups and quality circles.

OTED: One-touch exchange of dies. Uses a human touch to changeover one or more machines at the same time.

Overhead: Costs not directly tied to the product. Normally refers to all personnel who support the production process whether it is physical or transactional.

Overtime: Work beyond the traditional 40 hours usually results in a premium paid per hour.

Pareto chart: A vertical bar graph showing the bars in order to size from left to right. Helps focus on the vital few problems rather than the trivial many. An extension of the Pareto principle that suggests the significant items in a given group normally constitute a relatively small portion of the items in the total group. Conversely, a majority of the items in the total will, even in aggregate, be relatively minor in significance (i.e., the 80/20 rule).

Participative management: Employees collaborate with managers to work on improvements to the process. Basis for QC circles.

Pay for performance: Pay is tied to overall output by a team.

Perpetual inventory system: System designed to always have the correct amount of inventory in the system.

PFA: Process flow analysis, looks at the flow of just the product through the process using TIPS.

Phantom: A bill of material (BOM) or non-production work order used to determine if there are any parts shortages. How to create the phantom varies depending on the type of MRP or

ERP system. In general, a work order is created and then backed out of the system prior to MRP running again.

Physical layout: A means of impacting workflow and productivity through the physical placement of machinery or furniture. Production machinery should be grouped in a cellular arrangement based upon product requirements, not process type. In addition to this, in most instances, there is an advantage in having the workflow in counterclockwise fashion. Similarly, in an office environment, furniture should be arranged such that there is an efficient flow of information or services rather than strictly defined departments.

PDCA cycle: Plan-Do-Check-Act. The PDCA system, sometimes referred to as the Deming cycle, is the most important item for control in policy deployment. In this cycle, you make a plan that is based on policy (plan); you take action accordingly (do); you check the result (check); and if the plan is not fulfilled, you analyze the cause and take further action by going back to the plan (action).

Piece rate: Form of worker compensation based on individual output targets that vary by employee and process.

Pilot: Trying something out for one or several pieces in a controlled environment to test a hypothesis.

Plan: The means to achieve a target.

Planned downtime: Downtime that is scheduled for a machine or line.

Planner/buyer: Combines planning and buyer jobs.

Planner/buyer/scheduler: Combines planning, buying, and scheduling jobs.

Poka yoke: Japanese expression meaning *common or simple, mistake proof.* A method of designing processes, either production or administrative, which will by their nature prevent errors. This may involve designing fixtures that will not accept a defective part or something as simple as having a credit memo be a different color than a debit memo. It requires that thought be put into the design of any system to anticipate *what* can go wrong and build in measures to prevent them.

Policy: The company objectives are to be achieved through the cooperation of all levels of managers and employees. A policy consists of targets, plans, and target values.

Policy deployment: Hoshin Kanri—policy deployment orchestrates continuous improvement in a way that fosters individual initiative and alignment. It is a process of implementing the policies of an organization directly through line managers and indirectly through cross-functional organization. It is a means of internalizing company policies throughout the organization, from highest to lowest level. Top managers will articulate its annual goals that are then deployed down through lower levels of management. The abstract goals of top management become more concrete and specific as they are deployed down through the organization. Policy deployment is process oriented. It is concerned with developing a process by which results become predictable. If the goal is not realized, it is necessary to review and see if the implementation was faulty. It is most important to determine what went wrong in the process that prevented the goal from being realized. The Japanese name for policy deployment is Hoshin Kanri. In Japanese, Hoshin means *shining metal, compass,* or *pointing in the direction.* Kanri means *control.* Hoshin Kanri is a method devised to capture and concretize strategic goals as well as flashes of insight about the future and to develop the means to bring these into reality. It is one of the major systems that make world-class quality management possible. It helps control the direction of the company by orchestrating change within a company. The system includes tools for continuous improvement, breakthroughs, and implementation. The key to Hoshin planning is it brings the total organization into the strategic planning process, both top down and bottom up. It ensures the direction, goals, and objectives of the company are rationally developed, well defined, clearly communicated, monitored, and adapted based on system feedback. It provides focus for the organization.

POU: Point of use, designates location where product or tooling or information is used.

Preventative maintenance: Term given to duties carried out on machines in order to prevent a breakdown or unplanned stoppage.

Prioritization matrices: This tool prioritizes tasks, issues, product/service characteristics, etc., based on known weighted criteria using a combination of tree and matrix diagram techniques. Above all, they are tools for decision-making.

Problem-solving tools: These tools find the root cause of problems. They are tools for thinking about problems, managing by fact, and documenting hunches. The tools include check sheet, line chart, Pareto chart, flow chart, histogram, control chart, and scatter diagram. In Japan, these are referred to as the seven QC tools.

Process: A series of activities that collectively accomplish a distinct objective. Processes are cross-functional and cut across departmental responsibility boundaries. Processes can be value added or non-value added.

Process capability: See CPK.

Process control chart: Chart that represents tracking the sequence of data points over a number of or 100% samplings. It serves as a basis to define common cause versus special cause variation and to predict when a part or machine is likely to fail.

Process decision program chart: The process decision program chart (PDPC) is a method that maps out conceivable events and contingencies that can occur in any implementation plan. It, in time, identifies possible countermeasures in response to these problems. This tool is used to plan each possible chain of events that need to occur when the problem or goal is an unfamiliar one.

Process hierarchy: A hierarchical decomposition from core business processes to the task level. The number of levels in a hierarchy is determined by the breadth and size of the organization. A large enterprise process hierarchy may include core business processes, processes, subprocesses, process segments, activities, and tasks.

Process management: This involves focusing on the process rather than the results. A variety of tools may be used for process management, including the seven QC tools.

Process segment: A series of activities that define a subset of a process.

Product delivery process: The stream of activities required to produce a product or service. This activity stream encompasses both planning and execution activities to include demand planning, order management, materials procurement, production, and distribution.

Production control: Employee that tracks status of daily production; normally used in batch environments but sometimes in Lean environments.

Production schedule: Orders lined up in order of priority based on due date, promised date, or some other planning parameters.

Productivity: Productivity is the *amount* of products produced in a certain amount of time with a certain amount of labor. The products could be physical products or transactional such as processing an invoice or Internet blogs. Productive means getting things done, outcomes reached, or goals achieved and are measured as output per unit of input (i.e., labor, equipment, and capital).

Prototype: First piece on which new process is tried.

Pull production: In a pull process, materials are staged at the point of consumption. As these materials are consumed, signals are sent back to previous steps in the production process to pull forward sufficient materials to replenish only those materials that have been consumed.

Push production: In a push process, production is initiated by the issuance of production orders that are offset in time from the actual demand to allow time for production and delivery. The idea is to maintain zero inventory and have materials complete each step of the production process just as they are needed at subsequent (downstream) activities.

+QDIP: Acronym stands for safety, quality, delivery, inventory, and production. Ideally, parameters are set by the employees on the shop floor or in the workshop.

Quality: Refers to the ability of the final product to meet both the customers required specification and unspecified specifications.

Quality circles: Quality circles are an organizational tool that provides a team approach in which people get together to work on problems and to improve productivity. Their primary objective is to foster teamwork and encourage employee by involvement employing the problem-solving approach.

Quality function deployment: A product development system that identifies the wants of a customer and gets that information to all the right people so the organization can effectively exceed competition in meeting the customer's most important wants. It translates customer wants into appropriate technical requirements for each stage of product development and production.

Quality management: The systems, organizations, and tools that make it possible to plan, manufacture, and deliver a quality product or service. This does not imply inspection or even traditional quality control. Rather, it involves the entire process involved in bringing goods and services to the customer.

Queuing theory: Applies to manufacturing orders, people, or information that is waiting in line for the next process. Based on Little's law.

Queue time: Amount of time an order, people, or information is waiting for the next process.

Quick changeover: Method of increasing the amount of productive time available for a piece of machinery by minimizing the time needed to change from one model to another. This greatly increases the flexibility of the operation and allows it to respond more quickly to changes in demand. It also has the benefit of allowing an organization to greatly reduce the amount of inventory that it must carry because of improved response time.

Rate-based order management: This order management system employs a finite capacity loading scheme to promise orders based upon the agreed demand bound limits. These minimum and maximum demand bounds reflect potential response capacity limits for production and materials procurement.

Rate-based planning: A procedure that establishes a controlled level of flexibility in the product delivery process in order to be robust to anticipated variations in demand. This flexibility is achieved by establishing minimum and maximum bounds around future demand forecasts. The idea is that both the production facility and the material supply channels will echelon sufficient capacity to accommodate demand swings that do not exceed the established demand bounds. As future demand forecasts move closer to the production window, updated demand bounds are periodically broadcasted to the material suppliers. At the point of order receipt and delivery promising (within sales or customer service), demand bounding limits are enforced to insure that the rate-based production plan remains feasible.

Regression analysis: Statistical technique that determines or estimates the amount of correlation explained between two or more variable sets of data.

ROI: Return on investment, generally compares investment versus the return to determine the payback that is often stated in years and expressed as a percentage of earnings.

RONA: Return on net assets.

Root cause: The ultimate reason for an event or condition.

Run chart: A statistical problem-solving tool that shows whether key indicators are going up or down and if the indicators are good or bad.

Safety: Ensuring that the work environment is free of hazards and obstacles of which could cause harm.

Scanlon plan: A system of group incentives that measures the plant-wide results of all efforts using the ratio of labor costs to sales value added by production. If there is an increase in production sales value with no change in pricing, mix, or labor costs, productivity has increased and unit costs have decreased.

Scatter diagram: One of the seven QC tools. The scatter diagram shows the relationship between two variables.

Scheduled (planned) downtime: Planned shutdown of equipment to perform maintenance or other tasks or lack of customer demand.

Self-diagnosis: As a basis for continuous improvement, each manager uses problem-solving activity to see why he or she is succeeding or failing to meet targets. This diagnosis should focus on identifying personal and organizational obstacles to the planned performance and on the development of alternate approaches based on this new information.

Self-directed work team: Normally, a small group of employees that can plan, organize, and manage their daily responsibilities with no direct supervision. They can normally hire, fire, or demote team members.

Setup: The changing over of a machine or also the loading and unloading of parts on a machine.

Setup time: The amount of time it takes to changeover a machine from the last good part to and including the first good part.

Setup parts: Preparation, mounting and removing, calibration, trial runs, and adjustments.

Seven new tools: Sometimes called the seven management tools. These are affinity and relationship diagrams for general planning; tree systems, matrix, and prioritization matrices for intermediate planning; and activity network diagrams and process decision program charts for detailed planning.

Seven QC tools: Problem-solving statistical tools needed for customer-driven master plan. They are cause and effect diagram, flow chart, Pareto chart, run chart, histogram, control chart, and scatter diagram.

Seven wastes: Seven types of waste have been identified for business. They are as follows:

1. Waste from overproduction of goods or services
2. Waste from waiting or idle time
3. Waste from transportation (unnecessary)
4. Waste from the process itself (inefficiency)
5. Waste of unnecessary stock on hand

6. Waste of motion and effort
7. Waste from producing defective goods

The eighth waste: Waste of talent and knowledge

Shojinka: Means labor flexibility. The term means employees staffing the line can flex up or down based on the incoming demand, which requires employees to be cross-trained and multi-process/machine capable. It also means continually optimizing the number of workers based on demand. This principle is central to baton zone line balancing (bumping).

Shoninka: Means *manpower savings*. This corresponds to the improvement of work procedures, machines, or equipment to free whole units of labor (i.e., one person) from a production line consisting of one or more workers.

Shoryokuka[1]: Shoryokuka means *labor savings* and indicates partial improvement of manual labor by adding small machines or devices to aid the job. This results in some small amount of labor savings but not an entire person as in shoninka. Again this becomes a goal of all follow-up point kaizen events.

Simultaneous/concurrent engineering: The practice of designing a product (or service), its production process, and its delivery mechanism all at the same time. The process requires considerable up-front planning as well as the dedication of resources early in the development cycle. The payoff is in the form of shorter development time from concept to market, lower overall development cost, and lower product or service cost based upon higher accuracy at introduction and less potential for redesign. Examples of this include the Toyota Lexus 200 and the Ford Taurus.

SMED: Single-minute exchange of dies, 9 minutes 59 seconds or less setup time.

Smoothing/production smoothing: The statistical method of converting weekly or monthly schedules to level-loaded daily schedules.

SPC: Acronym for statistical process control.

Standard deviation: Statistical measurement of process variation (σ) which measures the dispersion of sample observations around a process mean.

Standard work: Standard work is a tool that defines the interaction of man and his environment when processing something. In producing a part, it is the interaction of man and machine, whereas in processing an invoice, it is the interaction of man and the supplier and the accounting system. It details the motion of the operator and the sequence of action. It provides a routine for consistency of an operation and a basis for improvement. Furthermore, the concept of standard work is it is a verb, not a noun. It details the best process we currently know and understand. Tomorrow it should be better (continuous improvement), and the standard work should be revised to incorporate the improvement. There can be no improvement without a basis (standard work).

Standard work has three central elements:

1. Cycle time (not takt time)
2. Standard operations
3. SWIP

Standard work (as a tool): Establishes a routine/habit/pattern for repetitive tasks, makes managing such as scheduling and resource allocation easier, establishes the relationship between man and environment, provides a basis for improvement by defining the normal and highlighting the abnormal, and prohibits backsliding.

Standard work in process: The amount of material or a given product that must be in process at any time to insure maximum efficiency of the operation.

Standardization: The system of documenting and updating procedures to make sure everyone knows clearly and simply what is expected of them (measured by daily control). Essential for application of PDCA cycle.

Statistical methods/tools: Statistical methods allow employees to manage by facts and analyze problems through understanding variability and data. The seven QC tools are examples of statistical tools.

Store, storage: Any time a product (part, information, or person) is waiting in the process.

Strategy: The business process that involves goals setting, defining specific actions to achieve the business goals, and allocating the resources to execute the actions.

Subprocess: A series of interrelated process segments that forms a subset of a total process.

Supplier partnerships: An acknowledgment that suppliers are an integral part of any business. A partnership implies a long-term relationship that involves the supplier in both product development and process development. It also requires a commitment on the part of the supplier to pursue continuous improvement and world-class quality.

System: A system is the infrastructure that enables the processes to provide customer value. Business systems comprise market, customer, competition, organizational culture, environmental and technological influences, regulatory issues, physical resources, procedures, information flows, and knowledge sets. It is through physical processes that business systems transform inputs to outputs and, thereby, deliver products and services of value in the marketplace.

Takt time: The frequency with which the customer wants a product or how frequently a sold unit must be produced. The number is derived by taking the amount of time available in a day and dividing it by the number of sold units that need to be produced. Takt time is usually expressed in seconds.

Target: The desired goal that serves as a yardstick for evaluating the degree to which a *policy* is achieved. It is controlled by a *control point, control item,* or *target item*.

Target costing: Method for establishing cost objective for a product or service during the design phase. The target cost is determined by the following formula:

$$\text{Sales price} - \text{target profit} = \text{target cost}$$

Target/means matrix: Shows the relationship between targets and means and to identify control items and control methods.

Target value: Normally a numeric definition of successful target attainment. It is not always possible to have a numeric target, and you must never separate the target from the plan.

Theory of constraints: A management philosophy first put forth in the book *The Goal* by Eliyahu Goldratt to identify bottlenecks in the process. In the book, he follows a young boy scout named Herbie. We call bottlenecks *Herbies* today in some cases. His approach was to identify the constraint, exploit the constraint, subordinate all non-constraints, elevate the constraint, and if the constraint is broken in step 4, then go back to step 1.

Throughput time: A measure of the actual throughput time for a product to move through a flow process once the work begins. Many people incorrectly label this measure as manufacturing lead time but it is actually a small subset and often has little to do with the total time from order inception to fulfillment.

TIPS: Acronym for parts of process flow analysis—transport inspect process store.

Total density: One of the eight Lean wastes is the *waste of motion*. One of the first things we advise when trying to identify wasted motions is do not confuse motion with work. In offices, this concept is revised slightly to the following: *do not confuse effort with results*.[2] Total density = work divided by motion. [3] Not all motion is work. It is important to separate needed motions versus wasted motions.

Total employee involvement (TEI): A philosophy that advocates the harnessing of the collective knowledge of an organization through the involvement of its people. When supported by the management, it is a means of improving quality, delivery, profitability, and morale in an organization. It provides all employees with a greater sense of ownership in the success of the company and provides them with more control in addressing issues that face the organization. TEI does not allow top management to abdicate its obligation to properly plan and set objectives. It does, however, provide more resources and flexibility in meeting those objectives.

Total labor time: The sum of labor value-added and labor non-value-added times.

Total productive maintenance: TPM is productive maintenance conducted by all employees. It is equipment maintenance performed on a companywide basis. It has five goals:

1. Maximize equipment effectiveness (improve overall efficiency).
2. Develop a system of productive maintenance for the life of the equipment.
3. Involve all departments that plan, design, use, or maintain equipment in implementing TPM (engineering and design, production, and maintenance).
4. Actively involve all employees—from top management to shop-floor workers.
5. Promote TPM through motivational management (autonomous small group activities).

The word total in *total productive maintenance* **has three meanings related to three important features of TPM:** total effectiveness (pursuit of economic efficiency or profitability), total PM (maintenance prevention and activity to improve maintainability as well as preventative maintenance), and total participation (autonomous maintenance by operators and small group activities in every department and at every level).

Transport: Any travel a part or information does throughout the process.

Tree diagram: The tree diagram systematically breaks down plans into component parts and systematically maps out the full range of tasks/methods needed to achieve a goal. It can either be used as a cause-finding problem-solver or a task-generating planning tool.

Value added: Must meet three criteria from the AMA video *Time The Next Dimension of Quality*: customer cares, physically changes the thing going through the process, and done right the first time. Value added was expanded for hospitals to physically or emotionally change the patient for the better in addition to the other two criteria.

Value-added work content ratio: The steps that actually transform and increase the value of the product or test requirements legislated by industrial licensing agencies. The value-added work content ratio is formed by simply dividing the sum of all value-added work steps by the product lead time for the total process. This ratio can also be used to evaluate waste only in the manufacturing process segment by dividing the numerator by the manufacturing flow time.

Vertical teams: Vertical teams are groups of people who come together to meet and address problems or challenges. These teams are made up of the most appropriate people for the issue, regardless of their levels or jobs within the organization.

Vision: A long-term plan or direction that is based on a careful assessment of the most important directions for the organization.

Visual management: The use of visual media in the organization and general administration of a business. This would include the use of color, signs, and a clear span of sight in a work area. These visuals should clearly designate what things are and where they belong. They should provide immediate feedback as to the work being done and its pace. Visual management should provide access to information needed in the operation of a business. This would include charts and graphs that allow the business status to be determined through their review. This review should be capable of being performed at a glance. To facilitate this, it is necessary to be able to manage by fact and let the data speak for it.

Water spider: New role for material handler. Water spiders can be a low-skill or high-skill job. The water spider job is to replenish empty bins on the line daily, plays a vital role in mixed model parts sequencing, should stay 15 minutes or more ahead of the line, can be utilized as a floater, can be utilized to release parts orders from suppliers, and should have standard work and walk patterns/milk runs.

Work groups: Work groups are an organizational tool providing a team approach in which people work together on problems to improve productivity.

World-class quality management: The commitment by all employees. It is a philosophy/operating methodology totally committed to quality and customer satisfaction. It focuses on continuous process improvement in all processes. It advocates the use of analytical tools and scientific methods and data. It establishes priorities and manages by fact. World-class quality management has perfection (world class) as its goal. We should benchmark to be better than the competition by a large margin, the best. To obtain this status, all employees must be involved, everyone, everywhere, at all times. The result will be products and services that consistently meet or exceed the customers' expectations both internal and external. This group is always passionate with respect to improving the customer experience.

Yo-i-don[4]: It means ready set go. It is used to balance multiple processes and operators to a required cycle time using andon. This means each station or line is station balanced to one cycle time. When each operator completes their work, they press the andon button. Once the count-down or count-up clock reaches the prescribed cycle time, any station not completed, immediately turns the andon light to red. At this point, the supervisor and other team members will come to help that station.

Yokoten[5]: It is a process critical for creating a true learning organization. Sharing best practices (successes) is critical across the entire organization. In kanji, yoko means beside, side, or width and ten has several meanings but here it would mean to cultivate or comment. Yokoten is a means of *horizontal or sideways transfer of knowledge*, that is, peer-to-peer across the company. People are encouraged to Gemba, to see the kaizen improvement made for them, and see if they can apply the idea or an improved idea in their area. At Honeywell, this is referred to as horizontal linking mechanisms (HLMs).

Notes

1. *Lean Lexicon*, John Shook, LEI, 2004.
2. Source unknown.
3. Kanban JIT at Toyota—Ohno, Japan Management Association.
4. Monden Yasuhiro, *Toyota Production System*, 3rd edition.
5. http://eudict.com/?lang=japeng&word=ten.

Index

Note: Locators in *italics* represent figures and **bold** indicate tables in the text.

Printed in the United States
by Baker & Taylor Publisher Services